Drive Around

Dordogne
and Western France

Thomas Cook

YOUR GUIDE TO GREAT DRIVES

Titles in this series include:

- Andalucía and the Costa del Sol
- Bavaria and the Austrian Tyrol
- Brittany and Normandy
- Burgundy and the Rhône Valley
- California
- Catalonia and the Spanish Pyrenees
- Dordogne and Western France
- England and Wales
- Florida
- Ireland
- Italian Lakes and Mountains with Venice and Florence
- Languedoc and Southwest France
- Loire Valley
- Provence and the Côte d'Azur
- Scotland
- Tuscany and Umbria
- Vancouver and British Columbia
  and
- Selected Bed and Breakfast in France (annual edition)

For further information about these and other Thomas Cook publications, write to Thomas Cook Publishing, PO Box 227, The Thomas Cook Business Park, 15–16 Coningsby Road, Peterborough PE3 8SB, United Kingdom.

Drive Around

Dordogne
and Western France

The best of the Dordogne's lofty
châteaux, fortified medieval towns
and green mountain slopes, plus
the vineyards of the Bordeaux
region and the beaches of Biarritz
and the Atlantic Coast

Eric and Ruth Bailey

Thomas Cook
Publishing

www.thomascookpublishing.com

Published by Thomas Cook Publishing,
a division of Thomas Cook Tour Operations Limited
PO Box 227
The Thomas Cook Business Park
15–16 Coningsby Road
Peterborough PE3 8SB
United Kingdom

Telephone: +44 (0)1733 416477
Fax: +44 (0)1733 416688
E-mail: books@thomascook.com

For further information about
Thomas Cook Publishing, visit our website
www.thomascookpublishing.com

ISBN 1-841574-64-3

Text: © 2005 Thomas Cook Publishing
Maps and diagrams:
Road maps supplied and designed by Lovell Johns Ltd., OX8 8LH
Road maps generated from Collins Bartholomew Digital Database
© Collins Bartholomew Ltd, 1999
City maps prepared by RJS Associates, © Thomas Cook Publishing

Head of Publishing: Chris Young
Series Editor: Charlotte Christensen
Production/DTP Editor: Steven Collins
Project Administrator: Michelle Warrington

Written and researched by: Eric and Ruth Bailey
Update research by: David Brown
Driving information: Michael Hafferty

About the authors

Eric and Ruth Bailey first met as trainee journalists on a provincial English newspaper. They went their separate professional ways until their paths converged some years later, when they married and formed a freelance travel-writing team that has so far produced 16 books and countless articles for magazines and newspapers. Their travels have taken them across Canada from coast to coast and along the Eastern seaboard of the United States from Maine to Florida. They have also travelled extensively in Ireland, Mexico and Southern Africa. They are inland waterway enthusiasts and are passionately interested in rural life and dogs.

Acknowledgements

The authors would like to thank Helena Aldis, the Comité Régionale de Tourisme d'Aquitaine, the French Government Tourist Office in London, Holiday Autos, London Stansted Airport, Ryanair, Geoff and Maureen Smith and the staff of tourism offices throughout the region who so readily assisted in the research for this guide.

Contents

About Drive Around Guides

Thomas Cook's Drive Around Guides are designed to provide you with a comprehensive but flexible reference source to guide you as you tour a country or region by car. This guide divides the Dordogne and Western France into touring areas – one per chapter. Major cultural centres or cities form chapters in their own right. Each chapter contains enough attractions to provide at least a day's worth of activities – often more.

Star ratings
To make it easier for you to plan your time and decide what to see, the principal sights and attractions are given a star rating. A three-star rating indicates an outstanding sight or major attraction. Often these can be worth at least half a day of your time. A two-star attraction is worth an hour or so of your time, and a one-star attraction indicates a site that is good but often of specialist interest.

Chapter contents
Every chapter has an introduction summing up the main attractions of the area, and a ratings box, which will highlight the area's strengths and weaknesses – some areas may be more attractive to families, others to wine-lovers visiting vineyards, and others to people interested in finding castles, churches, nature reserves or good beaches.

Each chapter is then divided into an alphabetical gazetteer, and a suggested tour. You can select whether you just want to visit a particular sight or attraction, choosing from those described in the gazetteer, or whether you want to tour the area comprehensively. If the latter, you can construct your own itinerary, or follow the authors' suggested tour, which comes at the end of every area chapter.

The gazetteer
The gazetteer section describes all the major attractions in the area – the villages, towns, historic sites, nature reserves, parks or museums that you are most likely to want to see. Maps of the area highlight all the places mentioned in the text. Using this comprehensive overview of the area, you may choose just to visit one or two sights.

One way to use the guide is simply to find individual sights that interest you, using the index, overview map or star ratings, and read what our authors have to say about them. This will help you decide whether to visit the sight. If you do, you will find plenty of practical information, such as the street address, the telephone number for enquiries and opening times.

Symbol Key

- ⓘ Tourist Information Centre
- ⮂ Advice on arriving or departing
- ⓟ Parking locations
- ⓠ Advice on getting around
- ⊙ Directions
- ⓣ Sights and attractions
- ◖ Accommodation
- ⓜ Eating
- ⊖ Shopping
- ⓟ Sport
- ⊙ Entertainment

Practical information

The practical information in the page margins, or sidebar, will help you locate the services you need as an independent traveller – including the tourist information centre, car parks and public transport facilities. You will also find the opening times of sights, museums, churches and other attractions, as well as useful tips on shopping, market days, cultural events, entertainment, festivals and sports facilities.

Alternatively, you can choose a hotel, perhaps with the help of the accommodation recommendations contained in this guide. You can then turn to the overall map on page 10 to help you work out which chapters in the book describe those cities and regions that lie closest to your chosen touring base.

Driving tours

The suggested tour is just that – a suggestion, with plenty of optional detours and one or two ideas for making your own discoveries, under the heading *Also worth exploring*. The routes are designed to link the attractions described in the gazetteer section, and to cover outstandingly scenic coastal, mountain and rural landscapes. The total distance is given for each tour, as is the time it will take you to drive the complete route, but bear in mind that this indication is just for the driving time: you will need to add on extra time for visiting attractions along the way.

Many of the routes are circular, so that you can join them at any point. Where the nature of the terrain dictates that the route has to be linear, the route can either be followed out and back, or you can use it as a link route, to get from one area in the book to another.

As you follow the route descriptions, you will find names picked out in bold capital letters – this means that the place is described fully in the gazetteer. Other names picked out in bold indicate additional villages or attractions worth a brief stop along the route.

Accommodation and food

In every chapter you will find lodging and eating recommendations for individual towns, or for the area as a whole. These are designed to cover a range of price brackets and concentrate on more characterful small or individualistic hotels and restaurants. In addition, you will find information in the *Travel facts* chapter on chain hotels, with an address to which you can write for a guide, map or directory. The price indications used in the guide have the following meanings:

€   budget level
€€   typical/average prices
€€€   de luxe

la Rochelle

Rochefort

Angoulême

Page 98

Saintes

Page 272

Page 108

Rovan

le-Verdon-
sur-Mer

Jonzac

Page 86

Perigueux

Page 11

Carcans

Page 42

Page 66

Page 142

Bordeaux

Bergerac

Page 262

Page 192

Page 232

Page 54

Marmande

Arcachon

Page 254

Page 222

Mimizan

Agen

Page 212

Moissac

Page 242

Mont-de-
Marsan

Dax

Auch

Bayonne

Orthez

Hendaye

Biarritz

Pau

St-Jean-
Pied-de-Port

Tarbes

Oloron

Limoges

Page 152

Brive-la-Gaillarde
●

Aurillac
●

Page 172

e 182

● **Figeac**

Mende
●

hors

Page 164

Rodez
●

ban

Albi
●

Nîmes
●

Castres

●Ar

louse

●

Montpellier
●

Béziers
●

Introduction

A favoured region

Some of the best things in life are found in Western France. Gourmet foods, fine wines, well-preserved history, prehistoric cave paintings, lofty châteaux, fortified medieval towns and villages, miles of beaches, deep forests, river valleys, farmland and a mix of beautiful scenery from the pastoral to the steep green slopes of the Midi-Pyrénées.

All this and more is what can turn a casual first-time visitor into a dedicated lifelong Francophile.

Certainly there are many aspects of the Dordogne and the Bordeaux region that can be addictive. Those who like to keep their feet on the ground, however, will be aware of some of those idiosyncrasies that set France apart.

The Southwest is one of the country's most tourist-favoured regions. The resident population is comparatively low – under 50 to the square kilometre in places – but in high summer every hotel, gîte, auberge, chambre d'hôte and campground is fully booked. Narrow roads are jam-packed with holiday traffic.

And yet… While private individuals offer the warmest of welcomes, accommodations and places of interest, how seriously does the French government take its tourist industry?

Without a doubt the nation has a beautiful and fascinating product for visiting holidaymakers to enjoy – a product that sells itself. Perhaps that is the key to the situation. The climate in France is more temperate and predictable than that of its northerly neighbours in Europe. The weather starts to warm up in March and the sun usually shines well into the autumn, give or take the odd short spell of rain or wind. The tourist season could profitably be extended to seven months, taking the pressure off the peak months in the baking heat of July and August.

Some of the attractions and activities get into gear only in these two months.

In a May heatwave you may want to hire a canoe or rowing dinghy and spend an hour or two on the river, then find that boats can be hired only from mid-June to mid-September. It would be good to have more of what's available more of the time.

You may strike lucky and find some attractions and activities operating from May to October, or even from Easter, but this is not the norm.

The long French lunch break continues to rule. Hardly a museum or gallery or even a tourist office can be penetrated between noon and 2 pm. However eager you are to complete a full itinerary you may just as well follow the French example and take a long, leisurely lunch break.

Of course this is exactly what appeals to many visitors, who go to the region with one specific aim: to relax. Campgrounds with amenities on site, somewhere to sunbathe and swim, a playground for the children and some music or entertainment at night provide a wonderful carefree holiday. It's the see-and-do visitor who is frustrated by restricted opening times.

Eating out in the West is a major delight. Duck appears on many a menu, the gizzard frequently getting star billing. *Foie gras* is popular among those without scruples about its origins; likewise veal. Rabbit, once a favourite in French eateries, is seen only occasionally in French restaurants, though it is still the basis of a good meal in the home, served with locally produced prunes.

The fixed-price menu is a boon, banishing the fear of the unintentionally daunting bill. You usually have a choice of three or four fixed-price menus. The higher-priced ones may include house wine – a consideration, as the days of ordering a carafe of wine for peanuts are long gone. Self-caterers, though, may find good low-cost wines on supermarket shelves.

If you plan to stay put in one place on holiday, which part of the Southwest offers the most? Impossible to say. There is great variety, scenic beauty, history and the alluring ambience and *je ne sais quoi* of France throughout the region. Just decide whether it's to be seaside or inland, town (Bordeaux? Biarritz?) or country, the gentle hills of the Tarn and Garonne, the forests and beaches of the Landes, the rural ambience of Gascony or the heights and valleys of the Dordogne and the Midi-Pyrénées. It's all enchanting.

Below
Village du Bournat museum

Travel facts

Accommodation

In Southwest France you'll find a wide range of accommodation, in all price ranges, from campsites and converted farmhouses to luxury hotels and even châteaux. Bear in mind, however, that the main resorts are heavily booked at the height of the summer, especially during the French holiday season (mid-July to mid-August) and that in winter many hotels and campsites close – so be sure of getting what you want by booking in advance, especially if you're travelling with the family. Prices are generally higher along the Dordogne Valley, in the fashionable resorts, in towns and along the Côte d'Argent.

Hotels

French hotels are graded from one to four stars and 'luxury'. Unstarred establishments are cheap but have few facilities – always inspect a room before taking it. Tariffs are posted in reception and in every bedroom. Prices are quoted for a double room with two people sharing (not including breakfast) – check whether the 15 per cent VAT is included in the price. Single rooms are thin on the ground, so expect to pay for a double even if you're travelling alone. Most rooms have showers (cheaper than baths) but in smaller hotels there may be only one bathroom per floor. Breakfast often works out quite expensive – you'll find it more economical to eat out in a local café.

Reservations should made in writing (letter or fax); you'll have to pay a deposit (usually the equivalent of one night or 25 per cent). If you cancel your stay after paying the deposit, the hotel may require you to pay the total cost of the reservation. If you call in person, tourist offices will make reservations for the coming week (for a small fee).

You will be expected to arrive at the hotel before 1900 and no room will be held beyond 2200. If you're planning to arrive later, make sure you inform the hotel in advance.

One of the best-known and most reputable groups of hotels is the **Fédération Nationale des Logis de France** tel: *France 01 45 84 83 84*. These are inexpensive, family-run hotels, often in attractive surroundings out of town. The restaurants are equally good value and usually feature regional specialities. They are classified by 'chimneys' (1–3).

Chambres d'hôtes
A green-and-white sign denotes *chambres d'hôtes* – accommodation in a private home, which can range from a château to a farm cottage. Rooms can be booked through local tourist offices, the French Tourist Office or through **Château Acceuil** *tel: 02 32 33 78 87*; **Bienvenue à la ferme** *tel: 01 53 57 11 44*; *e-mail: bienvenue-a-la-ferme@apca.chambagri.fr*

Bed and Breakfast
Thomas Cook Publishing, in co-operation with Bed & Breakfast (France), publish an annual directory (price £12.99 plus p&p), available from **Thomas Cook Publishing**, PO Box 227, The Thomas Cook Business Park, 15–16 Coningsby Road, Peterborough PE3 8SB, UK; *tel: 01733 416477*; *e-mail: publishing-sales@ thomascook.com*

Bed & Breakfast (France) has a website at *www.bedbreak.com*. You can book your bed and breakfast on the website or by phone or e-mail using a credit card; *tel: 020 8956 2390*; *e-mail: bookings@bedbreak.com*

Hotel chains

Accor (includes Ibis, Mercure, Novotel, Sofitel, Formule-1)
www.accorhotels.com.
Central reservation number:
UK tel: 020 8283 4500;
USA tel: 800 221 4542.

Best Western
www.bestwestern.com. UK
tel: 0800 39 31 30; USA tel:
800 780 7234.

Campanile
www.campanile.fr. UK tel:
020 8569 6969.

Choice Hotels (includes Comfort and Quality Inns)
www.choicehotels.com.
France tel: 0800 91 24 24;
UK tel: 0800 44 44 44; USA
tel: 800 424 6423.

Holiday Inn
www.sixcontinentshotels.com/
holiday-inn. UK tel: 0800 40
50 60; USA/Canada:
800–HOLIDAY (800 465
4329).

Relais et Châteaux
www.relaischateaux.com.
International HQ –
15 r. Galvani,
75017 Paris, France;
tel: 01 45 72 90 00; e-mail:
info@relaischateaux.com.
Central Reservations: 00800
2000 0002 (International
freephone).

There are dozens of hotel chains in France, offering a range of categories from three to four star to budget. The main chains are listed left.

Gîtes

A *gîte* is self-catering accommodation, often in a converted farmhouse or country cottage. Lists of the *gîtes* in the government-run scheme are available in *The Gîtes de France Handbook* or from the Internet – *www.gîtes-de-france.fr*

Lists are graded in 'ears of *Gîtes* wheat' (14). Traditionally they are booked by the week although some now offer weekends out of season. To book a *gîte*, contact the owner direct or go to the website of **Gîtes de France** (*www.gites-de-france.fr/eng/index.htm*). **Maison des Gîtes** 59 r. Saint-Lazare, Paris, tel: 01 49 70 75 75 (*e-mail: info@gites-de-france.fr*), is open Mon–Sat 1000–1830. Many holiday and travel firms also offer *gîtes* as alternatives to hotels. They go quickly so it's essential to book well in advance.

Campsites

Campsites are graded from one to four stars. All have clean water, a refuse collection and a telephone; many have swimming pools, restaurants, children's play areas, camp shops and fabulous outlooks, depending on the price. Most sites have fixed tents, caravans or holiday bungalows on offer as well as spaces for people bringing their own tent or caravan. Camping is very popular with the French, so book in advance. For more information, **Camping France**, *www.campingfrance.com/indexuk.htm* handles online bookings for a range of owners covering more than 1100 campsites in Southwest France. **Mistercamp** operates a free telephone call-back service for information about campsites in France, from a website at *www.mistercamp.com/uk/index.htm; e-mail: info@mistercamp.com.* **ABC Camping** at *www.abccamping.com/aquitaineuk.htm* is an online directory of campsites in the region. Another is Les Campings at *www.les-campings.com/gb/index.html*

Camping Card International is a very useful item to carry on a camping tour. It is a small plastic card available from the AA or RAC and is accepted as an identity card at campsites in France, so it is not necessary to hand over your passport when registering on arrival. The CCI also entitles you to privileges on insurance and discounts on travel goods and services.

Airports

There are international airports at Bergerac, Biarritz, Bordeaux, Carcassonne and Toulouse. The airport at Périgueux is for internal flights.

Children

Look out for the little puffin in a striped shirt and the greeting *'Salut les Enfants'* – this sign guarantees quality service and accommodation especially suitable for children. The French tourist board has awarded several resorts the accolade 'Station Kid' for their child-friendly facilities and activities. Many resorts also go out of their way to welcome children and babies with special menus, babysitting services and supervised beach clubs.

Electricity

The electric current is 220 volts (50 MHz). Plugs should be circular with two round pins. Take an adaptor for non-continental apppliances.

Entry formalities

All visitors require a valid passport. EU citizens as well as US, Canadian and Japanese visitors do not need visas for stays of less than three months; Australian, New Zealand and South African nationals need a visa and should apply to the nearest French consulate before entering the country.

Climate

The climate in Southwest France is generally clement. Summertime can be capricious in the Dordogne, with heavy rain often following a period of hot, windy weather. In winter, snow is rare, but temperatures can drop to very low levels. The Atlantic coast enjoys more than 2000 hours of sunshine a year, with the brightest days between May and September. Rain is more frequent around Biarritz because of the mountains.

Currency

The unit of currency, the euro (€), is divided into 100 cents. When sums are written, a comma rather than a decimal point is used to separate euros from cents.

Major credit cards are accepted (and sometimes preferred) by hotels, restaurants and petrol stations. They can also be used in multilingual cash dispensers (ATMs) known in France as *distributeurs*, found outside most banks. Cash advances can also be drawn against credit cards in any bank where you see the appropriate sign.

Customs regulations

There are no restrictions on goods brought to and from EU countries, provided they are for personal use (try to adhere to official guidelines: 10 litres of spirits, 90 litres of wine, 110 litres of beer and 800 cigarettes maximum). Goods purchased in duty-free shops are still subject to restrictions and visitors from outside Europe have to abide by stricter regulations – ask before you leave home. The import of weapons, drugs and pornography is prohibited. For prescription medicines, carry a copy of your doctor's note.

Drinking

Tap water is safe to drink, but many people prefer to drink mineral water, which is available under a wide range of product names at supermarkets and convenience stores. Wine is produced in many parts of the region, with those of the famous châteaux in the Bordeaux region heading the list. The area around Cahors produces a 'black' wine – deep red in colour and robust in flavour. From the vineyards of Bergerac come both red and white wines, with sweet Monbazillac taking pride of place – a wonderful wine to take at the start of a meal with *foie gras* or with the dessert. Gascony has never produced great wine, but the lip-pursing tingly output from the grapes there is put to good use by being distilled as Armagnac, believed by some people to be the world's finest brandy.

Eating out

Traditional mealtimes are 1200–1400 and 1900–2100. Restaurants are often pre-booked by French families for Sunday lunch, so be sure to reserve a table well in advance.

Bars and cafés sell snacks all day. It's often cheaper to stand at the counter and drink rather than sit on a terrace. *Salons de thé* are a more refined alternative if all you want is a light meal. *Crêperies* are everywhere but you'll find little on the menu besides pancakes and salads.

Restaurants and brasseries are comparable in terms of price and quality, but the latter stay open longer. Prices are generally posted outside and there is usually at least one fixed-price menu, often good value. *Servis compris* means that a service charge of 15 per cent has been included.

Most towns in Southwest France have a produce market so you can stock up on picnic fare. In some you can buy such delicacies as truffles, foie gras and oysters. Delicatessens (*charcuteries*) also sell prepared dishes and salads. Other useful food outlets are bakers (*boulangeries*) and *pâtisseries* specialising in cakes and pastries.

Food

So many excellent foods are reared or grown in Southwest France and its coastal waters that you could spend a couple of months touring in the region, living like a gourmet and gourmand combined and never have the same meal twice. Here the self-caterer may have the edge on the person who constantly eats out, because you can not only look avidly at the wonderful produce – poultry, fish, meats and cheeses in the markets and shops – you can also buy them and enjoy transforming them into really memorable meals in your holiday home. You can serve a breakfast of big fleshy *cèpes* (wild mushrooms) from the Dordogne with grilled sausages made from veal and lamb, or omelettes flavoured with black truffles from Périgord – truffles are very expensive but a little goes a long way in an omelette. You could have a light lunch of oysters from Arcachon, bought for absurdly low prices, or a supper of *lamproie* (lampreys) caught from the Garonne, the Gironde or the Dordogne rivers.

A restaurant meal can be a gastronomic treat. If you've promised yourself some high-fat holiday eating go for the *foie gras* or the duck conserve. The French do amazing things with goose gizzards, which are considered a delicacy. At a low cholesterol level you may prefer pheasant or woodpigeon, or maybe woodcock. The Landaise chickens that range freely in Europe's largest forest have a superb flavour. Lamb from Pauillac is delicious. Those who like eels will love the *piballes* from the Gironde. Basque country tuna and *koskera* cod are good choices.

One curious tendency in the classier restaurants seems to be to serve meat or fish artistically with sauce and garnish but with a minimum of

Conversion tables

Distances

Metric	Imperial
1m	3ft 3in
5m	16ft 6in
10m	33ft
50m	164ft
100m	330ft
1km	0.75 mile
2km	1.5 miles
5km	3 miles
10km	6 miles
20km	12.5 miles
50km	31 miles
100km	62 miles

Weight

Kg	Lbs
1	2
2	4.5
5	11
10	22
20	45
50	110
75	165
100	220

Fluid measures

Litres	Imperial gallon
5	1.1
10	2.2
20	4.4
50	11

Area

1 hectare = 2.471 acres
1 acre = 0.4 hectares

Museums

Opening times vary according to season – some museums close altogether in winter. Most have at least one closing day per week (often Mon or Tue) and few are open all day; lunch usually falls from 1200–1400, though it may be later. If in doubt, check at the local tourist office.

vegetables. You may have slices of duck arranged with one or two asparagus spears, half a mushroom, a sprinkling of chopped herbs, a cherry and a couple of tiny potatoes. The posher the establishment the lower the vitamin C content, it seems, or perhaps it's just a passing phase among trendy chefs.

You can compensate with fresh fruit for dessert – big beautiful plums from around Agen or the Lot Valley, or some of the sweet golden grapes of Moissac.

The French have their cheese course before the dessert and the cheese board usually has some goat's or sheep's milk cheeses among the selection. Some may be bland but many are beautifully flavoursome.

And dessert? You couldn't do better than Armagnac pie. It's a pudding for grown-ups.

Eating out in France can be a problem for vegetarians. The French are great meat-eaters and few restaurants understand the concept of a meal comprising only vegetables. Mashed potato and quiche often come loaded with *lardons*, tiny pieces of chopped pork or ham. The term *vegan* is virtually unheard of, and you may be offered cheese or egg dishes or even fish as substitutes for meat. The Dordogne is renowned for *foie gras*, a great delicacy consisting of duck liver paté, but this is particularly offensive to vegans because it is made by force-feeding the birds to enlarge their livers.

Nature parks

There are four regional nature parks in the area covered by this book: the Parc Ornithologique, where there are birdwatching and natural history activities on the edge of the Bassin d'Arcachon, and the Parc Régional des Landes, Europe's largest forest, which has an outdoor ecological museum, workshops and stages exhibitions, environmental studies and activity programmes including canoeing and cycling tours.

Opening times

As a general rule, food shops open Mon–Sat 0800–2030; other shops open 0900–0930 and close 1900–1930. Bakers (*boulangeries*) open on

Information

There are tourist offices (*Syndicats d'Initiatives* or *Offices de Tourisme*) in most towns. English is usually spoken and there is a comprehensive range of information on accommodation, local attractions, restaurants and other facilities.

Regional tourist office *Comité Regionale du Tourisme, 23, Parvis des Chartrons, Cité Mondiale 33074 Bordeaux; tel: (33) 05 56 01 70 00; e-mail: tourisme@crt.cr-aquitaine.fr; www.crt.cr-aquitaine.fr*

Regional tourist office *Comité Départemental du Tourisme de la Dordogne, 25 r. du Président Wilson, 24009 Périgueux; tel: 05 53 35 50 24; fax: 05 53 09 51 41; e-mail: dordogne.perigord.tourisme@wanadoo.fr; www.perigord.tm.fr/tourisme/cdt*

Regional tourist office *Comité Départemental du Tourisme de la Gironde, 21 cours d'Intendance 33000 Bordeaux; tel: 05 56 52 61 40; fax: 05 56 81 09 99; e-mail: tourisme@gironde.com; www.tourisme-gironde.cg33.fr*

Regional tourist office *Comité Départemental du Tourisme des Landes, 4 r. Aristide Briand, Mont-de-Marsan; tel: 05 58 06 89 89; fax: 05 58 06 90 90; e-mail: cdt.landes@wanadoo.fr; www.tourismelandes.com*

Regional tourist office *Comité Départemental du Tourisme de Lot-et-Garonne, 4 r. André Chénier, Agen; tel: 05 53 66 14 14, fax: 05 53 68 25 42; e-mail: c.d.t@wanadoo.fr; www.lot.et.garonne.com*

Regional tourist office *Comité Départemental du Tourisme Béarn-Pays Basque, 4, allé des platanes, Bayonne; tel: 05 59 46 52 52; fax: 05 59 46 52 46; www.tourisme64.com*

Health

There are no vaccinations specifically recommended for visitors to France. EU residents with an E111 form are entitled to reciprocal health treatment – however, this will only meet part of your expenses and is no substitute for adequate health insurance. American Express cardholders should apply to Global Assist *tel: (France) 01 47 16 25 29*, for any medical emergency. Pharmacies (marked with a green cross) will treat minor complaints. They will also direct you to a doctor or dentist.

Insurance

Adequate insurance is essential. Most package holiday companies offer policies, but you can make your own arrangements if you prefer. Some house contents and health policies cover losses and accidents abroad, so check your existing policies.

Maps

The best maps for drivers are the Michelin 1:200,000 maps of Aquitaine (No 234), Midi-Pyrénées (No 235) and Auvergne-Limousin (No 239). Town plans are issued free by French Tourist Information and vary in their quality and usefulness. Most offices also have maps showing local footpaths with suggested routes.

Sun mornings too. Lunchtime closing is 1200–1400, but supermarkets and shopping complexes stay open all day and sometimes later into the evening. Half-day closing is often Mon, but all these times are subject to seasonal variations.

Banks open Mon–Fri 0900–1200, 1400–1600. Some open Sat morning; some close Mon. They usually close early the day before a public holiday.

Packing

Shorts and a tee shirt will be perfectly adequate during the day in summertime, especially on the coast, but in the higher areas inland, where the weather is more variable and there can be sudden rainstorms, it would be wise to have a light raincoat or anorak and a cotton sweater handy. The sun's strength can be deceptive everywhere, so don't forget to pack or buy a high-factor protection lotion. Also, remember to bring insect repellent and any prescribed medicines.

Postal services

Post offices (*bureaux de poste*) are indicated by a yellow sign and the words *La Poste* in blue. They are generally open Mon–Fri 0800–1700 (or 1900), Sat 0800–1200. Smaller offices will close for lunch (1200–1430). Letters marked *poste restante* may be sent to any post office, to be collected on payment of a small fee (take your passport as proof of identity). Many post offices also have photocopying and fax facilities. Post boxes are yellow. Letters for abroad should be posted in the *départements étrangers* slot. Stamps (*timbres de postes*) can be bought from post offices, and shops and cafés displaying a red diamond (*tabacs*).

Public transport

Public transport is generally reliable and efficient. SNCF is the national rail system. Services are frequent and fares reasonable – Eurailpass, Flexipass and Saver Pass are all valid in France. SNCF also offers its own range of discounted tickets. Under-4s travel free on public transport, 4–11s travel half-price. For more information *tel: 020 7647 4900*. All train tickets must be validated with a date stamp in the orange automatic machines at the entrance to platforms. Rail maps and timetables are available at stations. TGV super-express services between large towns require reservations, especially at peak times. You are not allowed to take a bicycle on TGV services, only local trains (if in doubt look for the bike sign on timetables). Buses cover more towns than the train network and are a cheaper way of getting around. The central bus station is often next to the rail station; route maps and timetables can be picked up here and from tourist information. Bicycles may be taken on some bus services at the discretion of the driver.

Public holidays

New Year's Day
  1 January
Easter Sunday
  and Monday
Labour Day
  1 May
VE Day – 8 May
Ascension Day
Whitsunday and
  Monday
Bastille Day –14 July
Assumption Day
  5 August
All Saints' Day
  1 November
Armistice Day
  11 November
Christmas Day
  25 December

Safety and security

Southwest France is a safe place to holiday, but groups of tourists will always attract the opportunist thieves. Beware pickpockets, especially on public transport and in crowds – keep your money in a belt or other secure place and don't leave valuables lying about where they can be seen. Never leave luggage unattended. It is a good idea to have photocopies of your passport and records of your credit cards, traveller's cheques and insurance policies stored separately from the items themselves. If you do lose something, report it to the police immediately.

Emergency phone numbers:

Police and ambulance 17

Fire brigade 18

Reading

Fiction

The Three Musketeers – Alexandre Dumas. Dashing D'Artagnan was a man from Gascony. *Bonjour Tristesse* – Françoise Sagan, the author, was born at Cajarc in the Lot Valley. *Beloved Enemy* – Ellen Jones. A novel based on the life of Eleanor of Aquitaine.

History

Eleanor of Aquitaine: the Mother Queen – Desmond Seward. The fascinating tale of the most powerful woman in medieval England and France. *The Hundred Years' War* – Jonathan Sumption. Two volumes (so far!) on the complicated violence that rumbled on for more than a century, disturbing life across the whole of the region.

Wine

The Wines of Bordeaux – David Peppercorn. An authoritative survey by a top taster. *Enjoying Wine* – Don Hewitson. A handbook for aficionados of DIY (*drink* it yourself, that is). *The Winemasters* – Nicholas Faith. A look at 200 years of wine-making in Bordeaux.

Shopping

Ask a Frenchman or woman for advice on what to take home as a memento of your holiday and you'll never get them off the subject of food and drink. Certainly there are plenty of wonderful gastronomic treats that come from the Southwest and are canned or otherwise preserved in a way that makes them easy to carry and keep for a while. As for the wines…

But what of more permanent souvenirs and gifts?

Jewellery: Fine silver or gold chains and chunkier jewellery in the form of Celtic crosses.

Laguiole knives: This knife (pronounced lay-ole) is a true symbol of the plateau of Aveyron, used by shepherds and others.

Copperware: This has been made in the Montagne Noir region of the Midi-Pyrénées since the Middle Ages. Kitchenware – pots, pans and dishes – are still produced in local workshops. Ornamental beaten brass and copper items are also made.

Leatherware: Belts, purses, handbags and other leather goods can be found in distinctive designs. Specialised leatherware and glove-making by craftsmen in Millau, a small village at the foot of the Larzac plateau, is sought after by fashion designers.

Earthenware: Items with hand-painted flower and bird designs are traditional products of Martres-Tolosane, 50km from Toulouse.

Combs: These, made from the horns of young bulls, are a speciality of the Hers valley (Ariège) craftspeople.

Back to food and drink. Any of the wines of Bordeaux, Bergerac, Cahors, Fronton – red, white or rosé – will give great pleasure, and

Time

France is on Central European Time, 1 hour ahead of GMT; 6 hours ahead of US Eastern Standard Time; 9 hours ahead of Pacific Standard Time. French summertime begins on the last Sunday of March and ends on the last Sunday in September.

Tipping

Service charges (15 per cent) are automatically added to hotel and restaurant bills; it's at your discretion whether you leave an additional tip in restaurants (a couple of euros will suffice). Taxi drivers, doormen and petrol pump attendants, etc, may be tipped, again at your discretion.

Toilets

Public toilets can be found at shopping centres, petrol stations, etc. Standards vary; however, facilities in cafés, restaurants, hotels and museums are usually very good. *Messieurs* – men; *Dames* – women.

don't forget Armagnac. *Foie gras* and duck *confit* are obvious ideas. An extensive choice and good prices are available to visitors to the Labeyrie company's recently opened Pavilion du Foie Gras at St-Georges-de-Maremme in the south of the Landes, 30km from Biarritz. Take home some tinned truffles and the aroma will instantly evoke memories of your holiday.

Sport

You'll find all the literature you need on sports and outdoor activities in tourist offices.
Golf – Aquitaine has around 50 high-quality courses, many of them laid out by the best international golf course designers. The variety of the region's terrain has enabled courses to be set up in woodlands, close to vineyards, among dunes on plains, and in valleys and mountains. The Aquitaine Golf Pass covers five green fees on courses in Gironde and Biarritz/Landes.
Water sports – sailing, surfing, windsurfing, sand-yachting, canoeing, kayaking, whitewater rafting, diving and rowing are all widely available.
Other outdoor activities include fishing, walking, cycling and horse riding. The guide to the long-distance footpaths marked by red-and-white posts *Sentiers de grande randonnée* (GR) can be bought from tourist information or from the **Fédération Française de la Randonnée Pédestre**, *14 rue Riquet, Paris; tel: 01 44 89 93 90; e-mail: info@ffrp.asso.fr; www.ffrp.asso.fr*

Telephones

Public call boxes are in plentiful supply except in remote countryside. You'll need a phone card (*télécarte*) available from post offices, railway stations and *tabacs* in 50 or 120 units. Calls from a restaurant or hotel are usually subject to a surcharge. Mobile phones (cell phones) work in France, but you must check with your service provider at home that your handset is programmed for international roaming. You will be charged when you receive calls in France from people calling your usual mobile number.

Travellers with disabilities

Facilities for travellers with disabilities have improved in recent years, particularly in the main resorts. However, it's a different story once you venture into rural areas. Local police may be sympathetic to the parking needs of people with limited mobility, and the Blue Disabled Badge is recognized, but the steep cobbled streets in some medieval towns may make life difficult. More information can be obtained from the **Association des Paralysés de France**, *17 bd Auguste-Blanqui, Paris; tel: 01 40 78 69 00; fax: 01 45 89 40 57; www.apf.asso.fr*

Driver's guide

Accidents

Automobile clubs

Members of UK motoring organisations (AA or RAC) can extend their accident insurance and breakdown services to France. Both organisations offer a wide range of information and advice as well as suggesting itineraries and routes. *www.theaa.com* offers a free, turn-by-turn route map of your journey. See also *www.rac.co.uk www.viamichelin.co.uk*

Autoroutes

Most of the French autoroutes are toll roads. The commonest system of charging (*péage*) involves taking a ticket from a machine at the start of the toll section, which raises an automatic barrier. On leaving the system, or at an intermediate tollbooth, the ticket is presented and the amount to pay is displayed on an illuminated sign. Payment may be made in euros or by credit card. Signatures are not normally required. Traveller's cheques cannot usually be used for tolls. On autoroutes speed is sometimes automatically computed from time of entry and distance covered on arrival at the tollbooth. If a speeding offence is disclosed you may be prosecuted.

You must STOP after any accident. You can be in serious trouble if you don't. Call 15, 17 or 18 to alert the Ambulance, Police or Fire Service as appropriate, or use the EU universal emergency number 112. On an autoroute or main road, use one of the bright orange free SOS emergency roadside telephones located at frequent intervals.

Give whatever aid you are capable of to any person injured or in peril. It is an offence not to do this if it lies within your ability. This applies whether you are driver, passenger or witness. Safeguard against a secondary accident. Hazard lights – warning triangle – signal to other traffic. Exchange details of vehicles, drivers insurance etc. (French cars display insurance details on a windscreen sticker.) Complete a 'European Accident Statement' form – ask your insurers for this before you leave, the French driver will almost certainly have one. This forms a factual record. It is not an admission of fault. Note as many details as you can. Photographs? Witnesses? If someone has been injured, you must inform the police. If you have damaged someone else's vehicle or property and you are unable to give the owner your details, you must inform the police. The police will not usually take details where an accident involves material damage only, unless there is evidence of an offence such as dangerous or drink driving. Inform your insurers as soon as possible.

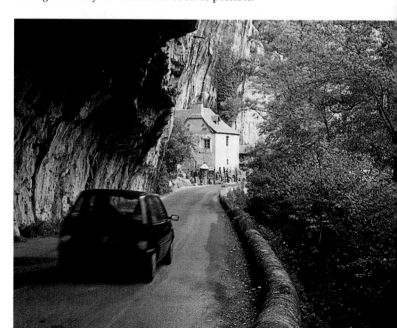

Documents

Members of EU countries and US citizens only need a valid national driving licence, but an international driving licence is essential for other nationals. Provisional licences are not valid and drivers must be over the age of 18. UK photo card licences are best. Paper licences are lawful but further proof of ID may be required. Registration papers (a logbook) and a letter of authorisation if the car is not registered in your name, insurance papers and Test Certificate (MoT) (originals – photocopies are not valid) and a nationality plate must be carried. The above documents must be produced at the time on request by police. An immediate fine may be imposed if they are not to hand. For UK drivers a 'Green Card' is not required in France for car insurance. Your certificate of insurance issued in Britain conforms to French legal needs. However, this is minimum legal cover. You should ask your insurers to extend your normal, full cover for use abroad for the period of your stay. Continental breakdown insurance is recommended. Should you visit the state of Andorra in the Pyrenees you will require a Green Card. Holders of US insurance must take out a European policy.

Breakdowns

If you are on an autoroute, stop your vehicle on the hard shoulder, getting it as far to the right as possible. On ordinary roads, consider using the verge but beware of roadside ditches. Hazard lights on. Place a warning triangle at least 30m from the scene, visible from 100m away. (Remember, it can be very dangerous to walk on the hard shoulder of any motorway.) You and your passengers are probably safer out of the vehicle and well up the verge away from the traffic.

If you need assistance on an autoroute you must use one of the free roadside telephones to connect you with the police. You cannot arrange recovery yourself, even if you are a member of a breakdown service. No garage will send a recovery vehicle onto an autoroute without police permission. There is a fixed scale of charges. (€72 by day, €108 by night.) You may not carry out a DIY tow on an autoroute and you may only do so on an ordinary road for 'a few metres' in an emergency. Makeshift towing is strongly discouraged and usually voids French car insurance.

Continental breakdown insurance is strongly recommended and one phone call is all it takes to hand the whole problem over to multi-lingual operators who are experts in sorting things out.

Caravans and camper vans (Trailers and RVs)

France is probably the most 'camping and caravanning friendly' country in Europe and there are numerous attractive campsites from economical to de luxe in the area covered by this guide. Booking ahead is really only necessary in the height of the season. The Alan Rogers' campsite guides are very useful. *Camping sauvage* ('wild' camping) is completely banned. Camping in State Forests or any wooded area is virtually always prohibited because of the serious risk of fire. Overnight parking of motorhomes is frequently permitted (and often free) in the central square of smaller towns and villages where water and toilet facilities are available. There are no formalities about bringing a caravan into France if your stay is for less than six months.

Motorhomes and cars towing trailers have to pay a higher toll on autoroutes. Some caravanners use the facilities of the autoroute *aires de repos* (rest areas) for an overnight stop. This is quite lawful, as your autoroute ticket lasts for at least 24 hours. If you do this, you are advised to use common sense and stop in a well-lit spot, in view of passers-by. Thefts and break-ins are, unfortunately, not unknown.

Speed limits for cars towing trailers or caravans are the same as solo vehicles. Occasionally, there may be a reduced speed limit for caravans on long declines. This is to reduce the danger of instability when the caravan is being neither pulled nor braked but is 'floating' behind the towing vehicle.

Drinking and driving

The French limit is 50mg of alcohol per 100ml of blood and penalties increase sharply if an 80mg limit is exceeded. There is a determined campaign to reduce incidents of drinking and driving, and penalties are severe, with heavy fines and imprisonment. Random breath tests are common and you should not underestimate the powers of the police or the consequences of failing a test. A large fine may be demanded on the spot and your vehicle may be impounded until it is paid. Any disqualification is immediate. If you are the sole driver, you will be stranded and any 'get-you-home' insurance will be invalidated by reason of you having committed an illegal act.

Essentials

You *must* have a red warning triangle and hazard lights in case of accident, a headlight dip adjusted to the right, a first-aid kit and spare bulbs. You'll also need nationality (GB, IRL, etc.) plates (or a sticker, usually supplied with Channel crossing tickets), a torch, and a petrol container.

Petrol = *Essence*
Unleaded = *Sans plomb 95 and 98 octane*
4-star = *Super*
Diesel = *Gazole, Gasoil or Diesel*
LPG = *GPL*

If you intend driving in the Pyrenees or the Alps (and particularly if you are towing a trailer) you should remember that engine efficiency decreases with altitude, by about 10% per 3000 feet. This can mean that a heavily laden non-turbo car just coping with the additional load at sea level, may not manage the incline as it climbs higher.

Driving in Dordogne

There are three classes of road – motorway (*autoroute* – A); main road (*route nationale* – RN or N); and secondary road (*route départementale* – D).

Autoroutes are of excellent quality with frequent rest and service areas, offering the fastest means of covering long distances by car. The exit slip roads tend to have very tight curves and should be negotiated at much reduced speed, especially if towing a trailer or caravan. Whilst there is no problem out of season, during the peak holiday periods they become overloaded.

Routes Nationales and Départementales. While the autoroutes offer virtually the shortest distance between two points, the RN and D roads tend to meander as they follow the geography of the region.

Driving rules

Traffic drives on the right in France. A fundamental driving rule is that traffic from the right has priority at junctions. In practice, priority from the right applies mostly in towns and on rural roads. Main roads are clearly signed as such by a yellow and white diamond sign which is repeated every 5km, or the conventional triangle showing a broad vertical black stripe with a narrow horizontal line crossing it (*see page 29*). Junctions marked with a simple X, or not marked at all, are governed by the 'Priority from the Right' rule. Any unmarked junction in a town or village must be treated as subject to this rule.

The rule applies to *junctions* and does not mean giving way to vehicles coming out of lay-bys, driveways, garages, parking spaces, etc. You should, however, give way to buses moving away from a bus stop.

Traffic on roundabouts has priority and drivers entering the system must wait for a safe opportunity. Unfortunately, French drivers are very haphazard about signalling their intentions on roundabouts and care is needed.

Pedestrians have right of way when on marked crossings, but the practice of stopping for a pedestrian waiting to use a crossing is unknown. If you decide to display such courtesy, remember that following drivers may not anticipate your action.

Fuel

Service stations are open all day but are normally closed on Sundays and public holidays. If a public holiday falls on, say, a Thursday, it is

Fines

The police/*gendarmes* have wide powers to impose on-the-spot fines for a variety of motoring offences. Speed checks are frequent and merciless. Payment must be in cash and should you not be able to pay there and then, for instance if the banks are closed and there is no ATM nearby, your vehicle and your passport may be impounded until you do. The fine is, in fact, a part payment (*amende forfaitaire*) and you may receive notification of a higher penalty later. At present such extra fines cannot be enforced abroad but EU legislation is being contemplated to make this possible.

Speed-trap detection devices are illegal, whether in use or not. The device is invariably seized and a heavy fine imposed.

In practice, if you drive sensibly, you are no more likely to be stopped or prosecuted in France than any other country. It is the *consequences* of such a prosecution that should be considered, especially when you are on holiday.

'Inforoute'

If your car radio is equipped with RDS this will work in France, interrupting radio programmes with road news flashes (in French). You may also receive traffic news on 'Inforoute' on 107.7 MHz FM. These low-power transmitters cover the motorway routes and provide local up-to-date traffic reports, in French.

common practice to take the Friday off as well, rather than spoil a good weekend. This can mean that petrol stations are closed for four days, especially in the country. In rural areas petrol stations can be few and far between, especially on *départementale* roads.

Fuel is cheapest at big supermarkets in out-of-town retail parks (*Centre Commercial*) and, not surprisingly, most expensive on motorways. Until the changeover of British credit cards to those incorporating a 'chip' is complete, 24-hour automatic pumps which require a credit card and PIN number, are very unlikely to work with British issued cards due to incompatible computing systems. Keeping the fuel tank well-filled is good practice.

Information

You should take an up-to-date map with you. Changes in road numbers and motorway interchanges can booby-trap old editions. The Michelin 1:200 000 'yellow' maps are ideal. Free *Bison Futé* (Crafty Bison) maps showing alternative routes using secondary roads to avoid traffic problems, are available from the French Government Tourist Office or information offices in France. These routes are well signposted, make a pleasant change from main roads and are a great help in avoiding the predictable traffic problem zones. If you want to be a 'Crafty Bison' yourself, you could try taking an early or late lunch and stay on the road between 1200 and 1400. The French drop everything for lunch and the roads become much quieter.

Parking

There is some free parking in Disc Parking zones, where the bays are marked out in blue. Purchase a disc (*Disque de stationnement*) at petrol stations or supermarkets. Setting your arrival time on the disc automatically displays the expiry time in a cut-out window. Meter or ticket parking follows the usual pattern. Very often parking is free 1200–1400. These times are displayed on the ticket machine.

If parking in the street, you *must* park facing the direction of travel, i.e. on the right in two-way streets. It is, in any case, bad practice to park on the left, as you may drive off forgetting to move to the correct side of the road.

It is illegal to leave a vehicle parked in the same place for more than seven days, and a lesser time in some cities. Obstructive or illegal parking, especially in cities, often results in the offending vehicle being uplifted and taken to a pound. Foreign number plates will not save you.

Some parking zones work on the basis of parking on the odd-numbered side of the street for the first fortnight of a month (1st–15th) and on the even-numbered side for the second. A special sign indicates the entry to the zone. (See page 29.) Changeover time is between 2030 and 2100 on the last day of each fortnight.

Lights

All traffic must use headlights in rain or poor visibility. Right-hand-drive cars must have their headlight beam modified to prevent dazzle. This can take the form of masking off part of the headlamps (which unfortunately reduces the light output) or stick-on optical beam deflectors which cause the headlight to dip to the right. Some vehicles which have quartz-iodine headlamps cannot be modified in these ways and you should check with the car dealer. Driving with defective lights can result in a fine. The fine is less likely if you can remedy the defect right away. It is a legal requirement to carry a spare set of bulbs. Motorcycles must display headlights at all times.

Mobile phones

The use of a hand-held phone when driving is specifically forbidden. The use of hands-free phones is strongly discouraged. The only safe and legal way for the driver to use a mobile is to stop and switch off the engine beforehand.

Seat belts

Wearing of seat belts for front and rear passengers is compulsory when the vehicle engine is running. Children under 10 must occupy the rear seats but an infant up to 9 months may travel in the front seat if secured in an approved rear-facing seat, *but not if a passenger air bag is fitted.*

Security

Sensible care should be taken, particularly where vehicles are left for long periods in vulnerable places such as tourist site car parks. Do not leave items on view inside the car, even if you know they are of little or no value, a potential thief does not.

In the large cities it is wise to keep car doors locked and windows up, if in slow-moving traffic or while stationary at traffic lights, as thieves on motorcycles occasionally reach inside to steal valuables. If hot weather means you must have the window open, be sure that handbags, wallets, cameras etc. are well out of sight and reach and, above all, never on a passenger's lap.

Should you have the misfortune to become a victim of crime, your insurers will require you to report the circumstances to the police and obtain a record that you have done so. In the country go to the *Gendarmerie* and in larger towns the *Commissariat de Police*.

Speed limits

Autoroutes – 130kph (110kph in rain). If windscreen wipers are needed it's 'raining'.
Dual carriageways – 110kph (100kph in rain)
Other roads – 90kph (80kph in rain)
All built up areas – 50kph on roads between the entrance sign to a town and
departure sign (place name crossed with diagonal bar).
There's a 50kph limit on any road when visibility is less than 50m.
Drivers with less than two year's experience must not exceed the 'rain' speed
limits even in fine weather.

Road signs

All major routes are clearly signed; even most minor roads have their destinations and route numbers marked. International European traffic signs are used throughout France

accôtement non-stabilisé – soft verge
aire – rest area
cédez le passage – give way
chaussée déformée – uneven surface
défense de stationner/stationnement interdit – no parking
dépassement interdit – no overtaking
déviation – diversion
gravillons – loose chippings
passage protégé – right of way
péage – toll
poste d'essence – petrol station
priorité à droite – priority to traffic from the right
priorité aux piétons – give way to pedestrians

ralentir – slow down
rappel – reminder of previous restriction
renseignements – information
rives dangereuses – dangerous roadsides
route barrée – road closed
sens interdit – no entry
sens unique – one way
seulement riverains – residents only
sortie de camions – HGV exit
stationnement gratuit – free parking
stationnement interdit – no parking
stationnement payant – paid parking
toutes directions – route for through traffic
un train peut en cacher un autre – one train may hide another
virage – bend
vous n'avez pas la priorité – you do not have priority

Right
Baynac-et-Cazenac

FRENCH ROAD SIGNS

Ⓐ
You have Priority at *all* junctions on this road.

Ⓑ *
You have Priority at *next* junction. (Note: important difference with A.)

Ⓒ *
Be prepared to *Give Way* to traffic from right at next junction.

End of Priority road.

CÉDEZ LE PASSAGE
'Give Way'.

*Signs B and C may indicate a junction from either side, not necessarily a full crossroads.

VOUS N'AVEZ PAS LA PRIORITE
You do not have Priority. *Give Way* at roundabout.

Signs attached to traffic lights are valid only if lights are OFF or yellow light is flashing.

Flashing yellow light = Proceed with caution. *Give Way* to traffic on right.

BERGERAC
The red border on a town sign *means start of 50km/h limit*. If surmounted by 'Priority' sign (as here), you are on the Priority road through the town.

PARKING

Disc Parking.

Parking on payment at meter.

Entry to zone where Parking is allowed first fortnight on odd-numbered side of street – second fortnight on even-numbered side.

WARNINGS

RISQUE DE VERGLAS
Risk of black ice.

Snow chains obligatory.

ALLUMEZ VOS FEUX
Switch on Headlights.

70m
Minimum distance between vehicles.

Itinéraire Bis
Alternative Route

Déviation
Diversion

Frequently found at tunnels

Getting to Dordogne and Western France

Eurostar *Tel: 08701 606 600; www.eurostar.com* – London Waterloo Intl to Paris (2 hrs 40 mins), also Lille Europe for connecting high-speed TGV trains to Bordeaux and Toulouse.

Eurotunnel *Tel: 08705 35 35 35; www.eurotunnel.com* – drive-on trains from Folkestone to Calais Coquelles through the Channel Tunnel (35 mins), direct access to the French motorway system. For more information contact **Rail Europe** *tel: 08705 848 848* (UK); or **Eurotunnel** direct reservations *tel: 08705 35 35 35*.

Brittany Ferries *Tel: 08705 360 360*, brochure line: *08705 143 537*; *www.brittanyferries.com* – Portsmouth to St-Malo (9 hrs) and Caen (6 hrs); Poole to Cherbourg (4 hrs), Plymouth to St-Malo (7½ hrs) and Cherbourg (12 hrs). Also Cork to Roscoff (13 hrs), summer only.

Flying

Southwest France is well-served by a choice of airline services, including scheduled flights and fly-drive packages with the national airlines and low-cost no-frills services. Your local travel agent will have information on all options, and all airlines have websites with online or phone booking facilities. There are scheduled flights from London to Toulouse, Bordeaux, Biarritz, Bergerac, Carcassonne and numerous internal flights with Air France from Paris. Contact **Ryanair** *tel: 0871 246 0016* (UK), *0818 30 30 50* (Ireland), *www.ryanair.com*; **Easyjet** *tel: 0871 7500 100* (UK), *www.easyjet.co.uk*; **Air France** *tel: 0845 359 1000* (UK) or *01 605 0383* (Ireland), *www.airfrance.com*; **British Airways** *tel: 0870 850 9850, www.britishairways.com*; **British European** *tel: 08705 676 676* (UK), *www.british-european.com*. Air France also operates a direct flight from Dublin to Bordeaux, British Airways flies from Birmingham direct to Bordeaux and British European has a direct service from Birmingham to Toulouse.

To get to Southwest France from the USA it is necessary to fly to Paris and change to an internal service or continue your journey by train or car.

Ferries

The ferry is still a popular way to take a car to France, so booking ahead is strongly recommended, especially in high season. Cross-channel passenger and car ferries and the SeaCat (catamaran) leave from various points along the south coast of England, also from Ireland. There's an equally good choice of destination ports: four in Normandy and two in Brittany.

Coaches

Coaches are a more economical way of travelling long distances than taking the train, but journey times are longer. Coach reservations can be made at any **National Express** travel office (*tel: 08705 80 80 80, www.nationalexpress.com*). **Eurolines** (*tel: 08705 143 219*) operates a network of Continental coach routes from London Victoria Coach Station, including a direct service to Tours (12 hours) with connections to Bordeaux, Brive, Cahors and Toulouse –

P&O Ferries *Tel: 08705 202020; www.poferries.com* – Portsmouth to Cherbourg 2 hrs 45 mins (fast ferry) or 4 hrs 45 mins (ship), Portsmouth to Le Havre 5½ hrs, Dover to Calais 1½ hrs, Rosslare to Cherbourg 19 hrs.

SeaFrance *Tel: 08705 711 711; www.seafrance.co.uk* – Dover to Calais 90 mins.

Hoverspeed *Tel: 08702 408 070; www.hoverspeed.co.uk* – Dover to Calais services by SeaCat fast catamaran (60 mins), also Newhaven to Dieppe by SuperSeaCat (2 hrs).

Speedferries *Tel: 01304 203000; www.speedferries.com* – Dover to Boulogne by large catamaran, 50 mins.

Condor Ferries *Tel: 0845 345 2000; www.condorferries.com* – Poole to St-Malo 5½ hrs; Portsmouth or Poole to Cherbourg 5 hrs (summer only).

Irish Ferries *Tel: 08705 171717 (GB), 0818 300 400 (Rep. of Ireland), www.irishferries.com* – Rosslare to Cherbourg 19½ hrs, Rosslare to Roscoff 17 hrs (summer only).

French Motorail *Tel: 08702 415 415; e-mail: motorail@raileurope.co.uk; www.raileurope.co.uk* – car-carrying train services operate in summer from Calais to Brive and Toulouse.

e-mail: welcome@eurolinesuk.com; www.eurolines.co.uk. There are also direct coach services from Dublin Busaras to Paris.

Rail services

Eurostar trains link London (Waterloo International) with Paris (Gare du Nord) and Lille Europe via the Channel Tunnel. The major railheads in Southwest France are Bordeaux, Brive and Toulouse and there are connecting services from Lille Europe by high speed TGV trains, so it's possible to avoid crossing Paris to Montparnasse or Austerlitz stations which serve the Southwest from the French capital. There are 15 TGV trips a day in each direction between Bordeaux and Paris and the journey time is less than three hours. There are Motorail services from Calais and Paris to Brive and Toulouse.

Rail Europe and Eurostar offer a through-ticket service. Contact main station Travel Centres or High Street travel agents for more details. Discounted tickets are available for students and young people under 26 and for InterRail pass-holders.

If you are planning to take your car through the Channel Tunnel, the entrance is off the M20 at junction 11A just outside Folkestone. After driving on to Eurotunnel the journey time is 35 minutes to Calais Coquelles and the terminal gives direct access to the A16 autoroute and the rest of the French motorway network. LPG or dual-fuel vehicles may not use the Tunnel.

Driving

If you are taking your own car, the autoroute system (mostly toll roads) is an excellent means of getting to your destination. Using the A16 from Calais to Paris and the A10 from Paris means it is possible to drive all the way from the Channel Tunnel to Bordeaux by motorway. The A10 and A20 provide an all-motorway route from Paris to Bordeaux and Brive. If you are taking your car through the Channel Tunnel, you join the French motorway network as soon as you drive off the train and out of the tunnel at Calais Coquelles. All main car manufacturers have service stations in France – obtain a list of addresses before you go.

You can avoid long-distance driving in France by using the French Motorail (www.raileurope.co.uk) which will transport your car and passengers to your destination overnight April to October in a purpose-built train. Services are from Calais to Bordeaux, Brive and Biarritz.

Car hire is expensive in France; it is normally cheaper to make arrangements before you leave, or consider an inclusive deal or fly-drive. You must be over 21 and have held a licence for at least one year, perhaps two. All the usual main car hire firms have offices in France, and often at airports, main railway stations and ferry ports. It is wise to book ahead for peak holiday periods.

Above
St-Céré fountain

Setting the scene

Landscapes

Anyone touring the entire area covered in this book will experience diverse types of landscape. Farmland with great acreages of sunflowers, vines, orchards, walnut groves, tobacco and many other fruit, vegetable and cereal crops. Rugged rocky hills, deep ravines, wide rivers, cliff-hanging villages, rolling hills – it's all to be found in the Southwest. There's also a long Atlantic coastline with sandy beaches and exhilarating surfing.

It is amazing, considering the long and terrible wars suffered by the French, how many buildings – indeed whole villages – have survived from the Middle Ages and earlier. The sculptured Romanesque capitals of the 11th-century cloisters at Moissac, with their biblical scenes and animal, bird and plant carvings, are worth crossing continents to see.

Prehistory also plays a major part in the enjoyment of the region. Some of the best-preserved examples of cave art in the world are in the foothills of the Pyrenees and the Dordogne, some dating from the last Ice Age. Limestone caverns thick with grotesque shapes and colourful 'curtains', pillars, stalagmites and stalactites can be visited in the Dordogne Valley. The gorges and *causses* (limestone plateaus) of the Aveyron are between the Dordogne and the Cévennes. The wide open contours are punctuated with villages of character from the Lot to the Tarn gorges.

The Dordogne

The Dordogne is one of the great hands-on holiday destinations in which people can hike, cycle, go on horseback or reach by car to stroll around châteaux and historic villages and sites of interest. Some take to the water, hiring canoes or kayaks either by the hour or for long-distance trips, or taking a more leisurely cruise by trip boat.

Until the late 18th century what we know as the Dordogne was called Périgord. In 1790 the French *départements* were formed, most taking the name of the most important river in the *département*. Geographically the *département* divides conveniently into four areas with the chief town, Périgueux, more or less in the middle. These areas are called Périgord Vert, Blanc, Noir and Pourpre (Green, White, Black and Purple).

Périgord Vert is the wide crescent in the north, crossed by the Dronne, Bandiat and Auvézère rivers, with lush valleys, woodlands and streams much loved by landscape painters. Périgord Blanc takes its name from the chalky limestone outcrops. Périgueux is here, and the village of Sorges, known for its 'black gold' (the truffle) and its

Truffle Museum. The lower section of this area is shared by Périgord Noir to the east, dotted with châteaux and with the Vézère and Dordogne rivers following historic courses, and Périgord Pourpre to the west contains the scenic wine-growing area around Bergerac. Here the Dordogne grows wider.

The Midi-Pyrénées is one of France's most varied regions, ranging from warm limestone plateaux in the north to the snowy peaks 270km south in the Pyrenees. Rolling farmland dotted with dovecotes is a feature of the area, with medieval towns and *bastides* (fortified towns) in its crests and valleys. *Foie gras*, Armagnac and the 'black' Cahors wines are some of the products of the Midi-Pyrénées.

The Bordeaux wine-growing area of the Gironde sustains many tiny villages. The great metropolis, Bordeaux city, is at the heart of the *département*. An hour's drive east takes you to the lovely up-market seaside resort of Arcachon, a yachting base and fishing harbour, with oyster beds, pine woods and the biggest sand dune in Europe.

South of Arcachon is the Landes *département*, with another superlative – Europe's biggest forest. Much of Landes is a great natural park, providing an opportunity for wildlife watching, rambling, fishing and canoeing along remote streams.

Gascony, in the Landes, has one of the lowest populations in France. Most of it is farmland and it is known for the great quantities of garlic grown there. Geese, ducks and other poultry, marketed in various forms, contribute to the local economy. Being so dependent on the land, the farmers of the Gers are adept at sticking up for their rights and defending their way of life. Local government offices and politicians have often been at the receiving end of a trailer-load of dumped cow dung or a well-aimed egg.

The ever-popular city of Biarritz, with its many golf courses and world-class surfing, is in the southernmost part of the region, in the *département* of Pyrénées-Atlantique. People come here for therapeutic seawater treatments and, inland, on the borders of Landes and Pyrénées-Atlantiques, mud and hot springs provide the basis for curative spa treatments.

Tarn et Garonne

East of Gironde and south of Dordogne is the Tarn et Garonne *département*, bisected by the Garonne river. In spring much of the countryside explodes into massed white and pale pink blossom as the orchards of many varieties of fruit promise a good harvest to come. Montauban, the county town, with its lovely ancient bridge over the Tarn, draws visitors to its Ingres Museum. Paintings by Montauban-born painter Ingres and other artists with local connections are exhibited on five floors of a historic building in which the Black Prince had a room.

Moissac, with its abbey, cloisters and exquisitely carved south doorway from the 11th century, is worth a night or two's visit. The

Canal Latéral à la Garonne goes through the town, with attractive moorings, and the River Garonne, on which boat trips are available, is nearby.

A drive east in this *département* takes you to the Aveyron Gorges, providing exciting landscapes. Medieval villages cling to cliff sides. The Causse de Quercy overlooks the gorges, and the daring will enjoy the challenge of potholing, climbing and hang-gliding. Canoeing, cycling and horse riding are also popular pastimes here. One of the old villages in the vicinity is Bruniquel, hanging down the southern slopes of an 80m cliff overlooking the Aveyron and Vere rivers. This area has an interesting prehistoric site rich in cave dwellings and rock shelters. The 12th-century castle sitting at the top of the cliff has been a classified Historic Monument since 1840.

Throughout the Southwest, towns and villages present a cheerful aspect of stone buildings with red crinkly-tiled roofs. Narrow side-streets and alleys paved in brick, with central runnels or gutters, reflect medieval charm.

The beginnings

Archaeologists and cave explorers have produced evidence that there were human beings in Southwest France as far back as 450,000 years ago. The earliest known settlers, *Homo erectus*, shaped pebbles of quartz, flint, jasper and other minerals into chopping and scraping tools. Neanderthal man, who appeared on the scene around 200,000 BC, had learned how to make and use fire.

The caves of the Dordogne and Lot valleys – sites such as Lascaux and Pech Merle – especially reveal how Cro-Magnon man, who replaced the Neanderthals in about 35,000 BC, soon learned to produce sophisticated works of art. Findings in the village of les Eyzies-de-Tayac, in the Vézère Valley, indicate continuous habitation of the caves there from the Stone Age to the 1950s.

No one knows for certain whether the paintings and etchings created on the walls of the caves were ceremonial, linguistic or purely artistic – but there is no questioning the skill and dynamism of the work.

The Romans

Aquitaine was conquered by Julius Caesar's forces in 56 BC, though not without a struggle. The inhabitants of today's Périgord and Quercy put up a ferocious fight, but their neighbours to the south, around the Tarn and Aveyron rivers, were more acquiescent and at last the region fell to the Roman raiders. Under the new rulers, however, trade flourished, and Cahors and Périgueux became very prosperous.

Visigoths and Franks

The good life under the Romans was shaken during the 3rd century AD by successive raids by Germanic tribes from the north and the Visigoths swept through Southwest France on their way to Spain. As

Above
Statue of a Neanderthal man,
Les Eyzies-de-Tayac

the Roman Empire crumbled, the Visigoths were able to establish a semi-Romanised kingdom, continuing the Latin culture and Roman law in the 5th century. Their rule did not last long. In 507 Clovis, king of the Franks, defeated the Visigoths in the Battle of Vouillé and took control of much of the Southwest. But there was further instability as Saracens invaded from the east and a succession of wars broke out among Clovis's successors.

Emperor Charlemagne
By the time he was crowned Holy Roman Emperor in 800, Charlemagne had already created the Kingdom of Aquitaine and he soon brought a fragmented France together, maintaining control by placing his most trusty supporters in positions of power. The counts of Toulouse and the dukes of Aquitaine emerged during this time as powerful barons.

Charlemagne's rule over Southwest France was soon to fail, destabilised by Viking raiders, who rampaged through the Dordogne and Isle valleys, and the increasing power of the barons. By the year 1000, the Count of Toulouse ruled over most of Quercy, while a smaller consortium of barons, including the Count of Périgord, were at least nominally part of Aquitaine.

Eleanor of Aquitaine
In 1137 Eleanor, only daughter of William of Aquitaine, married Louis, the Dauphin of France. She was aged 15 and her marriage took with it a dowry, which included the duchies of Aquitaine, Gascony and Périgord. Within a year her husband was crowned Louis VII, but theirs was not to be a lasting romance. In 1152 the marriage was annulled on grounds of consanguinity, and Eleanor retained all the lands in her dowry. In the same year Eleanor, a wily and powerful woman, married Henry Plantagenet, Duke of Normandy and Anjou, and between them the couple ruled over land extending from the English Channel to the Pyrenees, a territory as vast as that of the French crown's. Relations between France and England began to be

Right
La Roque-Gageac

strained and when Henry was crowned Henry II of England in 1154 the delicate thread holding the two countries together snapped, resulting in a struggle that was to continue off and on for the next three centuries.

Eleanor could not resist plotting. After separating from Henry she set up court in Poitiers and began a series of intrigues. When she encouraged her son Richard the Lionheart in the fight against his father, Henry had her imprisoned in London and she was not released until 15 years later – in 1189 – when her husband died.

The Hundred Years' War

Under the Treaty of Paris of 1259 the Plantagenets agreed to pay homage to the French king for their lands in Aquitaine, and in the following years *bastides* (fortified towns) were established as the French and English marked out their newly agreed territories. But there were too many complications for the fragile treaty, and Aquitaine changed hands repeatedly.

Edward III, who was crowned king of England in 1327, had a strong claim to the French throne because he was a grandson on his mother's side of Philip IV of France. In 1340 Edward put forward his claim and formally styled himself king of France. The stage was set for the Hundred Years' War.

The war started in 1345 in Brittany and Normandy and ended in 1453 when the English were defeated at the Battle of Castillon in the Dordogne Valley. The intervening 108 years saw much bloodshed and plunder and towns and territories changed hands repeatedly. Aquitaine, and especially the Dordogne, saw much violence.

The Wars of Religion

The next serious outbreak of violence came in 1562 with the outbreak of the Wars of Religion – a series of bloody conflicts that was to last for 37 years. It all came about as a result of the spread of Lutheran and Calvinist doctrines and by the middle of the 16th centuries Southwest France was split. Cahors and Périgueux were Catholic, while much of the old lands of the Count of Toulouse, including Montauban and Toulouse, were Protestant. Périgueux was taken by the Protestants in 1575. Cahors fell in 1578 after a siege that lasted three days.

As strife raked back and forth across the land, the old castles and fortified churches that had given the people some protection during the Hundred Years' War were brought into use again, but as before it was the villages and smallest towns that suffered most.

Peace came in 1598 when Henri IV proclaimed freedom of worship under the Edict of Nantes. There was more religious trouble in 1685 when Louis XIV revoked the Edict of Nantes, provoking a period of armed unrest and savage retribution. In the Protestant towns of Montauban and Bergerac hundreds of skilled workers were forced into exile.

The Revolution

By the 18th century France was firmly in the grip of a system that divided the country into three 'estates'. The first estate consisted of the monarchy and nobility, the second was the clergy and the third the rest – the middle classes and peasants. The first two estates paid no taxes, the third, especially the peasants, funded the excesses of what was seen as an arrogant and corrupt regime.

In rural Southwest France the Revolution was very much a peasants' revolt, but Bordeaux also played a major part, with the 'Girondin faction' actively seeking the setting up of a Federalist government. But their ideas were seen as effete and they were persecuted by more radical rivals. Two of their number hid in caves near St-Emilion but were found and executed.

The 20th century

The dawn of the 20th century saw the region's population diminishing rapidly. There were a number of reasons for the decline, but the main factors were the tiny landholdings, which made farming uneconomic, and job prospects in the expanding cities. In addition, World War I took a terrible toll of young men.

Following the capitulation of France in 1940, soon after the start of World War II, German troops marched into Bordeaux, but much of the rest of Southwest France remained unoccupied until 1942. Throughout the war the French Resistance was very active in the region, especially where forests and rugged countryside provided the ideal terrain for guerrilla warfare. The partisans' actions were a serious thorn in the Germans' side and there were terrible reprisals. The story

Architectural glossary

Apse – vaulted semicircular recess at east end of church.

Capital – decorated top of column.

Chancel – part of a church containing the main altar, choir and sanctuary.

Chevêt – highly ornamented east end of a French church.

Corbel – supporting piece of stone or timber used for carrying a beam, often decorated.

Crenellation – square indentation on battlement.

Dormer – brick or stone structure with gabled window projecting from sloping roof.

Flamboyant Gothic – elaborate style of church architecture, common in 15th-century France.

Flying buttress – brick or stone support for outside wall of building.

Gable – triangular section of wall between sloping ends of pitched roof.

Keep – main tower within the walls of a medieval castle.

Machicolation – opening in parapet through which missiles could be hurled.

of courageous men and women of the French Resistance is told in a number of museums throughout the region.

Heritage roads

Pilgrims have been flocking to Santiago de Compostela in northwestern Spain since the 9th century when the tomb of St James the Great, the first Apostle to be martyred, was rediscovered. St James – San Tiago in Spanish, St-Jacques in French – was beheaded in Jerusalem in AD 91 and his remains taken to Spain. Following the rediscovery of the tomb, a church was built nearby and soon people from all parts of Europe began flocking to the site, following specific routes, resting in hostels and visiting holy places along the way.

Those making the pilgrimage were easily identified. They wore a heavy grey cape and broad-brimmed hat, carried a long stave and used a scallop shell as a badge. Hostels and shrines along the roads often had the shape of a scallop shell carved above the main entrance. The shells are known to this day in France as *Coquille St-Jacques*.

Today, many people still follow in their footsteps and the 'Roads to Compostela' have been granted international heritage status by UNESCO, along with such wonders as the Great Wall of China and the Pyramids of Egypt. In Aquitaine, where many of the roads from around Europe converge, 16 sites have been listed as outstanding evidence of the pilgrims' paths.

The major site in the Dordogne is the ancient Cathédrale St-Front, in Périgueux. Some parts of the building date from before AD 1000.

The Gironde has three sites. At Bazas, 50km south of Bordeaux, the 13th-century cathedral is listed with the adjacent pilgrims' hospice. At Entre Deux Mers, 25km east of Bordeaux, are the considerable remains of the Abbey of Sauve-Majeure, built in the 11th century and in medieval times the seat of ecclesiastical authority over a vast area extending into Northern Spain. Some of the pillars from the abbey are exhibited in the Cloisters Museum in New York City.

At Soulac-sur-Mer, on the northern Côte d'Argent, Eglise Notre-Dame-de-la-Fin-Terres was built in the 12th century to replace an oratory where pilgrims gathered. Soulac was the start of what became known as 'the English route' because this was where many pilgrims from England landed to begin the European mainland stage of their journey.

Three of the heritage sites are in Bordeaux. The Basilica St-Seurin, an outstanding building, has parts dating from the 4th century. The Basilica St-Michel is an impressive monument in one of the city's oldest districts. The Cathédrale St-André dates from the 11th century, and was the scene of the marriage of Eleanor of Aquitaine to Henry Plantagenet.

Among the listed sites in the Landes are the Eglise Ste-Quitterie in Aire-sur-l'Adour, 30km southeast of Mont-de-Marsan, and the 10th-century abbey at St-Sever, 15km south of Mont-de-Marsan.

Architectural glossary (cont ...)

Pepperpot – conical roof common on castle towers in 15th-century France.

Retable – ornamental screen behind altar, usually decorated with paintings or religious carvings.

Romanesque – architectural style of 9th to 12th centuries featuring rounded arches, thick masonry walls and massive, rounded columns.

Rood screen – decorated wood or stone partition at the entrance to the chancel.

Transept – arms of cross-shaped church set at right angles to the nave.

Vault – arch forming roof or ceiling.

In Agen, the Cathédrale St-Caprais was built on the site of a 6th-century basilica.

The Cathédrale Ste-Marie in Bayonne, not far from the Spanish border, once welcomed many pilgrims and today is one of the city's major attractions.

Writers

The literary heritage of Southwest France stems from the 12th century when wandering troubadours (part musician, part poet, part jester) began travelling from court to court to entertain the nobility with music, songs and poems about love and war. Among the most famous of them were Bertrand de Gourdon, Almeric de Sarlat, Arnaut de Ribérac and Dormunda de Cahors, the latter being the only female troubadour to have established a niche in posterity.

With the establishment of new universities after the Hundred Years' War, intellectual activity flourished and the opening of printing houses in Bergerac, Cahors and Périgueux in the early 16th century provided wider scope for writers. Clément Marot (1496–1544) of Cahors composed epigrams and sonnets and became one of the great Renaissance poets. Etienne de la Boëtie (1530–63) from Sarlat (author of *Discourse on Voluntary Subjection and Against One*), Pierre de Bourdeille (the chronicler who wrote under the name of Brantôme), and Jean Tarde (a historian from la Roque-Gageac), became famous names in the 16th and 17th centuries. François de Salignac de Lamothe-Fénelon, author of *Télémaque*, was born near Carlux in the Dordogne Valley in 1651.

More recent writers from the region have included Eugène le Roy (1836–1907), author of the Périgord classic *Jacquou le Croquant*, and, of course, Françoise Sagan, famous for *Bonjour Tristesse*, whose birthplace is Cajarc on the River Lot.

Dominique Ingres

Said to be one of the finest draughtsman in the history of painting, Jean-Auguste-Dominique Ingres (1780–1867) was born in Montauban and studied in Paris with the famous neo-classical artist Jacques-Louis David for four years. Between 1806 and 1824 he studied and worked in Italy and he first won acclaim in 1824 when his altarpiece *The Vow of Louis XIII* was exhibited in Paris.

Although he is identified with neo-classicism, Ingres painted in a variety of styles. His famous painting, *The Dream of Ossian*, was created in the romantic style and several of his works reflect the influence of the Italian Renaissance artist Raphael, one of his favourite painters.

Ingres painted many historical, mythological and religious subjects, but is probably best known for his portraits and female nudes. A collection of his paintings and drawings is exhibited in the Musée Ingres in Montauban (*see pages 202–11*).

Touring itineraries

Wine

Days 1–2: **Bordeaux and the Médoc** – spend a day in Bordeaux (*see pages 42–53*), with a tasting at La Maison du Vin, shop window-gazing at places such as La Vinothèque, where they sell more than 200 Bordeaux wines, and a visit to Vinorama to learn some wine history; then take a day's tour of the Médoc and its famous châteaux (*see page 54*).

Days 3–4: **St-Emilion** – walk the hillside town's lovely streets, visit the church carved out of solid rock and take a tour of surrounding vineyards (*see page 60*).

Day 5: **Bergerac** – an interesting city, with interesting wines – red and white – produced in the area (*see pages 66–8*).

Days 6–7: **Cahors** – Lots to see and do here – and a 'black' wine to sample (*see pages 182–91*).

Family

Days 1–2: **Arcachon** – climb the dunes, visit the four 'seasonal' resorts, eat the oysters (*see pages 262–71*).

Days 2–3: **Mimizan-Plage** – more sun, sand and sea – plus a chance to visit the Ecomusée de la Grande Lande (*see page 234*).

Day 4: **Hossegor** – ride the surf that draws the champions or enjoy a more relaxing time on the beaches of the nearby lake (*see page 256*).

Day 5: **Bayonne** – try the ham, take a trip on the River Ardour, tour the old town (*see page 247*).

Days 6–7: **Biarritz** – bask in the Basque sunshine, have a casino flutter and enjoy yourself in the region's most fashionable resort (*see pages 242–5*).

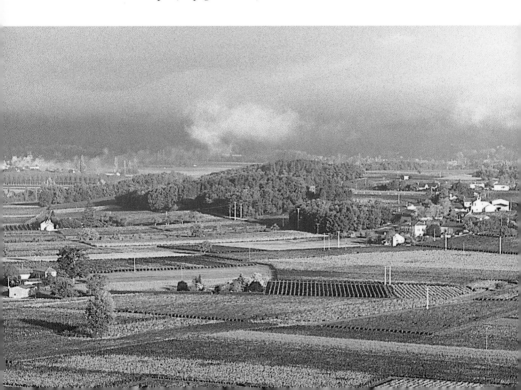

Castles and caves

Day 1: **Bergerac** – visit the châteaux of Lanquais and Monbazillac, where you can also try the wine (*see pages 71–2*).

Day 2: **St-Cyprien** – ideally placed for visits to Josephine Baker's les Milandes château, Castelnaud and the pretty village of Beynac-et-Cazenac (*see pages 69–70*).

Day 3: **Sarlat-la-Canéda** – châteaux galore and the Dordogne river are within easy reach of this lively town (*see pages 132–5*).

Days 4–5: **Les Eyzies-de-Tayac** – so much to see around this attractive village, including the Musée National de la Préhistoire and troglodyte caves (*see pages 120–3*).

Days 6–7: **Montignac** – leave plenty of time to visit Lascaux II, the ultimate painted cave experience (*see page 123*).

Top 10

Bergerac – lovely riverside town with an attractive medieval quarter (*see pages 66–8*).

Ecomusée de la Grande Lande – extensive open-air folk museum (*see page 234*).

Les Eyzies-de-Tayac – a cliff on one side, a river on the other (*see pages 120–3*).

Lascaux II – a superb reproduction of the most famous painted cave in France (*see page 123*).

Moissac – stunning cloisters, nearly 1000 years old (*see pages 212–21*).

Musée de Plain Air de Quercy – entertaining and informative open-air museum (*see page 167*).

Pont Valentré – remarkable 14th-century bridge (*see page 187*).

Rocamadour – the famed pilgrimage centre (*see pages 157–8*).

St-Cirq-Lapopie – a fairy-tale village hanging steeply over the River Lot (*see pages 168–9*).

St-Emilion – charming hillside town of narrow twisting streets (*see page 60*).

Below
Cahors vineyards

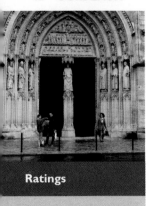

Bordeaux

Ratings

Architecture   ● ● ● ● ●

Museums   ● ● ● ● ●

Art   ● ● ● ● ○

Food
and drink   ● ● ● ● ○

Restaurants   ● ● ● ● ○

Shopping   ● ● ● ● ○

Entertainment
● ● ● ○ ○

Historical
sights   ● ● ● ○ ○

Bordeaux wears its history with pride. It was known as Burdigala before the Romans came and has played a major part in European, especially Anglo-French, politics and trade for more than a thousand years. Eleanor of Aquitaine and Henry Plantagenet, England's King Henry II, were married here, and from here the Black Prince set forth on his missions of terror. The city's wine industry has flourished since Roman times and the Plantagenets' penchant for 'claret', as they called the region's red wine, cemented a special relationship between the city and English consumers which has flourished over the centuries. Today, Britain is the leading customer for Bordeaux's wines. France's eighth-largest city, Bordeaux is an architectural treasure house, with whole streets standing as monuments to its lively past. But it is also a modern city with high-tech industries that keep its mind very much on the future.

ⓘ Town Centre *12 cours du XXX Juillet; tel: 05 56 00 66 00; fax: 05 56 00 6601; e-mail: otb@bordeaux-tourisme.com; www.bordeaux-tourisme.com. Open daily, all year. Closing times vary according to season. Information office also at Bordeaux St-Jean railway station, tel: 05 56 91 64 70.*

Getting there and getting around

Arriving and departing

The Bordeaux-Mérignac International Airport (*tel: 05 56 34 50 50; e-mail: info@bordeaux.aeroport.fr*) is 12km out of town. A shuttle bus operates to the city centre and the railway station.

Bordeaux has good road links in all directions. From the north the A10 brings traffic from Paris, Orléans, Tours and Poitiers. From the southeast, the A62 and A61 form the Autoroute des Deux Mers, linking the Mediterranean with the Atlantic. The A63 is the main link from Northwest Spain, Biarritz and Bayonne. (*Information and tolls www.asf.fr (Autoroutes du Sud de la France).*)

Trains run from the Gare Bordeaux-St-Jean, r. Charles Domercq.

Palais Gallien

Rue Émile Fourcand

Museum d'Histoire
Naturelle

Rue Docteur Albert-Barraud

Rue Turenne

Rue de l'Abbé de l'Épée

Rue St Fort

Rue Thiac

Seurin

Rue de Lurbe

Rue Castéja

Rue Rolland

Place des
artyrs de la
Résistance

Rue Judaïque

Rue du Palais Gallien

Rue Fondaudège

Rue Huguerie

Rue Cours G. Clémenceau

Place
de Tourny

Jardin
Public

Place du
Champs de Mars

Cours de Verdun

Cours du Mal Foch

Allées de Los Angeles

Allées de Tourny

Cours du XXX Juillet

Musée des
Chartrons

Rue Ferrère

Rue Foy

Croiseur
Colbert

Musée d'Art
Contemporain

Allées de Chartres

Allées de Bristol

Quai Louis XVIII

Allées de Munich

Allées d'Orléans

La Garonne

Maison
du Vin

Casa de
Goya

Église
Notre
Dame

Place et Marché
des Grands Hommes

Cours de l'Intendance

Place de la
Comédie

Le Grand
Théâtre

Rue Esprit des Lois

Cours du Chapeau Rouge

Place
Gambetta

Bonnac

Rue du Château d'Eau

Rue Ste-Sernin

Rue du Dr N Penard

Rue de la Porte Dijeaux

Rue Vital Carles

Rue de la Porte Grassi

Rue St Rémy

Rue d'Piliers de Tutelle

Place du
Parlement
Ste-Catherine

Place de
la Bourse

Quai de la Douane

Galerie des
Beaux-Arts

de-Bonnier

Musée des
Beaux-Arts

Musée des
Arts Décoratifs

Salle de Conférences
de l'Athénée Municipal

Centre National
Jean-Moulin

Musée National
des Douanes

St-Pierre

Rue du Pas St Georges

Rue des Bahutiers

Porte Cailhau

Quai Richelieu

Fleuret

Cathédrale
St-André

Rue des Frères Bonie

Rue de Loup

Cours d'Alsace Lorraine

Rue Ste-

Maréchal Juin

Rue Lecocq

Rue Servandoni

Cours d'Albret

Palais de
Justice

Place de la
République

Rue du Mal Joffre

Rue du Hâ

Rue du Cdt Arnould

R. D Duberger

Rue du Hâ

Rue de Cursol

Musée
d'Aquitaine

Cours Victor Hugo

Rue Sainte Catherine

Palais
des Sports

Grosse
Cloche

Rue St-James

Rue Buhan

Salinières

Cours Victor Hugo

0 ———— 250m

0 ———— 250 yards

Getting around

You can enjoy guided tours of the city on foot, bicycle, horse-drawn
carriage, vintage bus, tour coach, river boat, taxi, limousine and
helicopter: details of these are available from the tourist offices.

There are about 20 car parks in the city centre. The largest are at pl. de
Tourny, the Mériadeck Shopping Centre on r. Claude Bonnier and

Cité Mondiale, quai de Chartrons, but local drivers seem to prefer parking wherever they're not supposed to – even on the pavement. Best thing for visitors is to leave the car at the hotel, if possible.

CFGTE operates bus services within the city (*tel: 05 57 57 88 88*). The nearest terminus to the tourist office is pl. Jean Jaurès. One- and three-day bus passes are available. Out-of-town routes are covered by Transgironde (*tel: 05 56 43 68 43*); the nearest terminus to the tourist office is allées de Chartres.

There are 24-hour taxi ranks at r. Esprits des Lois (*tel: 05 56 81 99 15*), and cours G. Clémenceau (*tel: 05 56 81 99 05*). Both are close to the tourist office.

The Gare St-Jean, r. Charles Domercq (*tel: 05 56 91 64 70*) is open daily 0430–0000. The free Carte Bordeaux Découverte allows entry to museums, monuments and other places of interest at discount prices.

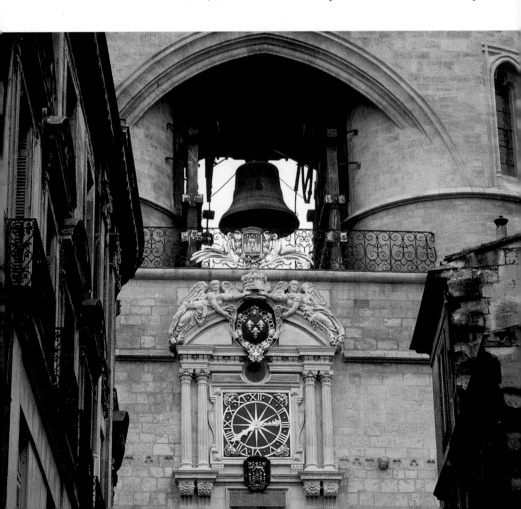

Must-see sights

Bordeaux is a fascinating city full of interesting streets and squares and historic buildings and sites. Here are some of the must-see locations.

Cours du Chapeau-Rouge: Running from Place de la Comédie to the river front, this wide elegant street owes its name to a tavern that stood here in the 15th century. In the 1600s it was a fashionable residential area.

Cours de l'Intendance: A continuation of cours du Chapeau-Rouge, travelling away from the river, this is the city's gold card shopping street – the place for high-fashion clothes and very expensive accessories.

Esplanade des Quinconces: Open space on a grand scale (when it isn't overrun by fairground rides and stalls selling *crêpes* and sticky sweetstuffs), the 12-hectare esplanade was laid out in the early 19th century. Its focal point is the massive Monument aux Girondins, 50m high, 65m long and 44m wide, a cornucopia of allegory with the Spirit of Liberty breaking free from the chains of oppression on top of a column surrounded by gushing fountains filled with statues. It honours the Bordeaux *députés* who went to the guillotine during the Revolution. There are also huge statues of the writers Montaigne and Montesquieu. At the riverside end of the esplanade two monuments in the shape of ships' figureheads symbolise Commerce and Navigation.

Jardin Public: Created in 1746 to link the suburbs of St-Seurin and Chartrons, the 10-hectare gardens were laid out in the English style in 1856 by the landscape artists Fisher and Escarpit. A collection of some 3000 plant species is housed in the Botanical Garden.

Place de la Bourse: This magnificent square flanked by the Garonne is the former Place Royale, designed by the architects Jacques and Jacques-Ange Gabriel and constructed 1731–55. The Stock Exchange, which gives it its present name, stands on the north side of the square, facing the former Hôtel des Fermes, the Customs Hall, which now houses the Musée des Douanes. The Fountain of the Three Graces was erected in place of a statue of Louis XV, which was removed during the Revolution.

Place Gambetta: Completed in 1747, when it was known as Place Dauphine, the square has a collection of pleasing façades surrounding an English-style garden that was the site of the guillotine during the Revolution.

Porte Cailhau: €€ (*pl. du Palais: tel: 05 56 00 60 00. Open Jul–Aug daily 1400–1800*) Standing at the river end of Place du Palais, this splendid tower, with its coned roofs and parapets, was completed in 1496 as one of the city's main gates. It was used as the entrance for visiting royalty. The history of Bordeaux is traced in exhibits on three floors inside the tower.

Porte du Grosse Cloche: The 15th-century gate, built on the site of one dating from the 13th century, has become an unofficial emblem of the city, thanks to the huge bell hanging in an arch beneath the tower's conical roofs. The bell was cast in 1775 and the clock underneath it was made in 1772. Another clock inside the building dates from 1592.

Sights

Cathédrale St-André *pl. Pey Berland; tel: 05 56 52 68 10. Open daily. Guided tours Wed 0730–1130 and 1400–1800; for information tel: 05 56 87 17 18.*

Centre National Jean-Moulin *pl. Jean Moulin; tel: 05 56 79 66 00; e-mail: cnjm@mairie-bordeaux.fr. Open Tue–Fri 1100–1800 and Sat–Sun 1400–1800. Closed Mon and public holidays. Free entry.*

Croiseur Colbert €€ *Port de la Lune, Quai des Chartrons; tel: 05 56 44 96 11; e-mail: colbert@mairie-bordeaux.fr; http://colbert.croiseur.free.fr. Open Apr, May, Sept daily 1000–1800; Jun 1000–1900 daily; Jul, Aug 1000–2000. Guided tour Sat 1430 (2hours 30min). Admission €7.50. Free entry on your birthday.*

Eglise Notre Dame *pl. du Chapelet; no tel. Open Mon 1430–1800, Tue–Sun 0800–1200 and 1430–1800.*

Le Grand Théâtre €€ *pl. de la Comédie; tel: 05 56 00 66 09. Guided tours all year, subject to rehearsals. Advance booking essential – contact tourist office.*

Musée d'Aquitaine €€ *20 cours Pasteur; tel: 05 56 01 51 00; e-mail: musaq@mairie-bordeaux.fr. Open daily 1100–1800. Closed Mon and public holidays. Free entry first Sun of the month.*

Cathédrale St-André**

A smidgin smaller than the Cathédrale Notre-Dame in Paris, the major and most imposing religious building in Bordeaux took more than 400 years to build – from the 11th to the 15th centuries. The many buttresses and flying buttresses were added to stave off imminent collapses during the years of construction. The Port Royale entrance, dating from the 13th century, is adorned with remarkable sculptures, including the Gothic *Last Judgement* on the tympanum.

Centre National Jean-Moulin**

Named in honour of the most famous of the French Resistance heroes, who was captured by the Gestapo, tortured and executed in 1943, the museum is devoted to World War II, the Resistance movement and the activities of the Free French Forces. Among the three floors of displays of illicit radio equipment, underground newspapers and photographs is a reconstruction of Jean Moulin's hidden office.

Croiseur Colbert**

Launched in 1959, the *Colbert* is to Bordeaux what HMS *Belfast* is to London. Designed as an anti-aircraft warship, the cruiser was converted into a missile-launcher. Among her more newsworthy missions were the rescue of Agadir earthquake missions in 1960 and Général de Gaulle's trips to South America (1964) and Quebec (1967). The Admiral's cabin, officers' and ratings' quarters, weapons and engine rooms and other parts of the ship are open to visitors.

Eglise Notre Dame*

Completed in 1707, the church has a wealth of stonework both outside and in. Its baroque-style exterior is decorated with a frieze of leaves, and carved ornamentation covers other surfaces. The interior contains barrel-and-groin vaulting, and elegant balconies flank the organ loft.

Le Grand Théâtre*

The name says it all. This imposing building, adorned with Corinthian columns and statues representing the Muses and goddesses, was completed in 1780 and echoes the high regard for culture in 18th-century France. The interior is superbly overblown, with lots of marble, carved wood, gilt and more statues. The auditorium has a magnificent frescoed ceiling from which hangs a huge chandelier with 14,000 glittering crystals.

Musée d'Aquitaine***

This excellently planned museum gives a very clear insight into the region's history from humankind's very beginnings. Exhibits range from Stone Age relics, through tools and jewellery from the Bronze

Musée d'Art Contemporain €€
Entrepôt 7 r. Ferrère; tel: 05 56 00 81 50; e-mail: capc@mairie-bordeaux.fr. Open 1100–1800 (2000 on Wed). Closed Mon, 25 Dec, 1 Jan, 1 May. Free entry first Sun of the month.

Musée des Arts Décoratifs €€ 39 r. Bouffard; tel: 05 56 00 72 53; e-mail: musad@mairie-bordeaux.fr. Open 1100–1800. Closed Tue and public holidays. Free entry first Sun of the month.

Musée des Beaux-Arts €€ Jardin de la Mairie, 20 cours d'Albret; tel: 05 56 10 20 56; www.culture.fr/culture/borde aux; e-mail: musbxa@mairie-bordeaux.fr. Open 1100–1800. Closed Tue and public holidays. Free entry first Sun of the month.

and Iron Ages, Roman coins and glassware and early Christian religious artefacts to sections on Bordeaux in the 18th and 19th centuries.

Musée d'Art Contemporain**

The museum is imaginatively housed in a converted early 19th-century quayside warehouse, which was rescued from demolition in the 1980s. It serves as a home for all forms of modern art and has a bookshop, library, restaurant and café.

Musée des Arts Décoratifs**

Collections of furniture, ceramics, glassware, gold plate and wrought ironwork are housed in a fine Louis XVI-style mansion designed for the Marquis de Lalande by the Bordeaux architect Etienne Laclotte in 1779. Examples of furniture, locksmithery, weapons, china and miniature paintings on ivory and paper are displayed in the lofts. There is also a restaurant and a tearoom.

Musée des Beaux-Arts***

Created in 1801, the Fine Arts Museum houses the tenth largest collection of paintings in France as well as drawings and sculptures. Among the most prestigious works on show are Titian's *Tarquin and Lucretia*, Brueghel's *Wedding Dance, Greece Expiring on the Ruins of Missolonghi* by Delacroix, *Martyrdom of St George* and *Jupiter Carrying Away Gannymede* by Rubens, and Ter Brugghen's *The Lute Player*. Three major Bordeaux painters are also represented: André Lothe, Albert Marquet and Odilon Redon.

Musée national des Douanes*

The clearance warehouse of the old royal customs hall is an appropriate setting for this museum, which tells the story of the French Customs Department through the ages. Documents, uniforms, weapons, models and equipment – including the latest computer technology – are displayed. A special section shows how aspects of the service have been portrayed in different media: film, literature, comic strips – and in Claude Monet's painting *The Customs Inspectors' Hut*.

Museum d'Histoire Naturelle**

A wide range of specimens from the flora, fauna, minerals and fossils of the world's continents and oceans illustrates the evolution of planet Earth. There are temporary exhibitions on a wide range of themes.

Musée des Vins*

The history of the maritime wine trade is outlined in the home of an early 18th-century Irish wine merchant. Among the collections on show are lithographed wine labels from the mid-19th century and wine bottles dating from the 17th century.

Vinorama de Bordeaux**

The history of Bordeaux wine from Gallo-Roman times to the present day is told by 75 costumed wax figures and a commentary in French, English, German and Japanese. The tour ends with a wine tasting.

Accommodation and food

Chateau de Lantic €€ *10 route de Lartigue, Martillac; tel: 05 56 72 58 68; e-mail: contact@chateau-de-lantic.com; www.chateau-de-lantic.com. Open all year.* Rooms in a restored 18th-century manor house in a village south of Bordeaux, off the A62 autoroute.

Hotel d'Aquitaine €€ *111 cours d'Albret; tel: 05 56 93 19 60.* Handy for the Musée des Beaux Arts, Cathédrale St-André and the main shopping streets, the hotel has 16 rooms with en suite facilities. No restaurant but breakfast is available.

Hotel Bristol €€ *pl. Gambetta; tel: 05 56 81 85 01.* Right in the thick of things, with 19 en suite rooms. No restaurant; breakfast available.

Hotel Burdigala €€€ *115 r. Georges Bonnac; tel: 05 56 90 16 16.* Quietly situated, yet within walking distance of pl. Gambetta and major attractions, the four-star establishment has 83 en suite rooms with television and telephones, garage parking and a restaurant (€€€).

Hotel Clémenceau €€ *4 cours George Clémenceau; tel: 05 56 52 98 98.* Just off the pl. Gambetta with almost everything Bordeaux has to offer

---

Musée national des Douanes € *1 pl. de la Bourse; tel: 05 56 48 82 82; e-mail: mnd.web@free.fr. Open daily 1000–1800, closed Mon and 25 Dec & 1 Jan.*

Museum d'Histoire Naturelle € *(free Wed) Hôtel de Lisleferme, Jardin Public; tel: 05 56 48 26 37; e-mail: museum@mairie-bordeaux.fr. Open 1100–1800 (1400–1800 Sat and Sun). Closed Tue and public holidays. Also free entry the first Sun of the month.*

Musée des Vins €€ *41 r. Borie; tel: 05 56 87 50 60; e-mail: info@musee-des-vins.com; www.musee-des-vins.com. Open Mon–Sat 1030–1730, first Sun of the month 1100–1700. Closed Sun, Mon and public holidays. Guided visits for groups.*

Vinorama de Bordeaux €€ *12 cours du Médoc; tel: 05 56 39 39 20. Open Tue–Sat 1030–1230 and 1430–1830 (Sun pm only). Closed Sun from Oct to May. Visit includes a tasting.*

Musée d'Aquitaine €€ *20 cours Pasteur, Bordeaux; tel: 05 56 01 51 00; e-mail dmb@mairie-bordeaux.fr. Open 1100–1800 daily. Closed Mon and public holidays. Free entry first Sun of the month and all year for students.*

Opposite
The Cathédrale St-André

The city's main shopping street – where you can buy almost anything you're likely to need – is r. Ste-Catherine, running through the heart of the old quarter from pl. de la Victoire to pl. de la Comédie, a distance of about 2km. The department stores Galeries Lafayette and Galeries Bordelaises are a few moments' walk from pl. de la Comédie. Another major shopping centre is in r. Claude Bonnier in the Mériadeck district. Traditional street markets are held on Sat in pl. Canteloup and pl. Maynard. Pl. St-Pierre is the scene of a market for organic produce on Thur and there's a flea market Sun–Fri in pl. Canteloup.

near at hand. Each of the 44 rooms has en suite facilities. No restaurant, but breakfast available.

Hotel La Méridienne €€ *153 r. Georges Bonnac; tel: 05 56 24 08 88.* In a quiet part of the Mériadeck district, this modern hotel has 40 rooms, half with air conditioning, and all with en suite facilities, TV and direct-dial telephones; there is also secure rooftop parking. No restaurant, but breakfast available.

Hotel de Normandie €€–€€€ *7 cours du XXX Juillet; tel: 05 56 52 16 80.* Close to the tourist office, with views over Esplanade des Quinconces and the River Garonne. 98 en suite rooms with TV and direct-dial telephones. No restaurant, but breakfast available.

Hotel des Quatre Soeurs €€–€€€ *6 cours du XXX Juillet; tel: 05 56 81 19 20. Closed two weeks Dec–Jan.* Similar location and facilities but cheaper and smaller than the Normandie, with 34 en suite rooms. No restaurant, but breakfast available.

Hotel de Sèze €€ *23 allées de Tourny; tel: 05 56 52 65 54.* As close to the centre of things as you could want. 24 en suite rooms. No restaurant, but breakfast available.

Baud et Millet €€ *19 r. Huguerie; tel: 05 56 79 05 77. Closed Sun.* Themed dinners are a speciality in this 80-seat air-conditioned restaurant, which boasts a stock of 200 different cheeses and a cellar of 950 bottles of wine from many parts of the world.

Le Bistrot des Quinconces €€ *4 pl. des Quinconces; tel: 05 56 52 84 56. Open daily 0730–0200. Closed 1 Jan.* Good food – including wonderful salmon and veal dishes – is served 18½ hours a day, 364 days a year in this centrally located bistro. Musical soirées are a feature.

Le Broceliande €€ *15 pl. des Martyrs-de-la-Résistance; tel: 05 56 96 38 93. Open Tue–Sun 1200–1415 and 1930–2230. Closed Sat lunchtime.* A good selection of wines is available by the glass. The chef's specialities include *escalope de foie gras* with apples and Calvados.

Café des Arts € *138 cours Victor Hugo and 184 r. Ste-Catherine; tel: 05 56 91 78 46. Open daily 0830–0200. Closed 25 Dec, 1 Jan.* Large and lively establishments serving simple but well-cooked dishes. Wine by the glass. Terrace dining available. Jazz concerts and traditional *chansons françaises* staged in the evenings.

Chez Brunet €€ *9 r. de Condé; tel: 05 56 51 35 50. Open Mon–Sat 1100–1430 and 1830–2230. Closed public holidays and weekends in Jul and Aug.* All types of oyster served every which way. Wines by the glass.

Chez Philippe €€–€€€ *1 pl. du Parlement; tel: 05 56 81 83 15. Open Tue–Sat 1200–1400 and 1930–2300. Closed 1 Jan, 1 May, the whole of Aug and 25 Dec.* In the pleasant heart of the city's old quarter, this is a

Above
The Esplanade des Quinconces

well-established and well-respected restaurant. Specialities include *fruits de mer* and grilled turbot. Wines by the glass.

L'Estaquade €€ *Quai des Queyries; tel: 05 57 54 02 50. Open daily 1200–1430 and 2000–2400.* Located on the east bank of the Garonne, in the city's La Bastide quarter, L'Estaquade is fairly new and deservedly fashionable, specialising in seafood dishes, especially those originating in Morocco and Mediterranean France.

La Tupiña €€–€€€ *6–8 r. Porte-de-la-Monnaie; tel: 05 56 91 56 37.* Authentic traditional cuisine, with the emphasis on specialities of the Southwest: The owner, Jean-Pierre Xiradakis, is probably Bordeaux's best-known chef.

Nightlife

Bordeaux is not one of the world's most swinging cities, but many late-night bars can be found around quai de Paludate, pl. de la Victoire and along r. des Pilliers de la Tutelle, off pl. de la Comédie. Many restaurants and bistros offer soirées of jazz, traditional *chansons* or –

mon Dieu! – karaoke. **L'Avant Scène** (*r. de la Borie; tel: 05 57 87 55 88*) is a simple bar where they dispense traditional jazz – and beer from a piano. For those with more highbrow tastes, there's a continuous programme of theatre, opera and classical concerts. Check the tourist office for the latest information.

Suggested walk

Total distance: About 4km, but because it's a circular route it can be shortened or terminated at any point.

Time: Allow 3 leisurely hours.

Route: Start at pl. de la Comédie, which is dominated by the colonnaded bulk of **LE GRAND THEATRE ❶**. Cross to **COURS DE L'INTENDANCE ❷** and within 150m turn right into Passage Sarget and follow it into pl. Chapelet. This gets its name from the bas-relief above the main entrance to **EGLISE NOTRE-DAME ❸**, which shows the Virgin handing a rosary (*chapelet*) to St Dominic.

After a tour of the church, retrace your steps to pl. de la Comédie and turn right into r. Ste-Catherine, a long pedestrianised street lined with shops large and small and with a warren of fascinating lanes and alleys leading from each side. This is the district known as Vieux Bordeaux.

Continue to cours d'Alsace et Lorraine, where a right turn leads to pl. Pey-Berland. Here, the Tour Pey-Berland, a 15th-century tower, stands apart from the main body of **CATHEDRALE ST-ANDRE ❹**, scene of the wedding in 1152 of Eleanor of Aquitaine and Henry Plantagenet, soon to become King Henry II of England. Opposite the tower, follow r. D. Dubergier into cours Pasteur and at the **MUSEE D'AQUITAINE ❺** bear left into cours Victor Hugo. Cross r. Ste-Catherine and opposite la **GROSSE CLOCHE ❻** take r. du Mirail, remarkable for its grand houses from the 17th and 18th centuries.

Next, turn left into r. St-Francois, which has a fine collection of 18th-century buildings. This leads to pl. Canteloup and **Basilique St-Michel ❼**. This impressive church took two centuries to complete from the start of construction in 1350, and has the second highest spire in France – a 15th-century structure 114m tall.

From the riverside end of the church, in pl. Duburg, follow r. de la Fusterie, where the Porte de Bourgogne, a triumphal archway built in 1755, stands on the site of a medieval city gate. Cross cours Victor Hugo and continue along r. de la Rousselle, where the family home of the 16th-century essayist Michel de Montaigne stands at Nos 23–25.

At the end of r. de la Rousselle, turn right and from r. Ausone cross cours d'Alsace et Lorraine into r. Chai des Farines, which leads into pl.

du Palais, where you can visit **PORTE CAILHAU** ❽. Follow r. des Agentiers, then r. du Parlement St-Pierre into pl. du Parlement, once a royal marketplace, now a pleasing cobblestoned square surrounded by Louis XV buildings. From here bear right along r. F. Philippart to **PL. DE LA BOURSE** ❾. Facing the river, turn left and a short walk along the quayside brings you to **COURS DU CHAPEAU-ROUGE** ❿. Another left turn here returns you to pl. de la Comédie.

Ratings

Cellar tours and tasting	●●●●●
Château vineyards	●●●●●
Architecture	●●●○
Food and drink	●●●●
Heritage	●●●●
Markets	●●●○
Scenery	●●●●
Walking	●●○○

Bordeaux vineyards

Even if your interest in wine has been restricted to its taste and its effect, a visit to Bordeaux, one of the great wine-growing regions of France, is almost sure to kindle a desire to learn more about one of nature's most delectable products. This is easy to arrange. Bordeaux has at least 5000 wine châteaux, many of which offer highly informative guided tours of their cellars, and a tasting. The Bordeaux region, in which the Garonne and Dordogne rivers flow, has up to 121,400 hectares of vineyards, with 57 appellations and six main families of Bordeaux wine. Villages of pale stone houses with crinkly-tiled red roofs punctuate the miles of farmland and the straight rows of vines. Visitors in winter and spring will see great spheres of mistletoe decorating leafless trees – sometimes half a dozen clumps of the parasite in one tree.

CHATEAU CORDEILLAN-BAGES✢

ⓘ **L'Ecole du Vin de Bordeaux €€€**
Château Cordeillan-Bages, Pauillac; tel: 05 56 59 24 24; e-mail: contact@cordeillanbages.com. Closed mid-Dec–Jan.

For tours and tasting information, contact **Conseil Inter-professionel des Vin de Bordeaux (CIVB)** *I cours du XXX Juillet, Bordeaux; tel: 05 56 00 22 66; e-mail: ecole@vins-bordeaux.fr*

How can a person interested in wine become a knowledgeable connoisseur in less than a week? The techniques and vocabulary used in tasting fine Bordeaux wines, the study of all aspects of wine production through visits to châteaux, vineyards and cellars, instruction from wine industry professionals and familiarisation with wine lists are achievements that can be acquired in a five-day residential course at a unique facility in Pauillac.

Professionals as well as amateurs sharpen their knowledge and experience at L'Ecole du Vin de Bordeaux, based at the Château Cordeillan-Bages, where most of the seminars and meals – perfect marriages of wine and food – are held. The course includes trips to a variety of cellars in the region, with tastings. In the cellar are 10,000 bottles of wine, some 75 years old.

Yellow rose

The yellow roses between the vine rows are not purely for decoration. Highly susceptible to vine diseases, the roses give early warning of any such problems affecting the vines.

Right
Look out for *dégustation* (wine-tasting) signs

CHATEAU LANESSAN❖❖

Château Lanessan
€€ *Domaines Boulaller, Cussac Fort-Médoc; tel: 05 56 58 94 80. Open all year. Visits daily 0900–1200 and 1400–1800.*

Guided tours of the grounds, gardens and the Dutch greenhouse are provided in this late 19th-century, Tudor-style château in the Médoc. An additional point of interest is the display of horse-drawn carriages from the early 1900s, tack room, stables and other items. The narration is in French and English.

CHATEAU LOUDENNE❖❖

Château Loudenne
€ St-Yzans-de-Médoc;
tel: 05 56 73 17 80; e-mail:
chateau-loudenne@
wanadoo.fr. Open daily all
year 0930–1230 and
1400–1730, by appointment
weekends and public
holidays.

Sloping gently down to the Gironde estuary is one of the vineyards that provides a useful initiation into the world of wine. An hour's tour culminates in a tasting. The 17th-century château is set in 120 hectares, of which 62 hectares are planted with vines – 48 hectares producing red wine and 14 producing white. The cellars were built by the Gilbey brothers in the 1870s.

Before the vines have grown to their full summer height, the visitor may experience the surreal sight of a ship apparently moving regally on a sea of vines: large commercial vessels cruise along the river estuary just beyond the vines.

The guided tour explains how the white wine grapes are mechanically stripped of stalks, pips and skin before fermentation. For red wine, pips and skin are needed to obtain tannin, so the whole berry is used. Average age of the vines at Château Loudenne is 25 to 30 years, the oldest being up to 60 years old.

Château Loudenne is one of the few châteaux in the Médoc producing white wine. It can be consumed young, but when aged its almond and honey flavours can be detected. Château Loudenne Red Cru Bourgeois wines are matured in the barrel for 15 months, then bottled and kept in the cellar for at least a year before being sold.

CHATEAU SMITH-HAUT-LAFITTE❖❖❖

**Château Smith-
Haut-Lafitte** €€
Martillac; tel: 05 57 83
11 22; e-mail:
smith-haut-lafitte@
smith-haut-lafitte.com;
www.smith-haut-lafitte.com.
Open daily by appointment
0900–1830. Visit to
cooperage. Free tasting.

In the Graves wine-growing region southeast of Bordeaux is the Château Smith-Haut-Lafitte estate, dating from the time of the Crusades – the fleur-de-lys features in its logo. It had become run down when, in 1990, it was bought by Daniel and Florence Cathiard (both of whom have skied for France), with its 18th-century château.

The property, in a beautiful tree-fringed setting with the Garonne river visible in the distance, devotes 44 hectares to red wines and 11 to white. By the mid-1990s the quality of the wine, which for years had ceased to be lauded by experts, had improved greatly and received rapturous attention.

In 1999 the estate was enhanced by the provision of a luxury hotel with 29 suites and rooms, and the introduction of a unique vinotherapy spa, a project of the Cathiards' daughter, Mathilde. Treatments include wine and honey wraps, barrel baths using micro-exploded chilled grapes, and Merlot wraps, using crushed grape pips, for anti-ageing.

In regenerating the vineyard, M. and Mme Cathiard got rid of the mechanised harvesting equipment and reverted to handpicking. They plough between the vine rows to clear weeds, enabling them to do without herbicides. They deliberately cut the yield, concentrating on quality rather than quantity. They installed a computerised weather station linked to sensors on the vines, monitoring humidity and weather conditions that could affect the vines, thus keeping spraying to a minimum. Also, they employed a cooper, an experienced craftsman following in his grandfather's footsteps, to produce 10 oak barrels a week.

The hotel has a restaurant and a brasserie serving lunch and dinner (*see Accommodation and food*).

PAUILLAC

ⓘ **Maison du Vins et du Tourisme du Médoc** *le Verrerie, Pauillac; tel: 05 56 59 03 08, offers a free video presentation on the local vineyard scene. Vineyard visits and tastings are organised mid-Jul–mid-Sept. Open daily 0930–1930; Sun and public holidays 1000–1800.*

A major centre of the wine trade in one of the Médoc's most prestigious wine-growing areas, Pauillac is on the Gironde river. It was once a busy port, with transatlantic steamers tying up at its quays. Today it attracts private yachts, cruisers and other pleasure craft. Famous châteaux (Premiere Grand Cru Classe) in the vicinity include Château Lafite-Rothschild (*tel: 05 56 59 26 83. Open for individual visits 1400 and 1530 with free guided tour and tasting by appointment with two weeks' notice. Closed public holidays and during grape harvest from Aug to end Oct*), Château Mouton-Rothschild and **Château Margaux**⁺. Free one-hour guides of the Château Margaux

Château Margaux
*Tel: 05 57 88 83 83;
e-mail: chateau-margaux@
chateau-margaux; www.
chateau-margaux.com/en.
Open for visits by
appointment only Mon–Fri.
Closed weekends, public
holidays, throughout Aug
and during the grape
harvest. Tasting reserved to
professionals. No direct sales.*

wine stores are available: book at least two weeks ahead. As well as the wine stores you will see various apparatus used in wine making and a collection of wine bottles from past ages.

Probably the most fascinating of these to visit from the tourist's point of view is the **Château Mouton-Rothschild✦✦€€** (*Pouyalet, Pauillac; tel: 05 56 73 21 29. Book two weeks ahead. Mon–Thur 0930–1100 and 1400–1600, Fri 0930–1100 and 1400–1500. Also weekends Jun–Oct. Open all year except 1 May and between Christmas and New Year*). Baron Philip de Rothschild, who died in 1988, was passionate about wine. He built his 'Great Cellar' in 1926 as a young man and went on to develop a museum of wine in art. The museum covers many centuries through paintings, tapestries, glassware and other exhibits from all over the world.

PLANETE BORDEAUX✦✦

This is a new centre 15km east of the city devoted to the 'Bordeaux' and 'Bordeaux Supérieurs' appellations, which make up half the Gironde vineyards and which provide a million bottles a year sold throughout the world. A film outlines the jobs carried out in the

Below
Plenty to spend your money on!

Planète Bordeaux
€€ *Maison des Bordeaux et Bordeaux Supérieurs, Beychac-et-Caillau; tel: 05 57 97 19 20; e-mail: contact@ maisondesbordeaux.fr. Open Mon–Sat Jun–Oct 0900–1730; rest of year Mon–Fri 0900–1230 and 1330–1700.*

vineyards during the year and an animated model illustrates the main production processes. A sound and light display staged in a fermenting room presents the transformation of grapes into wine.

Visitors' senses are put to the test in two other departments – identifying fruit and spice aromas introduced to some of the wine, and finally the tasting. A shop on the site sells wines of many châteaux in the region.

Right
A range of wines

Opposite
Bordeaux wine

St-Emilion✦✦✦

St-Emilion *pl. de Créneaux; tel: 05 57 55 28 28; e-mail: st-emilion.tourisme@ wanadoo.fr. Open year round. Guided tours €€.*

Fancy a change of pace? From Langon, southeast of Bordeaux, a barge carries up to 80 passengers for trips along the Garonne river. For information and reservations contact L'Escapade, 43 bis, r. des Salières, Langon; tel: 05 56 63 06 45.

It doesn't take long to realise why St-Emilion is such a favourite with visitors to the region. Sprawled over the slopes of two hills, it's a small but lively town of narrow, steep streets and ancient buildings, and its people are as proud of its history as they are of the renowned vineyards in the surrounding countryside. The town owes its name to an 8th-century hermit monk who settled in a grotto, which exists to this day.

The major attraction is the **Eglise Monolithe**✦✦, the largest troglodyte church in France. Carved out of solid rock between the 8th and 12th centuries, the huge structure contains three aisles and impressive vaulting and square pillars. Nearby, the **Chapelle de la Trinité**✦✦ is a small 13th-century sanctuary built by Benedictine monks. Below the chapel is the **grotto**✦✦ used by St Emilion, a small cell containing a natural spring and the hermit's chair, carved from rock. **Catacombs**✦✦ opening off a cliff facing the Chapelle de la Trinité connect with the troglodyte church. Guided tours of the chapel, catacombs and church can be arranged through the tourist office.

Accommodation and food

ⓘ Castillon-la-Bataille *pl. Marcel Paul; tel: 05 57 40 27 58. Open all year.*

ⓗ Les Sources de Caudalie, Vinotherapy Spa €€€ *Chemin de Smith Haut-Lafitte, Bordeaux-Martillac; tel: 05 57 83 83 83; e-mail: sources@sources-caudalie.com. Offers vinotherapy in the setting of a luxury hotel, with spa treatments for relaxation, anti-ageing, improved circulation and skin conditioning, using materials made from grape seeds and local spring water.*

Château Cordeillon-Bages €€€ *Pauillac; tel: 05 56 59 24 24, e-mail: contact@cordeillanbages.com*, has 25 individually furnished rooms available to the general public as well as those attending the wine school. Facilities include a babysitting service. A 10,000-bottle wine cellar supplies the restaurant.

Château Faugeres €€€ *St-Etienne-de-Lisse, St-Emilion; tel: 05 57 40 34 99, www.chateau-faugeres.com*. Overlooking 55 hectares of vines on south-facing slopes, the 10 guest rooms and sumptuously furnished lounge at this 18th-century château in St-Emilion provide charming accommodation. Also enjoy fine dining.

Clos Carré € *14 chemin de Carré, Libourne; tel: 05 57 51 53 01*, is an attractive old house with two double guest rooms and a family room, each with private facilities.

Hôtel de France et d'Angleterre €€ *3 quai Albert Pichou, Pauillac; tel: 05 56 59 01 20*. The hotel has 29 en suite rooms and a restaurant.

La Grande Vigne €€€ *Martillac; tel: 05 57 83 83 83*. Run by Didier Banyol, and awarded two Michelin stars, this new gourmet restaurant is at the four-star hotel on the Château Smith-Haut-Lafitte estate. M. Banyol also runs the country-style **Le Table du Lavoir €€** brasserie, where the décor is based on the place where grape pickers traditionally washed their clothes. In the hotel's tower is a cigar room, where guests can enjoy an aromatic cigar and a glass of cognac.

Le Médiéval €–€€ *pl. de la Porte Bouqueyre, St-Emilion; tel: 05 57 24 72 37*. Everybody's idea of the small-town French bar-restaurant: good food and service and an attractive setting with outdoor tables where you can watch the world go by.

Below
Wine and other gifts

Savour the flavour

For nearly 1000 years the extensive Bordeaux vineyards have been producing fine wines in a variety of landscapes. The region is mid-way between the North Pole and the Equator.

Placed between the Atlantic Ocean and the estuary formed by the Garonne and Dordogne rivers, it has a steady temperate climate and state of humidity. Europe's largest forest, the Landes Forest (11,000 sq km, or one-third the size of Belgium), forming a triangle between Bordeaux, Bayonne and Nerac, protects the wine region from the wind.

Experienced growers know which soil types and which grape varieties are the most appropriate, resulting in a whole range of flavours, each distinctively Bordeaux.

If it's a first-time experience, a visit to a château will open your eyes to the intricacies of wine production. Some people become so intrigued that they visit several wineries – all different in character – and are launched into a lifetime interest.

To ensure reliable quality, wine growers must adhere to strict rules relating to such considerations as a limit on the number of vines per acre, maximum permissible yields, pruning methods and percentage of alcohol. It is forbidden to irrigate the vineyard.

Rich soil is not necessarily a plus factor in the growing of wine. The poor, gravelly soil that produces the greatest Graves wines (hence the name) encourages the vines to push their roots deep to reach water and the elements of the subsoil, bringing richness into the grape. Vine roots can penetrate underground for 40 or 50 feet.

The huge cellars on the wine estates are an impressive site. The vat house or vat room contains great stainless steel vats in which the tannin is slowly extracted. Some vineyards have installed superbly made wooden vats.

The barrel room is even more memorable: hundreds of oak barrels mounted on their sides in straight rows. Each barrel contains 225 litres of wine.

At the end of the tour comes the tasting, bringing the eyes and nose into action as well as the taste buds.

🅗 Château de la Brède €€ Guided tours 1400–1700 Wed–Mon (Jul–Sept); weekends and public holidays rest of year.

Château des Ducs d'Epernon €€ Cadillac; tel: 05 56 62 66 95. Open daily Jun–Sept 1000–1800; Oct–May Tue–Sun 1000–1230 & 1400–1730.

Maison du Vin de Barsac pl. de l'Eglise; tel: 05 56 27 15 44. Open daily year round.

Restaurant La Maison du Douanier €€ *2 route de By, St-Christoly-Médoc; tel: 05 56 41 35 25; e-mail: maisondudouanier@wanadoo.fr; www.maisondudouanier.com. Closed Tue.* On the Gironde north of Pauillac, this restaurant, open all year, serves locally produced food and has a good wine list. English is spoken.

Suggested tour

Total distance: The main route covers a total of 145km. The detour adds 31km.

Time: Comfortable driving time for the main route is about 3 hours, with an extra hour for the detour. Set aside a full day to allow for sightseeing.

🅵 Maison du Vin de Castillon-la-Bataille
6 allées de la République;
tel: 05 57 40 00 88;
e-mail: contact@cote-de-castillon.com. Open daily
0830–1230 and 1530–1900
(summer); 0830–1230
(winter).

Maison du Sauternes
14 pl. de la Mairie; tel: 05
56 76 69 83. Open daily
year round.

🄲 Hostellerie St-Pierre €€ Verdelais;
tel: 05 56 62 02 03, is a
good place for lunch or an
overnight stop. One of its
walls bears a sketch by
Toulouse-Lautrec.

**🄳 To get maximum
benefit from the clear
air of the vineyards around
St-Emilion, you can hire a
bicycle from the town's
tourist office, pl. de Crenaux
(signposted); tel: 05 57 55
28 29; e-mail:
st-emilion.tourisme@
wanadoo.fr**

Links: From Langon the A62 continues south towards Agen, Moissac and Montauban. If you prefer not to drive on the autoroute, a toll road, take the N113, which follows much the same course – that of the River Garonne, in fact – as far as Moissac.

Route: From central Bordeaux join the Rocade ring road (this can be accessed at the riverfront about 1km downstream of Pont d'Arcins) and follow signs for the A62 – the Autoroute des Deux-Mers – to Toulouse. After 12km (toll-free section) leave the autoroute at Exit 1 and follow signs to **LA BREDE ❶**, where the moated château was the birthplace in 1689 of the writer–philosopher Baron Montesquieu. Take the D109 north for 4km to Martillac, home of the **CHATEAU SMITH-HAUT-LAFITTE ❷** vineyard, then head east for 3km, turning right on to the N113.

Continue south for 25km to **BARSAC ❸**, where half a dozen manor châteaux welcome visitors. From Barsac follow the D114 south for 10km to Budos then turn left on to the D125 to reach **SAUTERNES ❹** in 3km. Famous for its sweet white wines, the area around Sauternes also has a number of châteaux open to visitors. The D8 skirts the eastern edge of Sauternes and after 5km reaches the commercial town of Langon, where the N113 crosses the Garonne to the medieval village of St-Macaire.

Detour: From St-Macaire take the D19 north for 4km to the village of **VERDELAIS ❺**, where the painter Henri Toulouse-Lautrec died in 1901 at the age of 37. He lies in the local cemetery. Follow the D117 west for 3km to Ste-Croix-du-Mont, where there are extensive views across the river towards the far-off Pyrenees. Turn right here on to the D10 and continue for 5km to **CADILLAC ❻**, a riverside *bastide*

Côtes wines

Côtes wines – Côtes de Bourg, Premières Côtes de Bordeaux, Premières Côtes de Blaye, Côtes de Castillon and others – come from a vast area stretching from the edge of the Charentes in the northwest to the Périgord region in the east. This is a more hilly area than the Médoc and the vines are grown on wide slopes, some on clay soils which absorb sunlight. The Merlot grape is the basis of these wines from the right banks of the Garonne, Dordogne and Gironde rivers.

The vineyards producing Premières Côtes de Bordeaux are seen along a 60km-long, 5km-wide stretch along the right bank of the Garonne.

To the east, St-Emilion, heartland of the Merlot grape, is known as 'the hill with a thousand châteaux'. It certainly seems like it as you explore the narrow roads, punctuated by stone crosses, and pass château after château amid sloping vineyards around the ancient town.

Sweet and semi-sweet white wines, among them Barsac and Sauternes, are grown in the southern parts of the Bordeaux wine region. These wines spend two or three years in the cellar before bottling. Great vintages go on improving for several decades, developing concentration and power unequalled by other wines.

founded in 1280, where the large château was completed in 1620, ruined during the French Revolution and later restored.

From St-Macaire take the D672 northeast for 21km to Sauveterre-de-Guyenne, a 13th-century *bastide* surrounded by châteaux in the heart of the Entre-deux-Mers region. A 7km drive east along the D230 takes you to Castelmoron-d'Albret, distinguished as France's smallest municipality. It covers an area of 4 hectares and has a population of 64. Next, follow the D139 east for 6km to **St-Ferme**, where there is an interesting fortified church dating from the 11th century.

From St Ferme take the D16 north for 4km, turn right on to the D672 for 3km to Pellegrue, then head north on the D15 to reach **CASTILLON-LA-BATAILLE** ❼ in 19km. Located on the north bank of the River Dordogne, Castillon-la-Bataille is honoured in history as the place where the Hundred Years' War ended in 1453. To reach **ST-EMILION** ❽ take the D130 northwest from Castillon-la-Bataille for 9km, then turn left on to the D243 for a further 4km.

Ratings

Castles	●●●●●
Historical sites	●●●●●
Architecture	●●●●○
Food and drink	●●●●○
Scenery	●●●●○
Vineyards	●●●●○
Museums	●●●○○
Children	●●○○○

Bergerac–Castelnaud

The River Dordogne, upstream from Bergerac to the ancient fortress of Castelnaud, offers a good range of touring experiences and contrasts. Bergerac, where the river is wider and quieter than in its upper reaches, manages to be both a modern commercial centre and a labyrinthine medieval city, where you can walk safely through narrow, traffic-free streets. The area is noted for its wines and at least a dozen appellations provide subtle variations. Growers on the designated Route des Vins welcome visitors and are eager to offer tastings. Upstream, the countryside becomes more rugged, the river a little wilder and history, it seems, rather closer. The châteaux here were built to repel raiders rather than satisfy fashion. The character of the river changes with every turn – flowing serenely through meadows, plunging over foaming rapids, looping back on itself as it meanders grandly between soaring walls of rock.

BERGERAC✣✣✣

ⓘ Bergerac 97 r. Neuve d'Argenson; tel: 05 53 57 03 11; e-mail: tourisme-bergerac@aquinet.tm.fr; www.bergerac-tourisme.com. Open all year, but closed Sun from mid-Sept to mid-Jun.

ⓟ Périgord Gabares €€ Quai Salvette, Bergerac; tel: 05 53 24 58 80; e-mail: perigord.gabarre@worldonline.fr

Right
Bergerac

Capital of the Périgord Pourpre region, whose name derives from the rich, purple-hued wines of the area, historic Bergerac is surrounded by vineyards and farms where the principal crops are tobacco and cereals. The River Dordogne, an important trade route in the past, flows through the heart of the city, but the Ancien Port, where river craft loaded and unloaded their cargoes in the past, is now less picturesquely used as a car park. The old quarter is a labyrinth of medieval stone and half-timbered buildings, most of it mercifully barred to traffic.

Périgord Gabares✣✣ offers one-hour river trips aboard a replica traditional Dordogne craft. The story of the river's influence on Bergerac's social and economic development and the history of the region's wine trade are highlighted at **Le Musée du Vin et de la**

🅗 **Le Musée du Vin et de la Batellerie** €€
5 r. des Conférences; tel: 05 53 57 80 92. Open Tue–Fri 1000–1200 & 1400–1730, Sat 1000–1200, Sun 1430–1830 mid-Mar–mid-Nov.

La Maison des Vins €€
2 r. des Récollets; tel: 05 53 63 57 55. Open daily Easter–Oct 1000–1900.

Le Musée d'Intérêt National du Tabac €€
pl. du Feu; tel: 05 53 63 04 13. Open Tue–Sat 1000–1200 & 1400–1800 (1700 Sat), Sun 1430–1830. Closed public holidays.

Batellerie✦✦. To learn about the modern wine industry and taste some of its products visit **La Maison des Vins**✦✦. Headquarters of the regional wine council, it is entered through the tranquil Cloître des Récollets, part of a monastery dating from the 12th century. The city's association with tobacco is reflected at **Le Musée d'Intérêt National du Tabac**✦✦, which houses a unique collection of art and artefacts associated with smoking.

Accommodation and food in Bergerac

Le Family € *3 r. du Dragon; tel: 05 53 57 80 90.* This small (only eight rooms) but atmospheric hotel stands at the heart of the old quarter. Rooms are equipped with television, direct-line telephones and double-glazed windows. There is a terrace bar and a garage for guests' cars. **Le Jardin d'Epicure** €€, the hotel's restaurant, specialises in Périgord cuisine.

Hôtel de France €€ *18 pl. Gambetta; tel: 05 53 57 11 61.* Adjoining the pedestrianised streets of the old quarter, this modern but quiet hotel has 20 rooms equipped with satellite TV, double glazing and direct-line telephones. Amenities include a swimming pool and garage parking.

Camping Municipal de la Pelouse *r. J-J Rousseau; tel: 05 53 57 06 67. Open all year.* The site is on the south side of the Dordogne, facing the Ile Pelouse. 70 pitches.

Hôtel le Windsor €€ *route d'Agen; tel: 05 53 24 89 76.* On the city's southern outskirts, the hotel has 50 air-conditioned rooms with full amenities, a restaurant, sauna, garden, terrace and a bar.

Le Nautic €€ *12 promenade Pierre Loti; tel: 05 53 57 03 27; e-mail: nautic24100@aol.com.* With shady terraces overlooking the river, the restaurant specialises in fish and regional dishes.

The vanishing nose

Bergerac's most famous citizen, the long-nosed Cyrano, never existed. He was created in 1897 by the playwright Edmond Rostand, who named his character after the real Cyrano de Bergerac, an eccentric 18th-century philosopher who had no connections with the city. A statue of the fictional Cyrano, flamboyantly standing in pl. de la Myrpe, frequently loses its nose to souvenir-hunters.

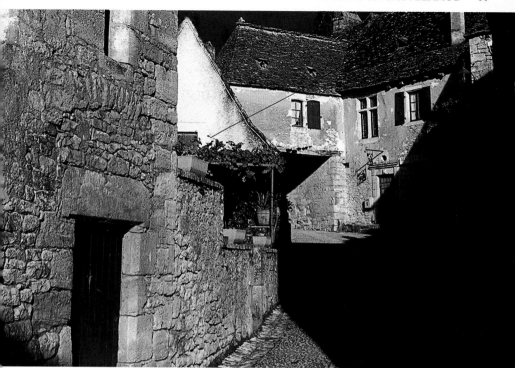

BEYNAC-ET-CAZENAC***

ℹ Beynac-et-Cazenac
la Balme; tel: 05 53 29
43 08; e-mail:
info@cc-perigord-noir.fr;
www.cc-perigord-noir.fr.
Open all year.

ℹ Le Musée de la
Protohistoire et
Parc Archéologique €€
La Tour du Couvent; tel: 05
53 29 51 28; e-mail:
parc.beynac@wanadoo.fr;
http://perso.wanadoo.fr/parc.
beynac. Open daily Jul–Sept.

Château de Beynac €€
Tel: 05 53 29 50 40. Open
all year; guided tours mid-
Mar–mid-Nov 1000–1200
and 1400–1830.

Above
Beynac-et-Cazenac

Rising steeply from the north bank of the Dordogne, Beynac-et-Cazenac is a pretty village of houses dating from the 15th century. Barge trips are available and canoes and kayaks may be rented. A combined ticket provides access to **Le Musée de la Protohistoire** and **Parc Archéologique****. The museum houses a collection of original and facsimile artefacts, including agricultural implements and iron-working tools dating from 2000 BC. The park contains reconstructed dwellings from as far back as the Neolithic period.

About 3km west of the village, at the top of a 150m cliff, is the **Château de Beynac****. Standing on the site of a much older fortress, the castle dates from the 13th century and was a focal point of exchanges between French and English armies during the Hundred Years' War.

Accommodation and food in Beynac-et-Cazenac

Hostellerie Maleville €–€€ *le Bourg; tel: 05 53 29 50 06; e-mail: hostellerie.maleville@wanadoo.fr.* Direct-line telephones and TV are installed in each of the 13 rooms in this delightful hotel overlooking the Dordogne. Home-made dishes are served in the riverside restaurant (**€–€€**), which is open to the public.

CASTELNAUD❖❖❖

Château de Castelnaud €€ *Tel: 05 53 31 30 00; e-mail: chateau@castelnaud.com; www.castelnaud.com. Open daily all year. Jul–Aug 0900–2000; May–Sept 1000–1900; Oct–mid-Nov 1000–1800; mid-Nov–Feb 1400–1700; Mar–Apr 1000–1800.*

An English stronghold during much of the Hundred Years' War, the **Château de Castelnaud** presents a belligerent face to the castle that was mainly held by the French at Beynac on the opposite side of the Dordogne. Today, you can enjoy one of the most stunning views of the Dordogne Valley from its terrace.

Abandoned at the beginning of the 18th century, but restored in recent years, Castelnaud now houses an imaginatively designed museum of medieval warfare. Audio-visual presentations outline the castle's colourful history and demonstrate the development of fortifications and battle tactics in the Middle Ages. Sound and light pageants highlighting historical events at the castle are staged Jul–Aug.

CREYSSE❖❖

Creysse *Syndicat d'initiative, Bella Riva; tel: 05 53 23 20 45; e-mail: port-de-creysse@wanadoo.fr; http://perigord.tm.fr/servtourisme/otsi/creysse. Open all year.*

Creysse Musée-Aquarium € *2bis Impasse Bella Riva; tel: 05 53 23 34 97. Open 1000–1800 all year (1900 Jun–Sept). Guided tours in the afternoon.*

This small community fronting the Dordogne river 8km east of Bergerac is worth a stop or an out-of-town trip. Surrounded by the Pécharmant vineyards, the oldest in the region, the village has a centrally located information centre, museum and a jetty for river barge trips – all on a compact site, Bella Riva, near the town hall.

The **Creysse Musée-Aquarium** displays fish belonging to 33 species which live in the Dordogne River including migratory fish such as salmon, sturgeon, trout and lamprey. In the cellars, an exhibition recounts the history of fishing from prehistoric times to the present day and there are exhibits of local, Stone Age flint tools. From the jetty outside the Aquarium, you can take a river cruise on a traditional Dordogne sailing barge, a *gabare*.

LANQUAIS❖❖

Château de Lanquais €€ *Tel: 05 53 61 24 24. Open daily Jul–Aug; rest of year closed Tue; open pm only Mar, Apr, Oct, Nov.*

Standing on a wooded hillside 15km east of Bergerac, the **Château de Lanquais** provides glimpses of the lives of its past inhabitants. The main part of the château, dating from the 14th century, has towers, machicolations and covered watchways for guards and served as a powerful fortress during the Hundred Years' War. A magnificent Renaissance palace was added by the same architect and craftsmen who built the Louvre in Paris. There are grandly furnished apartments, some with huge, superbly carved and decorated fireplaces.

LIMEUIL❖❖

Jardin-Musée, Limeuil €€ *signposted; tel: 05 53 63 32 06; www.limeuil-perigord.com/index1.htm. Open daily Jul–mid-Sept. Closed Mon mornings.*

An ancient fortified village and barge port, Limeuil is poised in picturesque tiers at the confluence of the Dordogne and Vézère rivers, each of which is spanned by a bridge from the town. The history of horticulture from prehistoric times to the present day is depicted in six gardens at the **Jardin-Musée❖**. Re-created by Michel and Véronique Guignard, the gardens contain flowers, vegetables and herbs grown as they were in the past and the appropriate tools for each age from as far back as Cro-Magnon times are displayed.

Accommodation and food in Limeuil

Hotel Domaine de la Vitrolle €€ *Tel: 05 53 61 58 58; e-mail: beaugier@perigord.com.* A small manor house at the centre of a large estate has been transformed into a stylish hotel/restaurant with spacious rooms.

LES MILANDES❖❖

Château des Milandes €€€ *les Milandes; tel: 05 53 59 31 21. Open Mar, Apr, Oct 1000–1815; Jul–Aug 0930–1930; May, Jun, Sept 1000–1830. Falconry shows daily at 1500 and 1630.*

On the south bank of the Dordogne, about 4km northeast of Castelnaud, the hamlet owes its fame to the late 15th-century **château** that became the home of the black American singer Josephine Baker (1906–75), who took the Parisian cabaret scene by storm in the years before World War II.

Star of the Folies Bergère, she became a French citizen in 1937 and during the war served with the Free French forces and the Résistance, work that earned her the Croix de Guerre. After the war she created a 'world village' at the château, providing a home and education for children of different nationalities and ethnic and religious backgrounds. Her story, and that of the château, is told through furnishings, photographs, a film and recordings of her songs.

A 7-hectare park surrounding the château contains 80 varieties of shrubs and there are demonstrations of falconry.

Opposite
Château de Castelnaud

Monbazillac✧✧

Château de Monbazillac €€
Tel: 05 53 61 52 52; e-mail: monbazillac@chateau-monbazillac.com; www. chateau-monbazillac.com. Open daily Apr 1000–1800; May, Oct 1000–1900; Jun–Sept 1000–1930; Nov–Mar 1000–1700. Closed mid-Jan–mid-Feb, lunch 1230–1400 except Jul–Aug and Mon Nov–Mar.

Only 5km south of Bergerac, the 16th-century **Château de Monbazillac**✧✧ stands on a hilltop grandly overlooking the vineyards that produce the Bergerac region's most famous wines. Monbazillac is a fine sweet white wine, which connoisseurs say goes perfectly with *foie gras*, blue cheeses, white meat and desserts. The wine is made only from grapes affected by *botrytis cinerea* – the 'noble mould'.

The château is a fortified Renaissance home surrounded by a moat, now drained. An imposing round tower with conical roof stands at each corner of the building. Highlights of the interior are the Great Hall – with its painted ceiling, massive Renaissance fireplace and beautiful Flemish tapestries – and the bedchamber of the Viscountess Monbazillac, furnished in Louis XIII style. Other rooms display rustic regional furniture.

Accommodation and food in Monbazillac

La Tour des Vents €€ *Moulin de Malfourat; tel: 05 53 58 30 10; e-mail: moulin.malfourat@wanadoo.fr; www.tourdesvents.com. Closed Jan.* At the highest point of the Monbazillac hills, the restaurant offers panoramic views of the Bergerac valley. The menu regularly features such regional specialities as *foie gras*, *cèpe* mushrooms, truffles and stuffed pigeon.

Tremolat✧✧

The attractive village of Trémolat is at the centre of what is almost an island where the Dordogne river sweeps in a majestic meander, a spectacle that may be viewed from a clifftop vantage point (signposted 'Route du Cingle de Trémolat'). From here you can see the entire loop. The main attraction in the village is the fortified church with high walls, a massive bell tower, four domes and a huge chamber where the entire population could seek refuge during an attack.

Suggested tour

Total distance: The main route, hugging the River Dordogne for much of the way, covers a little over 80km. The detour adds 35km.

Time: Driving time for the main route is about 1½ hours. Allow 2½ with the detour. If you decide to take in Eymet and Castillonès as a detour, picking up the main route again at Issigeac, the total driving time will be around 3½ hours. To take in all the sights allow a full day for the trip.

Above
Château de Monbazillac

Links: From Port-de-Couze, just west of Lalinde the D660 heads south across the river, passing through the *bastide* towns of Beaumont (*see page 142*) and Monpazier (*see page 147*). Limeuil marks the start of a trip through the Valley of Caves – a picturesque and absorbing

Issigeac may seem a sleepy sort of place, but it livens up with Sunday and evening markets and regular antique fairs.

Couze-et-St-Front has been a famous paper-making centre since the 16th century. At one time 13 paper mills operated in the Couze Valley – now only two are still working.

Le Moulin à Papier, *museum of paper-making, route des Guillaudoux; tel: 05 53 24 36 16; www. cyrano.online.fr/moulin.html. Open Apr–Oct 0930–1230 and 1430–1830.*

journey through pre-history (*see pages 118–131*). From Limeuil the D31 heads north to le Bugue from where a series of minor roads successively trace the winding Vézère river along the valley.

Route: From **BERGERAC** ❶ take the D13 south for 5km to **MONBAZILLAC** ❷. Less than a kilometre north of the château, turn left on the D14 to join the N21 (the main route to Agen). Head south for 4km then bear left on the D14 and continue for 8km to **Issigeac❖❖**, a quaint medieval village of stone and timber houses, many of them occupied by English expatriates. With its Bishop's Palace, Provost's House and quiet streets, Issigeac is a pleasant place to stop off for a stroll.

Leave the village on the D25 east and after 2km turn left on to the D22 to reach **LANQUAIS** ❸ in 13km. At Varennes, 1km further on, turn right on to the D37. **Couze-et-St-Front❖❖**, where you can cross the Dordogne to Lalinde, comes after 2½km.

Detour: From Couze-et-St-Front head south on the D660 for 6km, looking out for the remains of old paper mills on the river banks, then take the D27 east for 11km to **Moliéres** and a further 4km to **Cadouin**, two *bastides* (*see pages 144 and 146*). At Cadouin turn north on to the scenic D28 for 7½km, through Calès, then head west on the D29 for 2km to Badefols-sur-Dordogne, where the castle, now in ruins, was once the hide-out of a pirate gang who raided barges on the river. Continue west to **St-Front-de-Colubri**❖❖, where you can cross the river to Lalinde.

[Return to main route] From Lalinde, once an English *bastide* but now a workaday industrial town, head east on the D703 for 3km to the village of Sauvebœuf, where the D31 links up with the Route Cingle de Trémolat for spectacular views of the Dordogne. Continue to **TREMOLAT** ❹, where the D31 continues to **LIMEUIL** ❺, 7km away. The D51 follows the river upstream from Limeuil, reaching Coux-et-Bigaroque in 10km, and from here the D703 takes you upstream again to St-Cyprien (10km) and **BEYNAC-ET-CAZENAC** ❻ (another 10km). **CASTELNAUD** ❼ is 2km away on the opposite bank of the river.

Also worth exploring

From Bergerac take the D933 (Marmande route) to Eymet, 28km south, for a look at the vineyards and rolling countryside and at the *bastide* founded in 1271 and now renowned for *pâté de foie gras*, galantines and *charcuterie* products. Next, take the D18 and D111 to Lauzun then head east on the D1 to Castillonnès, another *bastide*. Then you can head north on the N21 to return to Bergerac, or join the D25 after 7km to reach Issigeac and follow the main route.

Opposite
Bergerac

Castelnaud–Carlux

Ratings

Historical sites	●●●●●
Scenery	●●●●●
Architecture	●●●●○
Castles	●●●●○
Caves	●●●●○
Food	●●●●○
Children	●●●○○
Outdoor activities	●●○○○

The area of the Dordogne Valley between Castelnaud and Carlux is great for those who love exploring old churches. There are half a dozen of them listed in this chapter, offering *aficionados* a wealth of architectural and artistic styles to enthuse over. There are also châteaux – some no more than romantic ruins – caves and two ancient towns to explore. Above all, there is splendid scenery to enjoy. Most of the places listed are close to the River Dordogne, meandering grandly through dramatic gorges and passing attractive villages, one of them officially named as the prettiest in France. In contrast, there's a sneak preview of the craggy Lot *département* during a visit to the hilltop town of Gourdon. Some of the riverside communities – especially Domme and la Roque-Gageac – can be rather crowded at times in summer, but there are many charming hideaways waiting to be discovered.

CARLUX❖❖

Carlux has nothing in the way of formal attractions and consequently does not draw the high-season crowds seen elsewhere in the Dordogne Valley. It is, nevertheless, a worthwhile stop for those who enjoy tranquillity and the magic of unrestored ancient ruins. The village is strategically placed, overlooking the valley, and some old houses and a small indoor market grace its pleasant streets. Its castle, burned out during the Hundred Years' War and now reduced to a couple of crumbling towers and a piece of wall, once belonged to the Vicomte de Turenne. A gorgeous view can be enjoyed from the old terrace. In the past, the nearby river crossing was guarded by the Château de Rouffillac, now also in ruins.

CARSAC-AILLAC❖❖

Barely 1km from the River Dordogne's north bank, the little community of Carsac-Aillac is easy to overlook as your eye scans the road map, but it is worth considering as an overnight stop. It has a couple of reasonable hotel/restaurants and three campgrounds and is handy the for best-known of the river's spectacular meanders, the Cingle de Montfort. The view of a perfect semicircle of water flowing between towering cliffs is made all the more stunning by the dramatic appearance of the Château de Montfort, seemingly clinging to the cliff edge.

The château has had a lively history. Originally a Cathar stronghold, it was seized and razed to the ground in 1214 by Simon de Montfort. During violent times in the following centuries it was rebuilt and destroyed again no less than three times. Its present appearance owes much to restoration work carried out in the 19th century. Carsac-Aillac itself has the charming l'Eglise St-Caprais, dating from the 12th century. In contrast to some superb medieval stonework and 16th-century vaulting, there are dramatic, modern stained-glass windows depicting the Stations of the Cross.

DOMME✧✧✧

ⓘ **Domme** *Maison des Gouverneurs, pl. de la Halle; tel: 05 53 31 71 00; e-mail: infos@domme-tourisme.com; www.domme-tourisme.com. Open all year (except Jan) 1000–1800.*

Standing majestically atop sheer cliffs, affording some of the most stupendous views in the entire valley, Domme is dubbed 'the Acropolis of the Dordogne' and like its Athenian counterpart it suffers at times from overcrowding – especially at weekends during the height of summer. The best times to visit the town, therefore, are early in the morning, in the evening, or out of season.

Founded in 1283, it differs from the traditional *bastide* because its location on a triangular site made it difficult for planners to follow strictly the usual gridiron pattern, though they did their geometric best. Nevertheless, its streets are a joy to explore and it's easy to see why the American writer Henry Miller thought that in Domme he'd found the closest thing to an earthly paradise.

There are three superb viewpoints on the river side of the town: the Jardin Public du Jubilé, on the site of the camp installed by Simon de Montfort after defeating the Cathars in 1214; the Promenade des

The captain's cunning

Domme's founders chose well when they decided to build their new *bastide* on a sloping triangular site high above the River Dordogne – a place that must have seemed impregnable, especially when its south side was protected by enclosing walls, towers, strong gatehouses and a moat.

Its commanding position made it the focus of attention in any conflict, and although it changed hands a number of times during the Hundred Years' War it suffered little damage. Then came the Wars of Religion and a cunning soldier who showed that complacency can be the greatest weakness in defending even the strongest fortress.

In 1588 Domme was an island of Catholicism in a sea swept by a Huguenot storm. Many places in Périgord had succumbed to the Protestants, but Domme, its back protected by those rocky cliffs, seemed secure – so secure that the defenders had not bothered to guard the river side of the town. That proved to be their Achilles' heel. Led by the Protestant Captain Geoffroi de Vivans, a party of 30 men scaled the precipitous la Barre cliff, created a noisy diversion and opened the town gates to their army outside.

Vivans burned down the church and priory, established Protestantism and occupied Domme for the next four years. In 1592 he saw that the tide was turning in the Catholics' favour – and again he had the last laugh. He offered to sell Domme back to the Catholics, took their money, then reduced the place to ruins before he left.

Domme caves €€
*pl. de la Halle; tel: 05
53 31 71 00. Open daily
0900–1900 (Jul–Aug);
0930–1200 and
1400–1800 (Apr–Jun and
Sept); 1400–1700 (mid-
Feb–Mar and Oct); school
holidays during rest of the
year.*

**Musée d'Art et de
Traditions populaires**
€€ *pl. de la Halle; tel: 05
53 31 71 00. Open daily
1000–1230 and
1400–1800 (Apr–Sept).*

Below
Domme

Falaises, a cliff-side walk overlooking the river; and Belvédère de la Barre, an attractive esplanade where you will find a bust commemorating Jacques de Maleville (1741–1824), who helped to draw up the Napoleonic Code.

On the south side you can take a walk along the Promenade des Ramparts and through the well-preserved 13th-century Porte des Tours, a defensive gateway once protected by a double portcullis and flanked by two stone circular towers. Between these two parts lies a network of attractive streets, including Grand'Rue, the main shopping thoroughfare. In pl. de la Halle, the main square, is the 16th-century Maison des Gouverneurs, housing the tourist information centre, and a 17th-century covered market, which provides access to the **Domme caves**✦✦, some 450m of galleries and low passages – some with stalagmites and stalactites and the bones of prehistoric animals – in which the population sought refuge during conflicts in the Hundred Years' War and the Wars of Religion. Views of everyday life at different stages of the town's past are presented in the **Musée d'Art et de Traditions populaires**✦.

Chateau de Fenelon✦✦

Château de Fénelon €€ *Ste-Mondane; tel: 05 53 29 81 45. Open Jun–Sept daily 0930–1900; rest of year daily 1000–1200 and 1400–1800.*

Just off the D50, close to the village of Ste-Mondane on the south bank of the Dordogne, the Château de Fénelon has three lines of fortified walls and dates from the 15th century, although considerable changes were made in the 17th century. Overlooking the river, the château was the birthplace in 1651 of François de Fénelon, author and tutor to the Duke of Burgundy, Dauphin of France. His tract *Télémaque*, addressed to the student duke and critical of Louis XIV, has become a classic of French literature. The author's bedroom, the château's chapel, a kitchen carved from solid rock and a military museum are open to the public.

Gourdon✦✦✦

Gourdon *24 r. du Majou; tel: 05 65 27 52 50; www.quercy-tourisme.com/gourdon. Open all year 1100–1800; Sun Jun–Sept only.*

Eglise des Cordeliers €€ *av. Gambetta. Guided tours organised by the tourist office.*

Grottes de Cougnac €€ *D70 road, 3km north; tel: 05 65 41 47 54. Guided tours Jul–Aug daily 0930–1800; daily Jun & Sept 0930–1100 and 1400–1700.*

Chapelle de Notre-Dame-des-Neiges € *Off D704 1½km southeast; tel: 05 65 41 12 90. Visits by arrangement with the presbytery in Gourdon.*

Gothic church € *le Vigan; tel: 05 65 41 12 90. Open Jul–Aug Mon–Sat 1000–1200, 1400–1900; rest of year contact Gourdon presbytery.*

Musée Henri-Giron €€ *le Vigan; tel: 05 65 41 33 78. Open Jul–Aug Tue–Sun 1000–1800; May–Jun and Sept–Oct 1000–noon and 1500–1800.*

Spilling around the summit of a rocky conical hill on the borders of Périgord and Quercy, Gourdon is a medieval market town serving a forested region known as Bouriane. Its old streets – including one appropriately named rue Zig-Zag – follow the lines of the old fortified town walls. Steeper, narrower lanes, such as rue du Majou and its ancient houses with overhanging upper storeys, head uncompromisingly for the summit. Here panting visitors may enjoy a superb view of the surrounding countryside from the site of the old castle, which was demolished in the 17th century.

Immediately below the summit, dominating a small cobbled square, is the 14th-century Eglise St-Pierre, whose huge buttresses and machicolations echo its beginnings as a fortified church. Its elegant west door is flanked by tall twin towers. Inside, there are carved and painted wooden panels dating from the 17th century.

Nearby, the Hôtel de Ville, built as a consulate in the 13th century, has arcades that serve as a covered market. Further down the hill, on the southern side of the town, is **Eglise des Cordeliers✦**, also from the 13th century, although the bulky belfry porch was added in the 19th century without regard to the slender Gothic lines of the original building.

Just north of the town, **Grottes de Cougnac✦✦** are twin caverns connected by a network of galleries and containing a treasure house of superb rock formations and outstanding prehistoric paintings of animals and human figures. Unlike some other caverns in the Dordogne region, these are rarely overrun with visitors.

Less than 2km to the southeast, **Chapelle de Notre-Dame-des-Neiges✦** is a 14th-century pilgrimage centre with a spring said to have miraculous qualities flowing through its chancel. At le Vigan, 5km east of Gourdon, is a **Gothic church✦**, all that remains of a prosperous 11th-century abbey that was sacked by the English during the Hundred Years' War. The **Musée Henri-Giron**, also at le Vigan, houses a collection of works by the contemporary Belgian painter.

LA ROQUE-GAGEAC❖❖❖

Les Caminades €€
*Tel: 05 53 29 40 95;
e-mail: bestofperigord@
perigord.com. One-hour boat
trips with commentary depart
daily 0930–1800 (mid-
Mar–Oct).*

Les Norberts €€ *Tel: 05
53 29 40 44; e-mail:
gabares-norbert@norbert.fr;
www.norbert.fr. One-hour
boat trips with commentary
depart Jul–Aug 1030–1800;
Apr–Jun & Sept 1400–1700;
Oct 1130, 1400 and 1500.*

Above
La Roque-Gageac

People argue over which is the most attractive village in France: la Roque-Gageac or St-Cirq-Lapopie in the Lot Valley. Well, officially the title goes to the village on the Dordogne and there seems to be no argument over its popularity. After Brittany's Mont-St-Michel and nearby Rocamadour, la Roque-Gageac is the country's third most-visited sight. In the summer, therefore, you're unlikely to take a photograph with no one in it.

It's easy to see what draws the crowds. The village is set tightly between the river and the craggy face of a sheer cliff and its picturesque streets are a pot-pourri of houses humble and grand. Until recently, it was a busy port for river barges carrying iron, salt, timber and wine, but historically it has always been something of a backwater. It was never ruled by an overlord and never taken in battle. Today, it earns its living from tourism and the main river traffic is canoes, which may be hired in the village. Two companies – **Les Caminades**❖❖ and **Les Norberts**❖❖ – operate barge trips.

Accommodation and food

Camping Aqua Viva *Carsac-Aillac; tel: 05 53 31 46 00; e-mail: aquaviva@perigord.com; www.aquaviva.fr/gb/presentation.htm. Open mid-Apr–Sept.* As well as 160 pitches, the site has chalets and motor homes for hire. Amenities include restaurant, takeaway food, grocery store, bar and launderette. Swimming, tennis and golf available.

Camping Beaurivage *la Roque-Gageac; tel: 05 53 28 32 05; e-mail: camping.beau.rivage@wanadoo.fr; www.camping-beau-rivage.com.* 200 pitches, with tents, chalets and mobile homes for hire. Full range of amenities, including hook-up facilities for motor homes.

La Belle Etoile €€ *la Roque-Gageac; tel: 05 53 29 51 44; e-mail: hotel.belle-etoile@wanadoo.fr. Open late Mar–Oct.* Right at the water's edge and offering a superb view of the Dordogne river, this 15-room hotel has a shady terrace for dining or cocktails and the menu features traditional cuisine.

Hostellerie de la Bouriane €€ *pl. Foirail, Gourdon; tel: 05 65 41 16 37. Closed mid-Jan–mid-Mar.* Each of the 20 rooms is equipped with TV and direct-dial telephones and the restaurant is air conditioned. There is a garden.

Hôtel Delpeyrat €–€€ *la Tavernerie, Carsac-Aillac; tel: 05 53 28 10 43; e-mail: hotel.rest.delpeyrat@wanadoo.fr. Open mid-Nov–Sept.* Terrace dining and a garden are features of this quiet 13-room hotel/restaurant, which is located 1km from the River Dordogne. Private parking.

Domaine du Berthiol €€ *D704, 1km east of Gourdon; tel: 05 65 41 33 33; e-mail: domaine-du-berthiol@wanadoo.fr. Open Apr–Oct.* Swimming and tennis are available at this 27-room hotel–restaurant, which stands in a rural setting with extensive views. The restaurant is air conditioned and the rooms have TV and direct-dial telephones.

Hôtel l'Esplanade €€–€€€ *Domme; tel: 05 53 28 31 41; e-mail: esplanade.domme@wanadoo.fr. Open mid-Feb–Oct. Closed all day Mon until Easter, then closed Mon and Wed lunchtime.* The 25 rooms in this comfortable hotel in the heart of the medieval city are equipped with telephones and television, and there is dining outdoors as well as in the restaurant, which is open to the public. Specialities include dishes featuring truffles and duck. The cellar features Bergerac and Pécharmant wines.

Le Nouvel Hôtel €–€€ *r. Malleville et Grand'Rue, Domme; tel: 05 53 28 38 67. Open Apr–Oct.* The proprietor/chef of this 15-room hotel–restaurant specialises in regional dishes. There is terrace dining and the restaurant is air conditioned. Rooms have en suite facilities and direct-dial telephones.

Below
La Roque-Gageac

Camping les Ombrages de la Dordogne *Carlux; tel: 05 53 28 62 17; e-mail: ombrages@perigord.com; www.ombrages.fr/engels. Open Jun–Oct.* The site has 80 pitches and offers tents for hire. Takeaway food is available and there is a bar and a launderette. Swimming and tennis available.

Camping le Pech de Caumont *la Burague, Cénac; tel: 05 53 28 21 63; e-mail: info@pech-de-caumont.com; www.pech-de-caumont.com. Open Apr–Sept.* 100 pitches. Tents and chalets for hire. Takeaway food, bar, grocery store, launderette. Swimming.

Hôtel le Périgord €€ *Port de Domme, la Roque-Gageac; tel: 05 53 28 36 55.* Standing in 2 hectares of parkland, the hotel has a gastronomic restaurant and its 40 rooms are equipped with TV and telephones. Swimming and tennis are available and there is ample parking for guests and diners.

Camping le Perpetuum *Domme; tel: 05 53 28 35 18; e-mail: luc.parsy@wanadoo.fr.* 120 pitches. Tents, chalets, mobile homes for hire. Restaurant, takeaway food, bar, groceries, disco, launderette. Swimming.

Les Quatre Vents €€ *Domme; tel: 05 53 31 57 57.* In a wooded setting with panoramic views, the hotel–restaurant has 26 rooms with TV and telephones. There are two swimming pools and a shady terrace. Canoeing, golf, tennis and horse riding are available.

Relais du Touron €€ *Route de Sarlat, Carsac-Aillac; tel: 05 53 28 16 70. Open Apr–mid-Nov. Restaurant closed Tue and lunchtime daily except Jul–Aug.* This simple hotel–restaurant has 12 rooms, a dining terrace, swimming pool and guest parking.

Les Près Gaillardou €–€€ *la Roque-Gageac; tel: 05 53 59 67 89.* The surroundings are rustic but comfortable and the cuisine inventive in this splendid little restaurant.

Suggested tour

Total distance: The route covers only 75km, but it offers spectacular views of the River Dordogne and a trip through craggy countryside for a foray into the Lot *département*.

Time: Non-stop, you can cover the route in less than 2 hours, but allow at least half a day for sightseeing – more if you want to make the most of Domme and Gourdon.

Links: From la Roque-Gageac you can follow the D46 north for 5km to reach Sarlat-la-Canéda, start of the route to Souillac (*see pages 135–6*). At Gourdon you are only 37km from Cahors (*see pages 182–91*), focal point of the Lot and Célé valleys: travel south on D704 for 12km, then on the N20 for 25km.

L'Eglise de Cénac
€ *Tel: 05 53 29 8145.*
Open daily Jun–Sept
1000–1800; rest of year by
appointment.

Route: From Castelnaud *(see page 70)* cross the bridge over the Dordogne, turn right and follow the D703 for 5km to the pretty riverside village of **LA ROQUE-GAGEAC ❶**, where you cross the river again on the D46 to **DOMME ❷**. The road also passes through Cénac, an interesting place for a short break.

In the 11th century Cénac was important enough for a large priory to be built there. Today, all that remains of those heady days is **l'Eglise de Cénac***, a small Romanesque church, once part of the priory, and even that suffered damage at the hands of the Protestants in 1589 during the Wars of Religion, which swept back and forth across the Dordogne region in the 16th and 17th centuries. Much of the church was rebuilt during the 19th century, but the east end, which was undamaged in the conflict, is in its original state. A good view of this part of the building, with its splendid stone roof, can be enjoyed from the churchyard. Inside, there are fine carved capitals decorated with biblical scenes, including Jonah and the Whale and Daniel in the Lions' Den.

Continue south for 16km, then turn left at the village of Pont-Carral on to the D673 to reach **GOURDON ❸** in a further 9km for a brief introduction to the Lot *département*. Heading north from Gourdon on the D704 provides an opportunity to stop off after 3km for a visit to the impressive **Grottes de Gougnac**. Continue north for a further 11km to Groléjac. From here you can turn right on to the D50 and travel 6km to visit **CHATEAU DE FENELON ❹**. Continuing north from Groléjac on the D704 will take you to **CARSAC-AILLAC ❺**, 2km away on the opposite side of the Dordogne and handy for a superb view of the **Cingle de Montfort**. From here you can turn right on to the D703, following the river upstream for 8km to Rouffillac, where a left turn on to the D61 will take you to **CARLUX ❻** in under 3km.

Périgueux

Ratings

Food	●●●●●
History	●●●●●
Architecture	●●●○
Art	●●●●○
Markets	●●●●○
Museums	●●●●○
Scenery	●●●○○
Children	●○○○○

Well named the City of Art and History, Périgueux is the compact little capital of the province of Périgord. The Musée de Périgord takes you back through prehistory. You can see the shell of a round tower of the Gallo-Roman era from the 1st century AD. You can wander through the medieval city and touch stonework that generates a feeling of affinity with people from centuries past who touched the same stonework: or perhaps that is fanciful. Périgueux, with its 12th-century cathedral, its lingering remnant of the medieval walls and its ancient courtyards and archways, hones the imagination and you feel assured that nothing will change in the next 1000 years. Back to earth! Périgueux is a market town with world-famous delights spread out before you. Truffles and *foie gras* from November to March, *charcuterie* and cheeses, pâté and pies all year.

History

ⓘ **Périgueux** *26 pl. Fencheville, Périgueux; tel: 05 53 53 10 63; e-mail: tourisme.perigueux@perigord. tm.fr; www.ville-perigueux.fr. Open in summer season Mon–Sat 0900–1900, Sun 1000–1800; rest of the year Mon–Sat 0900–1800. Closed Sun.*

Two thousand years ago the Gauls, living in the hills, got together with the Romans and built Vésunna, or Vésune. The city had public baths, temples, an amphitheatre accommodating 20,000 people and smart villas decorated with frescoes and mosaics. Traces of Vésune can still be seen in Périgueux. The Musée de Périgord exhibits items from the Gallo-Roman period found locally. It also has exhibits from many thousands of years before that period: its prehistory department is one of the largest in France.

The Cathédrale St-Front, dating from the 12th century, with 19th-century reconstruction work and embellishments, is one of the largest in France. Périgueux is rich in medieval and Renaissance architecture; careful restoration work has been going on since 1971. Much of the town's charm lies in its beauty, providing the sort of sightseeing that is mainly free. You stroll around encountering narrow medieval alleyways, nail-studded doors, archways, courtyards and corners. Guided walks of varying themes are worthwhile.

Surrounded by agricultural terrain, Périgueux is renowned for its gastronomic attractions. You can buy tins of Pâté de Périgord made from pork meat, goose or duck liver and a modicum of the precious truffle. Walnut cake is another enticing speciality.

Sights

Cathédrale St-Front pl. de la Clautre; tel: 05 53 53 23 62. Open 0800–1900 (in winter closes at dusk). Free entry but donations are welcome.

Cathédrale St-Front**

The 12th-century cathedral, built in the Roman-Byzantine style, replaced a mid-11th-century church that burned down. Dedicated to St-Front, a former Bishop of Périgueux, the building forms a combination of a Latin cross and a Greek cross, separated by a tower. Its domes are more than 36m high and 24m wide. Substantial reconstruction and adaptation work was carried out from 1850 by Paul Abadie, who went on to design the basilica of the Sacré-Cœur in Paris. It was the latest of several restorations – work that some people feel

Château Barrière
€ r. de Turenne. Freely accessible.

Le Tour de Vésune €€
Guided tour from the tourist office Jul–Aug Mon–Fri 1030. Variable times during the rest of the year, mainly in school holidays.

Jardin des Arènes *Public garden built on the site of a Roman amphitheatre. Open daily May–Aug 0730–2100, Sept–Apr 0800–1800. Free entry.*

Below
Cathédrale St-Front

considerably altered the cathedral's appearance, and not for the better. The domes and pinnacles were added at this time.

The semi-Roman, semi-Gothic cloisters, dating from the 13th to 16th centuries, remain in their original state. However, the cathedral is splendidly floodlit at night. In the Middle Ages the Cathédrale St-Front was an important resting place for pilgrims making the long trek through France to Compostela in Spain to pay homage at the shrine of St James.

Château Barrière*
Named after the family who owned it in medieval times, the Gallo-Roman castle, with a 12th-century keep, caught fire in 1575 during the Wars of Religion and was never rebuilt. The ruin stands formidably against the skyline. The sculpted door to the stair tower, added in the Renaissance period, is in a well-preserved state.

La Cité***
This is the site of the Gallo-Roman city of Vésune, built 20 centuries ago, prospering for many years, but declining in the 3rd century after suffering barbarian invasions. The **Tour de Vésune**** (Vésune Tower) is an impressive sight. Although a chunk of the cylindrical building has gone, the major part of the tower remains and much detail is still visible. The tower, the most sacred part of a temple, is 27m high and 20m in diameter. Its walls were covered in marble plates fastened by iron hooks which can still be seen.

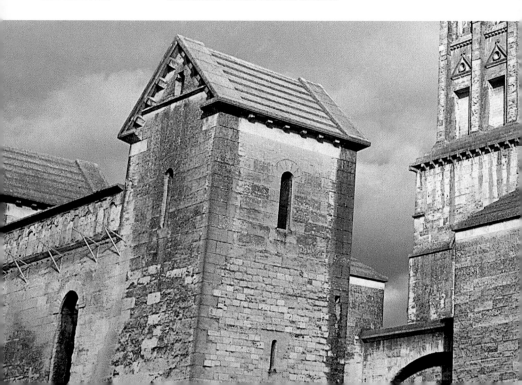

Nearby, the **Jardin des Arenes**✦✦ (*r. de l'Amphithéatre, freely accessible*) is a public garden on the site of the huge amphitheatre where up to 20,000 citizens watched sporting events. Although demolition of the amphitheatre began in the 3rd century – it was turned into a fortification when Vésune came under attack – it is still recognisable as an arena.

Porte Normande✦✦ (*r. Chanzy, freely accessible*), or the Normandy Gate, was built from enormous stones taken from tombs, temples and other sources. Its exact date of origin is not known, but it is thought to be from the 3rd century. The Vikings set fire to it in the 9th century.

La Maison Gallo-Romaine✦✦ €€ (*between r. de Turenne and r. Claude Bernard, may be visited on a themed walk organised by the tourist office Jul–Aug Mon–Fri 1000. Variable times rest of year, mainly in school holidays*) is from the 1st century but underwent rebuilding more than once until the 4th century. Its remains were discovered in 1959. It had living rooms and a bath: its heating system, by which hot air was carried through pipes, is well preserved. The villa would have been occupied by the wealthy and powerful Pompeius family.

Eglise de la Cité✦✦ (€, *donations welcome, pl. de la Cité; tel: 05 53 53 21 35. Open daily 0830–1830, except Sun and public holidays*). Built in the 11th century in the Romanesque style, the church is dedicated to St Etienne. During the Wars of Religion it was partially destroyed, losing its belfry.

Galerie Daumesnil
corner of r.
Limegeanne and r. de la
Misericorde. Freely
accessible.

Tour Mataguerre €€
r. de la Bride, Périgueux.
The tower is outside the
Périgueux tourist office,
which organises discovery
visits to it in Jul and Aug
Mon–Fri 1030, enabling you
to see the view from the top.

Musée Militaire €€ 28 r.
des Farges, Périgueux; tel: 05
53 53 47 36. Open
Mon–Sat Apr–Sept
1000–1200 and
1400–1800; Oct–Mar
Mon–Sat 1400–1800.
Closed Sun and public
holidays. 90-minute guided
tours available.

Musée de Périgord €€
cours de Tourny, Périgueux;
tel: 05 53 06 40 70. Open
weekdays except Tue
1000–1700, Sat, Sun
1300–1800. Closed public
holidays. Free entry
1200–1400 on weekdays
mid-Sept–mid-Jun.

**Vesunna Musée Gallo-
Romain** Parc de Vésone;
tel: 05 53 53 00 92; e-mail:
semitour@perigord.tm.fr;
www.best-of-perigord.tm.fr/
sites/semitour/vesunna/
vesunnafr.html. Open daily
except Monday 1000–1800.
A new museum built
over an archaeological
site in old part of
Périgueux, devoted
to exploring everyday
life in ancient times.

Opposite
Rue des Fages

Galerie Daumesnil✦✦

This is an example of restoration work in the old part of Périgueux. It involved demolishing some centuries-old houses, but it has resulted in a series of shady courtyards and attractive little squares. Façades from the 1400s to 1600s have been revealed. Walk through r. Limegeanne, a picturesque narrow street with some interesting shops.

Maison des Dames de la Foi✦✦ (€ 4–6 r. des Farges)

This 13th-century house is said to be among the oldest in Périgueux. It was named after the Ladies of the Faith when it became a convent in the 17th century.

Tour Mataguerre✦✦

The walls that fortified Puy St-Front, the medieval predecessor to Périgueux, had 28 towers, and the Mataguerre Tower is the last remaining one. The round tower has been rebuilt several times, the last occasion being in the 1470s, when the fleur-de-lys of the king of France added ornamentation.

Musée Militaire✦✦

Exhibits here, in France's most important military museum, take you from the Middle Ages to World War II. Weapons, gun carriages, uniforms and many aspects of warfare and defence through the ages make for an interesting visit. One section deals with the work of the Resistance Movement in Southwest France in World War II.

Musée de Périgord✦✦✦

Allow plenty of time to browse in all the departments of the museum. Périgord has yielded an enormous wealth of archaeological finds and relics of the past, and the museum's remarkable prehistoric section is one of the most important in France. Here you find yourself in the company of a well-preserved fossilised Neanderthal skeleton from 70,000 years ago. It is in the foetal position and was found at Montignac, in the Vézère Valley, in the 1950s. There is a skeleton from the palaeolithic period, about 12,000 years old, found at Chancelade. A casting of a 27,000-year-old skeleton found at St-Avit-Sénieur, is also displayed. Mammoths' tusks, engraved bones, and cutting and polishing stone tools are shown.

An incredible array of exhibits from the Gallo-Roman era in Périgueux and the department of Périgord make fascinating viewing. They include an oak pump found in 1975 in La Maison Gallo-Romain (see page 89), frescoes and mosaics, earthenware and jewellery, domestic items in terracotta and ivory, bone and bronze objects. An altar with a sculpture of a bull's head, used for the sacrifice of bulls, is one of the larger exhibits.

During his alterations to the Cathédrale St-Front in the 19th century, Abadie removed carvings of the medieval Romanesque façade, and these are displayed in the museum's arcaded gallery. Also

Themed walks €€
These are priced from just over €1 to just over €5. Except in peak season, times are variable: enquire at the tourist office. In Jul and Aug guided walks (discovery visits) depart from the tourist office at 1030 Mon–Fri (Gallo-Roman circuit) and 1430 Mon–Fri (Medieval/Renaissance circuit).

in the Middle Ages collections is the diptych of Rabastens – the rare 13th-century illuminated manuscripts on parchment.

The Fine Arts sections include paintings by French, Spanish, Italian and Flemish artists from the 15th to the 19th centuries. Among these is Canaletto's *Le Grand Canal et le Pont Rialto*, *La Pierre de Folie* of Pieter Huys and *Port de Honfleur* by Othon Friesz. Enamels, carved furniture, portraits and popular arts are in the former chapel, representing periods from the 13th century onwards. Don't miss the cloisters, with sculptures, a 12th-century altarpiece, Renaissance exhibits, Gallo-Roman relics and pieces from miscellaneous periods in history.

Perigord Gabarres❖❖ (€€ *Quai de l'isle Périgueux; tel: 05 53 53 10 63; e-mail: perigord.gabarre@worldonline. Open Easter–Oct daily 1000–1800*). Boat trips where visitors can get an introduction to the city and 2000 years of its history by taking a narrated cruise on the River Isle aboard the *Vesuna*: departures from the town-centre quay.

Themed walks❖❖
You can choose from more than a dozen guided walks organised by the Office of Tourism. They last from 45 minutes to two hours, with guides provided by the Ministry of Culture. Themes include the Gallo-Roman, medieval and Renaissance periods, the Cathédrale St-Front, l'Eglise de St Etienne de la Cité and a gastronomic tour, with or without a tasting.

Below
Old houses in Périgueux

Accommodation and food

Antonne-et-Trigonant € *la Pradelle, Antonne; tel: 05 53 06 17 88; e-mail: aufildel.eau@wanadoo.fr. Open mid-Jun–mid-Sept.* Just east of Périgueux by the River Isle, the two-star campground has 50 pitches for tents and caravans, a food store, bar and launderette.

Atur Le Grand Dague €–€€ *tel: 05 53 04 21 01; e-mail: camping.legranddague@wanadoo.fr; www.francecom.com/aft/camping/ le.grand.dague.* South of Périgueux on the RN89, the campground is open Apr–Sept with 93 places for tents, mobile homes and chalets. Amenities include a restaurant, bar, food store, launderette, swimming and mini-golf.

Auberge Notre-Dame €–€€ *56 av. Jean et Léonce, Route de Vergt, Notre-Dame-de-Sanilhac; tel: 05 53 07 60 69. Open daily in summer, closed Sat rest of year.* Set in the countryside 8km from Périgueux, the seven-room *auberge* has an extensive terrace for outdoor dining, and private parking. Horse riding and tennis are available.

B&B Le Pontet € *Rond-Point Agora, Boulazac; tel: 05 53 06 61 61.* Rooms sleeping two, three or four people, all at very modest prices. Breakfast is similarly inexpensively priced: English breakfast of cereals,

Markets You can find market stalls in one or other of the city's various squares every day. The main market at pl. de St Louis is especially busy on Wed and Sat. The truffles and *foie gras* offered Nov–Mar attract people from many miles away. Stalls sell meat, poultry, cheeses, flowers and fresh produce, household goods, clothes and other goods.

eggs and sausages is available. Rooms have TV and direct-dial telephones. The B&B is about 4km from Périgueux centre.

Hôtel Bristol €€ *37–39 r. A. Gadaud, Périgueux; tel: 05 53 08 75 90.* The 3-star, town-centre property has 29 spacious air conditioned en suite rooms. English and German are spoken. Private parking.

Hôtel Chateau de Reynats €€€, *av. des Reynats, Chancelade; tel: 05 53 03 53 59; e-mail: contact@chateau-hotel-perigord.com; www.chateau-hotel-perigord.com. Open all year.* Near the Abbey of Chancelade, less than 3km from the centre of Périgueux, the fully renovated 19th-century castle is a 4-star hotel with 13 guest rooms in the castle and 24 in the Orangery building. It has a heated pool, tennis and a restaurant (**€€–€€€**).

Hostellerie de l'Ecluse €€ *route de Limoges, Antonne; tel: 05 53 06 00 04; e-mail: beaugier@perigord.com; www.ecluse-perigord.com.* Beside a lock on the River Isle to the east of Périgueux, this 45-room, 3-star property is in parkland. Its 2-star restaurant (€€) is known for its regional cuisine.

Hôtel du Périgord *€€ 74 r. Victor Hugo, Périgueux; tel: 05 53 53 33 63.* Centrally situated, this 2-star hotel has 20 rooms and a restaurant.

Hôtel Tallyrand Périgord *€€ 21 pl. Francheville, Périgueux; tel: 05 53 54 37 70; e-mail: hotel.tallyrand@infonie.fr. Open all year.* In the heart of the city and close to the old town, this 3-star hotel offers a friendly welcome. It has 20 comfortable and stylish rooms, some with a view of the old town.

Brasserie Café de Bordeaux *€–€€ 3 r. du President Wilson, Périgueux; tel: 05 53 53 41 72. The brasserie is open daily 0800–2400.* The air conditioned restaurant, run by the third generation of the same family, serves Périgord specialities.

Restaurant de Clos St-Front *€ 5 r. de la Vertu, Périgueux (access through r. St-Front); tel: 05 53 46 78 58.* Near the Musée de Périgord, the restaurant has a shady terrace for outdoor eating.

Le Rocher de l'Arsault *€€–€€€ 15 r. de l'Arsault, Périgueux; tel: 05 53 53 54 06. Closed for second half of Jul.* The air conditioned restaurant with Louis XIII décor is run by a mother and daughter, Marie and Valerie, who take pride in serving fresh products from the land and sea.

Opposite
Place Bugeaud

Sharp shopping

Plenty of attractive little shops vie with the historic buildings for the tourists' attention in Périgueux. If you're self-catering you may want to stock up with ready-to-eat meats and pies at the *charcuterie* A La Cathédrale in *r. des Chaînes.* Try choosing from 75 sorts of chocolate at La Chocolatheque Philippon, *r. Taillefer.*

One of the pleasures of shopping on holiday – even window shopping – is finding things you don't see at home. Périgueux has some fine cutlery shops, or *coutelleries.* There's one in *r. Taillefer* and another in *r. Limogeanne.* Look for the neat little truffle knives, made in Périgord – a speciality of the region.

Bookshops – antiquarian and modern – are interesting in any language, and Périgueux has several. For gifts or something for yourself, browse around the leather goods at Maroquinerie St-Front, *av. Daumesnil,* near the cathedral. Maison Léon at *pl. de la Clautre* will also provide ideas for gifts and souvenirs, including *foie gras,* wines and liqueurs of the region. Cartier, Gucci and other world-famous names are represented at Bouix jewellers in *pl. de la Clautre.* The products of prestigious perfume houses can be found at Parfumerie Bleue, *pl. Francheville.* For paintings and other works with a local flavour, take a look into the gallery at *4 r. St-Front* – Créateurs et Artisans d'Art du Périgord.

From April to September visitors can tour some of the sights of Périgueux by a jolly little tourist train. The ride, with a commentary, takes about 35 minutes. *For information tel: 05 53 04 33 39.*

Half-day or full-day minibus tours of the countryside around Périgueux can be booked two days ahead. Tours are in air-conditioned vehicles. *Details from the tourist office or contact Allo Taxis, Périgueux; tel: 05 53 09 09 09 or M. Flanchec; tel: 05 53 53 70 47.*

Château de l'Herm
€€ la Bouderie; tel: 05 53 05 46 61; e-mail: mariepalue@aol.com; http://chateaudelherm.free.fr. Open Apr–Nov daily 1000–1900.

Above
Cathédrale St-Front

Suggested tour

Total distance: The main route covers 65km. The detour adds 40km.

Time: In theory you should be able to cover the distance comfortably in well under 2 hours, but much of the route is on winding rural roads through some very scenic countryside, so allow for 3 hours' driving time, plus another hour if you follow the detour.

Links: On the main route, from Thenon you can take the N89 east for 49km to Brive-la-Gaillarde (*see pages 152–3*), a major motorail terminus with important road links in all directions, notably south by way of the N20 and N140 to Figeac (*see pages 172–6*). On the detour, les Eyzies-de-Tayac has road links to Montignac (*see pages 123–4*) and Sarlat-la-Canéda (*see pages 132–5*).

Route: From **PERIGUEUX** ❶ head south on the N2089 for 5km. At Niversac continue south on the D710 to les Versannes, where you should pick up the D6 and travel east for a further 9km to la Bouderie.

It's worth stopping here to take a look around **Château de l'Herm****, an atmospheric ruin on top of a wooded hill. Surrounded by a weed-choked ditch that was once a moat the château was built in the 16th century on the site of a 12th-century structure and has a history of bloody family feuds of Shakespearean magnitude.

Continue on the D6 to Rouffignac ❷, a small town that was rebuilt after being burned down in an act of reprisal by the Germans in 1944. The 16th-century church was the only building to survive. The town's

Grotte de Rouffignac €€ *Tel: 05 53 05 41 71; e-mail: grottederouffignac@ wanadoo.fr; www.grottederouffignac.fr/ p_fr/uk_rouf.html. Open Jul–Aug daily 0900–1130 and 1400–1800; Apr–Jun and Sept–Oct daily 1000–1130 and 1400–1700 (1-hour guided tours by electric train).*

Just outside Plazac, the leaning Tour de la Vermondie is said to have stooped so that an imprisoned prince and his lover could exchange kisses. Nearer the truth, perhaps, is the belief that the tower was damaged by the Saracens in the 8th century.

main claim to fame, however, is the **Grotte de Rouffignac**, 5km to the south. The cave has some 8km of galleries and chambers decorated with more than 150 engravings of prehistoric animals from about 13,000 years ago. Depressions in the soft floor of the cave were created by hibernating bears, whose claw marks can be seen on the walls.

From Rouffignac follow the D32 south for 7km, then turn left on to the D47 and continue for a further 7km to **les Eyzies-de-Tayac** ❸, an attractive little town lying below an imposing line of cliffs riddled with troglodyte dwellings (*see pages 120–3*). Leave les Eyzies on the D706 and travel east for 5½km to Tursac, where scenes from the daily life of Neanderthal and Cro-Magnon people have been re-created in the **Préhistoparc** (*see page 127*).

After another 3½km the road reaches **la Roque St-Christophe** ❹, where more than 100 carved-out dwellings have been found in the 80m-high cliff, which dominates the landscape (*see page 124*). Cross the River Vezére to le Moustier and head north on the D6 for 5½km to **Plazac** ❺, where the Romanesque church with a 12th-century belfry-keep overlooks the village from a cypress-fringed hillock. From Plazac the D6 continues for 6½km to return to Rouffignac.

From Rouffignac follow the D31 northeast for 13km through the unremarkable town of Thenon, where the N89 will speed you back to Niversac on the outskirts of Périgueux in 24km.

The Isle Valley

Ratings

Food and drink	●●●●●
Historical sights	●●●●
Restaurants	●●●●
Villages	●●●●
Architecture	●●●
Scenery	●●●
Shopping	●●●
Museums	●●

The valleys of the River Isle and its tributary, the Auvézère, are by no means the best-known parts of the Dordogne to tourists, but they are never far from the thoughts of the food-loving French. The two rivers take us through three of Périgord's four regional colours: Périgord Pourpre (purple), Périgord Blanc (white) and Périgord Vert (green). The area may lack the dramatic gorges, cliffs and caves of the Dordogne and Lot valleys to the south, but that's not to say they lack interest. There are stunning châteaux and brooding ruins, history in abundance and fascinating villages hidden in the extensive forests of la Double and Landais. In some woodland areas – local inhabitants will not reveal exactly where – the elusive, delicious and highly-prized truffle may be uncovered. Add another regional speciality – *foie gras* – and you have the ingredients for a gourmet's paradise.

HAUTEFORT✦✦✦

Ⓘ Château de Hautefort €€ *Tel: 05 53 50 51 23; www.finest.tm. fr/chateau_hautefort. Open for guided tours (45 mins) Apr–Oct 0900–1200 and 1400–1900. About half the château is accessible to visitors with disabilities, who pay a reduced admission charge. Grounds and château may be visited separately; combined admission available.*

Among the gentle, thinly wooded hills of the Auvézère Valley this small village huddles beneath the grandeur of the **Château de Hautefort✦✦✦**, whose massive bulk is extended by two wings ending in towers resembling the matching pieces of an old-fashioned cruet.

The castle is the latest development of fortifications that have stood on the site since the 9th century. Its most notorious medieval occupant was Bertrand de Born, aka Bertrand the Troubadour, who seems to have been as good with a sword as he was with a song. A family feud kept him on his toes, defending the castle against raids by his brother, Constantine. In 1185 Bertrand secured an endorsement of his claim to the family home by Henry II, but a year later Constantine came back and burned the place down. Bertrand retired to a monastery where he died some time before 1215.

Rebuilt, the castle was strengthened during the 16th century to thwart attacks during the Wars of Religion. A century or so later, Marie de Hautefort was born there. She became lady-in-waiting to Anne of Austria and earned a place in history by her outrageous and unsuccessful flirting with Louis XIII – even inviting him to retrieve letters 'posted' down the front of her dress, but to no avail.

In 1630 Jacques-François de Hautefort began a reconstruction programme that was to last 40 years. In 1968 the château was badly damaged by fire. Careful restoration work began a year later and the place is now much the same as it was before the disaster, filled with wonderful collections of furniture, tapestries, paintings and porcelain and surrounded by 40 hectares of parkland, which include terraced and formal gardens.

Overleaf
Jumilhac-le-Grand

JUMILHAC-LE-GRAND***

Château de Jumilhac €€ *Tel/fax: 05 53 52 42 97, out of summer season 05 53 52 58 62; e-mail: ch.de.jumilhac@wanadoo.fr; www.best-of-perigord.tm.fr/ sites/chateaux/jumilhac/ jumilhac_uk.html. Open all year, Jun–Sept 1000–1900; rest of year open only at weekends and on public holidays in the afternoon. Guided tour 50 mins.*

Musée de l'Or €€ *tel: 05 53 52 55 43. Open mid-Apr–mid-Oct Sun and public holidays 1500–1800; Jul–Aug daily 1030–1830.*

The village is an outpost of Périgord Vert, almost at the head of the Isle river and on the edge of the Limousin Plateau. It is dominated totally by the huge **Château de Jumilhac***. The 19th-century illustrator Gustave Doré described the castle as the most romantic in France, but he was inspired more by the fairy-tale conical roofs of the main building than by the rather militaristic style of the whole complex.

The original castle was ruined by Richard Cœur-de-Lion's troops but was rebuilt around 1580 by Antoine Chapelle, the first Count of Jumilhac. Flanked by two wings added in the 17th century, the château encompasses a grand staircase, state drawing room, dining room and kitchens and collections of fine furniture and paintings. Terraced gardens enclose the buildings.

Housed in the old cellars of the castle is the **Musée de l'Or**, the only museum in France dedicated to gold and gold-mining. The story of gold is told from the extraction and treatment of the ore to the metal's applications as jewellery, in industry and as currency.

MUSSIDAN**

Tourist Office *pl. de la Répubique; tel: 05 53 81 73 87; e-mail: ot.mussidan@perigord.tm.fr; www.chez.com/otmussidan*

Musée des Arts et Traditions Populaires du Périgord €€ *Tel: 05 53 81 23 55; www.museevoulgre.cjb.net. Open Jun–mid-Sept Wed–Mon 0930–1200 and 1400–1800; Mar–May and Oct–Nov weekends and hols 1400–1800. Closed last two weeks Sept, and Dec–Feb. Guided tour 1hour 30min.*

Château de Mont-Réal €€ *Issac; tel: 05 53 81 11 13. Open Jul–Sept daily 1000–1200, 1430–1830.*

Château du Mellet €€ *Neuvic; tel: 05 53 80 86 65. Open for guided tours Apr–Sept, 1330–1830. Mornings and rest of year visits by appointment.*

Although it stands well downstream of the Isle Valley's most scenic and interesting parts, and is more involved in industry than tourism, Mussidan is neatly placed as a gateway to two of the Dordogne region's most extensive forest areas: Forêt de la Double and Forêt du Landais. An old Huguenot city, it was besieged a number of times during the Wars of Religion. The most horrendous siege – that of 1569 – inspired Michel de Montaigne to write *L'heure des parlements dangereuse*, one of his famous *Essays*.

Today, Mussidan's major attraction for visitors is the **Musée des Arts et Traditions Populaires du Périgord**, an eclectic collection of furniture, artefacts and machinery housed in a handsome mansion. Reproduced bedrooms, a kitchen, dining room and drawing room provide a glimpse of 19th-century bourgeois life in the region. There are reconstructions of rural crafts workshops, and a collection of agricultural tools and machinery is housed in a barn. Brass and pewter artefacts, glazed earthenware and examples of the taxidermist's skills are displayed in a large exhibition area.

At Issac, 7km southeast of Mussidan, the **Château de Mont-Réal** provided a name for the Canadian city. There are double-fortified curtain walls dating from the 12th century, but the château and chapel, surrounded by formal gardens, are 16th century.

The handsome **Château du Mellet** at Neuvic, 12km northeast of Mussidan, dates from the 15th century and is noted for its ornate machicolations, frescoes and Louis XVI salon. An 18th-century chapel and botanical gardens may also be visited.

SORGES✦✦✦

ⓘ Ecomusée de la Truffe €€ Tel: 05 53 05 90 11; e-mail: si.sorges@perigord.tm.fr. Open Jul–Aug daily 0930–1230 and 1430–1830; rest of year Tue–Sun 1000–1200 and 1400–1700. 'Truffle Trail' tours Tue and Thur 1530.

This modest but pleasant little market town is the capital of what many people believe is Périgord's most valued activity: the gathering of that 'black diamond of gastronomy', the truffle. The story of this odd and mysterious fungus is told in the **Ecomusée de la Truffe✦✦✦** with the aid of a diorama, photographs and documents. Twice a week you can join a guided group on a 'truffle shuffle' along a 3km trail outside the town. A find might recover the cost of your entire trip...

THIVIERS✦✦

ⓘ Thiviers Syndicat d'Initiative, pl. Foch; tel: 05 53 55 12 50. Open daily all year.

ⓘ La Maison de l'Oie et du Canard €€ pl. Foch, Thiviers; tel: 05 53 55 12 50. Open daily 1000–1200 and 1400–1800; Jul–Aug Mon–Sat 1000–1800. Closed Sun.

A bustling town on the main route between Périgueux and Limoges and Paris, Thiviers is devoted to the production and marketing of *foie gras*, the fattened liver of force-fed ducks and geese: so devoted, in fact, that a special museum – **La Maison de l'Oie et du Canard✦** – takes pride of place next to the Syndicat d'Initiative, which doubles as tourist office. The museum traces the history of domesticated ducks and geese from prehistoric times, and documents the methods used today in raising and fattening the birds.

Gourmands will doubtless be attracted to the *foie gras* market staged every Saturday morning, Nov–Mar, in the square in front of the museum. Guided tours of the town take place Jul–Aug Tue–Sat 1000–1130 and 1500–1730.

VILLAMBLARD✦

Just off the N21, about halfway between Bergerac and Périgueux, Villamblard may be a worthwhile stop-off for those who enjoy poring over old ruins – in this case, those of a massive fortress. There's a 15th-century castle at the nearby village of St-Jean-d'Estissac.

VILLEFRANCHE-DE-LONCHAT✦✦

ⓘ Musée d'Histoire Locale €€ r. de la Liberté, Villefranche; tel: 05 53 80 77 25. Open Sat–Sun 1000–1200 and 1400–1800.

Left Thiviers

About 17km northeast of St-Emilion, this large village is the western gateway to the Forêt du Landais, an area with many very attractive villages, some – such as St-Martin-de-Gurçon and Montpeyroux – with Romanesque churches or ruined castles. At **Carsac-de-Gurson✦**, 3km east of Villefranche, you can see the ruins of a château built by England's King Edward I. In Villefranche itself the **Musée d'Histoire Locale✦✦** concentrates on life at the time of the 16th-century essayist Michel de Montaigne. There are collections of paintings and earthenware pottery.

Land of the enlarged liver

Everyone eats well in Périgord, and it isn't only the force-fed ducks and geese who are likely to finish up with enlarged livers. The region is famous throughout France for its highly individualistic cuisine, much of it based on the flesh or innards of those unfortunate domesticated waterfowl.

After three months of free-range living, during which they are fed on a diet of alfalfa and grains, the birds are placed singly in cages and massively overfed for two to three weeks on ground meal and whole corn. A *gaveuse*, a type of funnel, is used to force-feed the birds. The ideal weight for a duck's liver is considered to be 450–500g (about 1lb) and 800–900g for a goose liver, three or four times the normal weight in each case.

You can buy *pâté de foie gras* and other duck and goose products directly from farms throughout Périgord and Quercy, and in many places they are only too pleased to show visitors around.

Truffles, the 'black diamonds' of Périgord, are regarded as the peak of gourmet experience – a fact that is reflected in the prices they command. A century or so ago they were plentiful, but today the entire output for the region amounts to a mere 4 tonnes a year.

The truffle is a strange black fungus, weighing some 100g and about the size of a Brussels sprout. Talented sniffer dogs or specially trained pigs are used to find truffles, which grow underground at the base of a tree, usually an oak. Truffle-hunters are notoriously secretive about the sources of their finds.

Despite its mundane appearance, the truffle has a superb aroma and even a few specks or fine slices introduce a unique flavour to many dishes, especially pâtés, *foie gras* and omelettes.

Accommodation and food

Auberge de la Belle Isle €€ *route d'Excideuil, Corgnac-sur-l'Isle; tel: 05 53 62 00 80; e-mail: info@la-belle-isle.com; www.la-belle-isle.com. Open all year.* Situated 5km from Thiviers on the D76, the hotel has five rooms and a restaurant specialising in traditional Périgord cuisine.

Auberge du Parc €€ *Hautefort; tel: 05 53 50 88 98. Open all year.* Five en suite rooms and a restaurant.

Auberge de la Truffe €€ *av. de Limoges, Sorges; tel: 05 53 05 02 05. Open all year.* With a swimming pool, billiard room, sauna, garden terrace and 18 en suite rooms, the *auberge* is ideal for those seeking a quiet holiday. The restaurant serves modern and traditional cuisine.

Camping la Chatonnière *Jumilhac-le-Grand; tel: 05 53 52 57 36; e-mail: camping@chatonniere.com. Open mid-Jun–mid-Sept.* Only 50 pitches but facilities include a waterside setting, tents for hire, places for motor homes, grocery store, takeaway meals, launderette and swimming pool.

Hôtel de France et de Russie €€ *51 r. du Gal. Lamy, Thiviers; tel: 05 53 55 17 80. Open all year.* The hotel has nine en suite rooms. No restaurant.

Hôtel du Grand Café €€ *1 av. Gambetta, Mussidan; tel: 05 53 81 00 07. Open all year.* Six of the hotel's ten rooms have en suite facilities. There is a restaurant and breakfast is available.

Camping de Gurson *Base de Loisirs, Carsac-de-Gurson; tel: 05 53 80 77 57; e-mail: lac-de-gurson@wanadoo.fr. Open Apr–Oct.* The site has 80 pitches and mobile homes and chalets to let. There is a restaurant, disco and bar and takeaway meals are available. Tennis and mini-golf.

Hôtel Lou Boueiradour €–€€ *pl. du Château, Jumilhac-le-Grand; tel: 05 53 52 50 47. Open all year.* Seven en suite rooms and a restaurant. Breakfast available.

Hôtel de la Mairie €€ *pl. de l'Eglise, Sorges; tel: 05 53 05 02 11.* The hotel has eight en suite bedrooms and a restaurant. Guests have use of the facilities at Auberge de la Truffe (*see opposite*).

Hôtel du Midi €€ *av. de la Gare, Mussidan; tel: 05 53 81 01 77. Closed mid-Oct–mid-Nov.* This small hotel (nine en suite rooms) has a swimming pool and a restaurant. Breakfast available.

Camping Municipal le Pontillou *Villamblard; tel: 05 53 81 91 87. Open mid-Jun–mid-Sept.* This small, simple site has 40 pitches, including places for motor homes.

Camping Municipal le Port *RN 89, Mussidan; tel: 05 53 81 20 09. Open mid-Jun–mid-Sept.* This small waterside campground has 25 pitches with facilities for motor homes; swimming pool.

Camping Municipal le Repaire *Thiviers; tel: 05 53 52 69 75. Open May–Sept.* Places with facilities for motor homes are among the 100 pitches on this waterside site, which also has a grocery store, bar and launderette. Swimming and tennis available.

Camping Plein Air Neuvicois *route de Planeze, Neuvic; tel: 05 53 81 50 77; e-mail: camp.le.plein.air.neuvicois@libertysuyrf.fr. Open Jun–Sept.* With 121 pitches, the riverside site has a restaurant and bar and offers takeaway meals. There is a launderette, and tennis and swimming are available.

Hôtel des Voyageurs €€ *r. Pierre Semard, Thiviers; tel: 05 53 55 09 66. Open all year.* Centrally located, the hotel has 30 rooms, only one of which has en suite facilities. There is a restaurant and breakfast is available.

Opposite
Hautefort

Suggested tour

Total distance: The main route covers 234km. The detour adds 26.5km.

Time: The route traverses some very pretty countryside, which means winding, hilly roads in places, so allow a good 4½ hours for driving alone – a pretty full day's trip, allowing for stops.

Links: From Mussidan the D709 heads south for 25km to Bergerac (*see pages 66–8*) and north for 24km to Ribérac on the River Dronne (*see pages 111–12*). The Dronne Valley can also be accessed from Thiviers by way of the D707/78 to Brantôme (*see page 109–10*).

Route: From **MUSSIDAN** ❶ head southeast on the D38, passing through **ISSAC** ❷ after 7.5km. After another 5.5km turn left on to the D4 to reach **VILLAMBLARD** ❸ in a further 3km. Continue on the D4 for 4.5km to Sargaillou then turn right on to the D42, which meets the N21 after 3.5km. Take the N21 north towards Périgueux for 23.5km.

Head east on the bypass for 4km then join the D5, travelling through Bassilac after 5km. The confluence of the rivers Isle and Auvézère comes about 2km east of Bassilac and the road continues to follow the Auvézère, passing through le Change after 7.5km and Cubjac (6km), where it crosses the river. After another 4km the road crosses the river again, at la Barge, and after a further 4.5km reaches the attractive village of **Ste-Eulalie-d'Ans**, which has an old mill by the river.

Continue on the D5 for a further 8.5km then join the D62 to reach **HAUTEFORT** ❹ in 5.5km. From Hautefort travel north on the D704, which reaches Cherveix-Cubas, where the river passes through an impressive gorge, in 5km. Another 5km along the road, turn left on to the D76, which reaches **Excideuil** in 6km. The village has a château with 12th-century towers.

Detour: From Excideuil head north on the D67, climbing steadily, passing through Dussac after 8.5km and reaching Sarrazac in a further 8.5km. At Sarrazac turn right and follow the very scenic D79 for 9.5km to **JUMILHAC-LE-GRAND** ❺.

On the main route, leave Excideuil on the D705 east and return to the D704 in 5.5km. Head north again for 9.5km and at Angoisse turn left on to the D80 to reach Jumilhac-le-Grand in 12.5km. From there take the winding, undulating D78 west to join the N21 in 14.5km, then head south for 4.5km to **THIVIERS** ❻. Continue on the N21 for 14km to **SORGES** ❼.

0   10km

Marthon
D16
Piégut-Pluviers
Augignac
Javerlhac-et-la-Chapelle-St-Robert
St-Martial-de-Valette
Nontron
St-Saud-Lacoussière
Mialet
La Coquille
Chaleix
Ladignac-le-Long
St-Yrieix-la-Perche
Glandon
D18
ac
St-Pardoux-la-Rivière
Jumilhac-le-Grand
5
D708
D675
Dronne
D12
Mareuil
Monsec
Villars
Champagnac-de-Belair
Thiviers
6
Sarrazac
Angoisse
D704
D78
D79
D80
D707
D67
Payzac
Lanouaille
St-Mesmin
D939
Brantôme
St-Pierre-de-Côle
N21
Dussac
D67
Excideuil
Verteillac
La Tour-Blanche
Bourdeilles
Sorges
7
Agonac
D106
Savignac-les-Églises
Coulaures
Tourtoirac
Hautefort
4
Cherveix-Cubas
Salagnac
Badefols-d'Ans
Auvézère
Montagrier
Lisle
Sarliac-sur-l'Isle
La Barge
Ste-Eulalie-d'Ans
D704
érac
D710
Tocane-St-Apre
Mensignac
D3
Antonne-et-Trigonant
La Barge
Cubjac
D5
Villac
Chancelade
Trélissac
Périgueux
Bassillac
Le Change
Ste-Orse
Ste-Orse
D3
Coulounieix-Chamiers
Le Lardin-St-Lazare
St-Astier
Atur
Boulazac
Ajat
Thenon
Coursac
E70
N89
Isle
Neuvic
St-Pierre-de-Chignac
Montignac
PÉRIGORD BLANC
D710
oux
Sourzac
Manzac-sur-Vern
Sargaillou
Rouffignac
Plazac
Vergt
D47
D704
lussidan
D4
Villamblard
3
N21
Vézère
Issac
Cendrieux
Les Eyzies-de-Tayac-Sireuil
2
PÉRIGORD
Ste-Alvère
Journiac
D709
Maurens
Pezuls
D710
Le Bugue
Campagne
Sarlat-la-Canéda
Liorac-sur-Louyre
Lembras
Bergerac
D660
Mouleydier
Trémolat
St-Cyprien
Beynac-et-Cazenac
D703
D936
Lalinde
D51
Le Buisson-de-Cadouin
Dordogne
Monbazillac
Couze-et-St-Front
D29
D25
Cénac-et-St-Julien
Domme
Faux
Beaumont
Belvès
St-Martial-de-Nabirat
igoulès
Bouniagues
PÉRIGORD NOIR

The Dronne Valley

Ratings

Villages	●●●●●
Architecture	●●●●○
Museums	●●●●○
Restaurants	●●●●○
Scenery	●●●●○
Art	●●●○○
Caves	●●●○○
Historical sights	●●○○○

The Dronne is a gentle, slow-moving river, with none of the dramatic scenery found in other parts of the Dordogne region. It passes through quiet meadows and broad-leafed woodlands, whose trees cast cool shadows over the water on tranquil summer days. This is an area for those who like the quiet, contemplative life – a place for relaxed walks and cycle rides; a place where you can find a shady spot beside the river and read a book, or slumber shamelessly. The major tourist attractions are well to the south, but there are still sights to be seen: the ancient abbey at Brantôme, the superb châteaux at Bourdeilles and Villars, where you can also visit one of the largest caves in France, with prehistoric art, stalactites and fantastic rock formations. Ribérac, a lively market town, is at the heart of an area rich in fortified churches.

BOURDEILLES✦✦✦

ⓘ Bourdeilles Syndicat d'Initiative *pl. des Tilleuls; tel: 05 53 03 42 96; e-mail: s.i@bourdeilles.com; www.bourdeilles.com. Open all year.*

ⓖ Château de Bourdeilles €€ *Tel: 05 53 35 50 10. Open for guided tours (45 mins) daily Jul–Aug 1000–1900; rest of the year 1000–1200 and 1400–1830. Closed Tue.*

Set on a gentle curve of the River Dronne, against a backdrop of a cliff bearing two castles in one, compact Bourdeilles (pop. 800) is a gem. Its houses, reaching up to the dominant château, cry out for photography. The **château✦✦✦** is in two quite distinctive parts: an austere feudal fortress dating from the 13th century and a much more relaxed Renaissance palace. The old castle, actually named *château neuf* ('new château') because it was built on the site of an even earlier fortification, has a 14th-century keep with walls 2.4m thick. There are wonderful views to be enjoyed from the top of the keep.

The newer building was created by Jacquette de Montbron, a gifted woman who studied geometry and architecture, in preparation for a visit by Catherine de Medici. As it happened, Catherine failed to appear and Jacquette did not live to see the building completed. Pierre de Brantôme, soldier, adventurer – he accompanied Mary, Queen of Scots, to Scotland in 1561 – abbot and writer of some pretty spicy stories, was born here in 1540.

A splendid collection of furniture from the 16th to the 19th centuries is housed in the Renaissance château, which has an extravagantly decorated *salon doré* with a painted ceiling, monumental chimney pieces and a superb tapestry: this is the room in which Catherine de Medici was to stay.

BRANTOME✦✦✦

ℹ **Brantôme** Abbaye, Boulevard Charlemagne; tel: 05 53 05 80 52; e-mail: si@ville-brantome.fr; www.ville-brantome.fr. Open all year. Guided tours of the town and boat trips.

🏛 **Abbaye de Brantôme** including the **Clocher**, the oldest bell tower in France (11th century), and a passage in the rock leading to the Cave of the Last Judgement; tel: 05 53 05 80 63. Open all year but closed on Tue Apr–Jun.

Brantôme is charmingly draped along both banks of a picturesque loop in the Dronne: the mellow buildings of the old abbey on one side; the balconied houses, colourful gardens and cafés and bars of the little town on the other. The two sides are connected by a 16th-century arched bridge. Brântome proclaims itself the Venice of the Périgord.

Brantôme Abbey✦✦ was founded by Charlemagne in 769, sacked by the Normans and rebuilt in the 16th century. Its most famous abbot was the chronicler Pierre de Brantôme (*see opposite*). The present buildings are from the 18th century. The baptistery in the abbey church has a 14th-century stone relief depicting the Baptism of Christ. Another, from the 13th century, shows the Massacre of the Innocents.

The **clocher**✦ (belfry) stands apart from the church on a 12m-high rock over an area riddled with caves, which were used by monks

Caves tour €€ *Tel: 05 53 05 80 63. Open Jul–Aug daily 1000–1900; rest of the year check with the tourist office for opening times.*

before the abbey was built. Dating from the 11th century, the gabled belfry is one of the oldest in France. Visitors may join a **guided tour of the caves**✢✢, including what was once the abbey mill, a dovecote and the Cave of the Last Judgement, a sombre place with a sculpted mural of *The Triumph of Death*.

The old convent buildings of the abbey now house the **Musée Fernand Desmoulin**✢✢ €€ *(tel: 05 53 05 80 63. Open Jul–Aug daily 1000–1200 and 1400–1900; Apr–Jun and Sept Wed–Mon 1000–1200 and 1400–1800)* which has collections of prehistoric art and the works of local painters. The **Musée Rêve et Miniatures**✢ €€ *(8 r. Puyjoli; tel: 05 53 35 29 00. Open Jul–Aug daily 1030–1800; Sept–mid-Nov Sat–Thur 1400–1700; early Apr–Jun Sat–Thur 1400–1800)* traces the development of French domestic furnishings from the Middle Ages to the present day in a series of houses built to a scale of 1:12. Meticulously detailed from cellar to attic, the houses even have tiny artefacts fashioned in silver, glass and china. One exhibit, especially for children, depicts an imaginary world of animals.

NONTRON✢✢

Nontron *5 r. de Verdun; tel: 05 53 56 25 50; e-mail: ot-nontron@wanadoo.fr. Open all year.*

Musée des Poupées et Jouets d'Antan €€ *Château de Nontron; tel: 05 53 56 20 80. Open daily in summer season 1000–1900; Mar–May and Oct 1000–1200 and 1400–1800; rest of the year 1400–1700. Closed Tue except in high season.*

Little remains of old Nontron, the most northerly town in Périgord. There are a few medieval houses, but its château dates only from the 18th century. Here, you will find the **Musée des Poupées et Jouets d'Antan**✢✢, an extensive collection of dolls from the past and present, also including such toys as fire engines, sea planes and toy soldiers. There is also a display of games of chance, including board and card games and roulette. Nontron claims to have France's oldest continuously operating cutlery forge. Wood-handled knives have been made by craftsmen in the village for over 500 years, using tools and methods that have changed very little in that time. Each knife is original and the handle is made from wood grown locally and air-dried for at least five years before being carved, shaped and finished with an unusual decorative design.

According to legend, the old castle, which no longer exists, was once terrifyingly attacked by raiders who sent in a herd of goats with flaming torches tied to their horns.

Left
Brantôme

RIBÉRAC✢✢

Ribérac *pl. Charles de Gaulle; tel: 05 53 90 03 10; e-mail: ot-riberac@wanadoo.fr. Open all year.*

Ribérac is noted as the centre of a region of churches with domed interiors. From outside, the churches look more like fortresses – and this, indeed, is what they were during times of conflict. The bell towers would have served as lookout posts and the domed construction kept vulnerable windows to a minimum. It also allowed a maximum of interior space – a necessity when the entire population of a village or small town might need to shelter from marauders.

Collégiale Notre-Dame €€ *Tel: 05 53 90 03 10. Open mid-Jun–mid-Sept daily 1400–1900; by appointment through the tourist office during the rest of the year.* Includes modern art exhibitions.

Most of these churches are very ancient, dating from the 11th and 12th centuries: Ribérac's own Eglise Notre-Dame was built in the year 1000, but suffered badly over the centuries. In 1568, during the Wars of Religion, it was burned down by Huguenot troops, and only the bell tower, the choir and part of the apse survived. Badly restored, it was battered again during the Revolution, when even the vaults were raided and lead coffins used to manufacture ammunition. Today, the church has been completely and more tastefully restored, using some of the original 11th-century stones, and the building is known as the **Collégiale Notre-Dame de Ribérac**, an exhibition centre and concert hall. It contains a collection of 17th-century paintings and has modern stained-glass windows designed by Henri Guerin.

Ribérac tourist office has published a leaflet giving details of a self-guided tour taking in more than 30 domed and fortified churches in the surrounding area. The leaflet, which has a map, is entitled *Le circuit des églises romanes à coupoles du Ribéracois.* A shopping and social centre, especially for many British people who have made their home in the area, the town has a large and lively street market every Wednesday and Friday.

Below
Horses and their riders cooling off in the River Dronne

St-Pardoux-la-Riviere✥✥

Located in a very picturesque part of the Dronne Valley, this small town was once an important stage in the Dordogne–Périgord postal

Musée de la Carte Postale €€ 46 av. de la Séparation; tel: 05 53 60 76 10; e-mail: bestofperigord@perigord.com. Open Apr–Oct daily 1400–1800. Closed Mon except in Jul–Aug.

system, a fact that is marked today by the **Musée de la Carte Postale Ancienne du Périgord** €€. Until 1750 St-Pardoux was the system's fourth most important station, after Périgueux, Bergerac and Sarlat-la-Canéda. Created in 1994, the museum has a collection of postcards and other documents representing the 557 *communes* in Dordogne–Périgord. A philatelic section traces the history of postal services in the region up to 1920. The museum is housed in a former police station and courthouse dating from 1680.

TEYJAT

Espace Muséographique €€ Le Bourg, Teyjat; tel: 05 53 56 23 66. Open all year, but closed Tue, 25 Dec, 1 Jan.

Away from the classic prehistoric sites found elsewhere in the Dordogne, the village of Teyjat proudly displays its own *grotte* – under the town hall. Stuffed with palaeolithic engravings and artefacts from around 10,000 BC, the cavern was discovered towards the end of the 19th century. For conservation reasons, access to the original engravings of bison, bears and other animals is restricted but the **Espace Muséographique** adjoining the site showcases the highlights and portrays the everyday life of Stone Age people.

VARAIGNES

Here's another unexpected discovery in the northwestern edge of rural Périgord: The village is home to **Atelier-Musée des Tisserands et de la**

Atelier-Musée des Tisserands €€
Château Communal, Varaignes; tel: 05 53 56 35 76. Open all year daily except Tue 1000–1200 and 1400–1800 (Sun pm only). Closed 25 Dec, 1 Jan.

'Charentaise', a working museum of the textile industry located in the Renaissance Château de Varaignes. Examples of the weaver's art are on show and there are demonstrations of processes from spinning fibres to the production of 'Charentaise' slippers, a regional speciality. Textile products are on sale in the museum shop. Aspiring weavers can join courses lasting from one to five days.

VILLARS✦✦

Château de Puyguilhem €€ *Tel: 05 53 53 44 35. Open daily in summer; daily except Mon in winter.*

La Grotte de Villars €€ *Tel: 05 53 54 82 36. Open for 1-hour guided tours Apr–Nov 1000–1900.*

Two attractions just outside the village draw visitors to tiny Villars. The first is the very striking **Château de Puyguilhem✦✦**, a 16th-century structure more typical of the Loire Valley than the Dordogne region. Deserted for many years, the château has none of its original furnishings, but there are magnificent chimney pieces, carved panels depicting the Labours of Hercules, coffered beams and massive chestnut beams. The exterior of the building presents a fairy-tale appearance, with towers, conical roofs, sculpted chimneys and balustrades and there are superb views of it from the surrounding grounds.

The second attraction is much older. **La Grotte de Villars✦✦** (*www.grotte-villars.com*) an underground network covering some 13km, contains prehistoric paintings said to be around 18,000 years old. Some of these have been covered by a thin translucent film of calcite, which has helped to prove their age. The network also contains impressive calcite streams, fine stalactites and draperies in yellow and ochre.

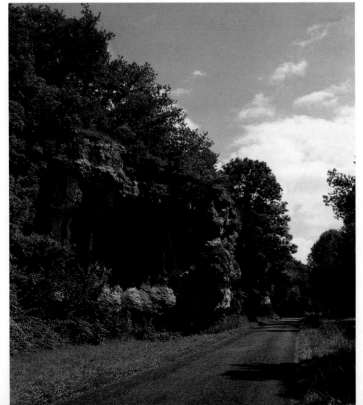

Left
Rock formation, Villars

Accommodation and food

Hôtel Chabrol €€–€€€ *57 r. Gambetta, Brantôme; tel: 05 53 05 70 15. Closed mid-Nov–mid-Dec.* Overlooking the River Dronne, opposite the town's 16th-century bridge, the Chabrol has 20 en suite rooms with direct-dial telephones and TV. The adjoining restaurant, les Frères Charbonnel, serves traditional Périgord fare and has a riverside terrace.

Domaine de la Roseraie €€€ *route d'Angoulême, Brantôme; tel: 05 53 05 84 74; e-mail: domaine.la.roseraie@wanadoo.fr; www.domaine-la-roseraie.com. Open Apr–mid-Nov.* The scent of roses pervades the air around this renovated 17th-century farmhouse, converted into a nine-room hotel. Each room has en suite facilities, direct-dial telephone and TV. The hotel stands in 4 hectares of wooded parkland and there is an outdoor swimming pool. Meals may be taken in the dining room or on the outdoor terrace.

Hôtel le Donjon €–€€ *pl. de la Halle, Bourdeilles; tel: 05 53 04 82 81; www.hotel-ledonjon.com. Open May–mid-Oct.* Only 25m from the château, the hotel has seven en suite rooms, a garden and courtyard. Private parking. Swimming, tennis and horse-riding available nearby.

Les Ecuries de Puynadal *Brantôme; tel: 05 53 06 19 66. Open Apr–Sept.* The campground has 30 pitches, with places for motor homes. Mobile homes and chalets may be rented. Bar; takeaway meals available; launderette; swimming; mini-golf.

Hôtel de France €€–€€€ *3 r. Marc Duffraise, Ribérac; tel: 05 53 90 00 61. Closed mid-Nov–mid-Dec and last two weeks of Jan.* A friendly, family-run hotel with an attractive restaurant and a relaxed garden dining area. There are 20 en suite guestrooms with direct-dial telephones and TV, and parking is available in the nearby marketplace.

Grand Hôtel Pelisson €€ *3 pl. A. Agard, Nontron; tel: 05 53 56 11 22. Open all year.* An outdoor swimming pool is the focal point of the hotel, which has 25 en suite rooms with direct-dial telephones and TV. Lunch and dinner may be taken on the poolside terrace.

Hostellerie Les Griffons €€€ *le Bourg, Bourdeilles; tel: 05 53 45 45 35; www.griffons.fr. Open mid-Apr–Sept.* Located at the water's edge, at the foot of the Château de Bourdeilles, the hotel is a 16th-century house with 10 rooms overlooking the River Dronne. Beams and ancient chimneypieces grace each of the en suite rooms, which are furnished with antiques. Modern amenities include direct-dial telephones, television and private parking. Fine dining is available in a magnificent dining room or on the flower-bedecked terrace.

De Masvicontaux *Nontron; tel: 05 53 56 02 04. Open Jun–mid-Sept.* Unsophisticated municipal campground with 70 pitches. Swimming.

Hôtel le Moulin de l'Abbaye €€€ *1 route de Bourdeilles, Brantôme; tel: 05 53 05 80 22; e-mail: moulin@relaischateaux.fr; www.relaischateaux.fr/moulin. Open May–Oct.* Charmingly situated, with a dining terrace right beside the River Dronne, the hotel has 19 luxurious en suite rooms with direct-dial telephones and TV. Private parking and garaging. The restaurant has a Michelin star.

Peyrelevade *av. André Maurois, Brantôme; tel: 05 53 05 75 24. Open May–Sept.* A municipal campground with 170 pitches, including places for motor homes. Launderette.

Relais de l'Archerie €€ *le Bourg, Villars; tel: 05 53 54 88 64. Open Mar–Dec.* The hotel has seven en suite rooms and a restaurant.

Rev'Hotel €–€€ *route de Périgueux, Ribérac; tel: 05 53 91 62 62. Open all year.* A new hotel in a garden setting, with 17 sound-proofed rooms, each with en suite facilities. Private parking. There is a restaurant and an outside dining terrace.

Hôtel Tilleuls € *Bourdeilles; tel: 05 53 03 76 40. Open Apr–mid-Oct.* Handy for the Château de Bourdeilles, this small hotel–restaurant (six rooms) offers simple but comfortable accommodation and traditional cuisine.

Suggested tour

Total distance: The main route covers 135km. The detour total is 33.5km.

Time: Allow 3½ hours for the main route and 1 hour for the detour.

Links: From Brantôme the D939 heads south for 22km to Périgueux (*see pages 86–97*). From Ribérac the D709 runs south through the Fôret de la Double to Mussidan (*see page 101*) in 24km. Here, the N89 runs east to Brive-la-Gaillarde (*see pages 152–3*) and west to Bordeaux (*see pages 42–53*).

Route: From **NONTRON** ❶ follow the D707 southeast for 10km to **ST-PARDOUX-LA-RIVIERE** ❷ and on for another 7km (to 2km beyond Milhac-de-Nontron), then head southwest for 6km to **VILLARS,**❸ passing the access to **Grottes de Villars** on the way. Continue southwest on the D82 for a further 6km and at Champagnac-de-Belair follow the D83 for 6km into **BRANTOME** ❹. Take the D78 west, reaching **BOURDEILLES** ❺ after 9.5km and Tocane-St-Apre after a further 14km. From here the D710 continues west to **RIBERAC** ❻, 14km away.

Detour: Head west out of Ribérac on the D708 and after 2km turn right on to the D5. After 6km the road reaches the village of **Festalemps**, where the domed church of St-Martin is marked by a sculpted Maltese cross on an exterior wall. The church bell dates from

1512. Continue for a further 5km to **St-Privat-de-Prés**, where the fortified church, with defences built above arches, is held to be one of the most beautiful Romanesque buildings in Périgord. Take either of the two roads north out of the village and in 2km turn left on to the D43 for 5km to **St-Antoine-Cumond**, which has a domed church with a 12th-century portal bearing sculpted geometric designs. Continue on the D43 to reach Aubeterre-sur-Dronne in 4km, then turn right on to the D17, which reaches St-Séverin in 9.5km.

Leave Ribérac on the D708 north and at la Borie, after 2km, turn left on to the D709 to reach St-Séverin in 10km. Head north on the D17 and after 4km, at Palluaud, turn east on to the D97, reaching Verteillac in 11.5km. From here head north again, this time on the D708, which continues through Mareuil to bring you back to Nontron in 35km.

Also worth exploring

The wooded countryside north of the River Dronne at **Bourdeilles** is well worth exploring. On the D106, just east of the town, is a rock formation known as **la Forge du Diable** (the Devil's Forge). Any of the unclassified lanes near here will take you into a fascinating area of small villages and hamlets ideal for ramblers and cyclists. **St-Julien-de-Bourdeilles** has a Gothic church with painted wooden statues and the remains of a 17th-century altarpiece. **Boulouneix** has a Romanesque chapel with a domed belfry and 17th-century paintings of St Jerome and Mary Magdalene. A fortified church with a painted wooden sculpture of Christ is at **Paussac-et-St-Vivien**, which also has a number of 16th-century houses.

The Valley of Caves

Ratings

Art	●●●●●
Caves	●●●●●
History	●●●●○
Museums	●●●●○
Scenery	●●●●○
Children	●●●○○
Food and drink	●●●○○
Villages	●●●○○

The Vézère river cuts its way from the rugged Corrèze down to the gentler Périgord. In the region known as the Périgord Noir, between Montignac and le Bugue, it passes through a stunningly rustic landscape punctuated by massive limestone cliffs. The cliffs are riddled with caves and rock dwellings carved by prehistoric people and continuously occupied for thousands of years. Here, humanity's beginnings are revealed in archaeological finds of ancient artefacts and bones – and in the large natural caves and grottoes through astonishingly sophisticated paintings and engravings of long-extinct animals created millennia ago with a skill that brings an irony to the word 'primitive'. Among these prehistoric art galleries is the greatest of them all: Lascaux, a treasure house discovered by accident, threatened by curiosity and saved by technology. The Valley of Caves completes the story of human ingenuity.

LE BUGUE✦✦✦

ℹ Le Bugue *Porte la Vézère; tel: 05 53 07 20 48; e-mail: bugue@perigord.com; www.perigord.com/bugue. Open Apr–Jun and Sept–Oct Mon–Sat 0930–1230 and 1430–1830, Sun and public holidays 1000–1300; Jul–Aug daily 0900–1300 and 1500–1900; Nov–Mar Tue–Sat 0930–1230 and 1430–1830.*

🅰 Aquarium du Périgord Noir €€€ *Le Bugue; tel: 05 53 07 10 74; http://aquafish.free.fr/ perigord/perigord.htm. Open mid-Feb to mid-Nov. Times*

A gateway into Périgord Noir, the busy market town of le Bugue stands on the north bank of the River Vézère, and as the western gateway to the Vézère Valley it has more than enough attractions to give a foretaste of what lies ahead.

A change from going underground, the **Aquarium du Périgord Noir✦✦** gives you the chance to see what life is like underwater. Looking through large windows set well below the water line, you can observe freshwater fish and crustaceans in surroundings made as natural as possible. There are massive catfish – some more than 1.5m long – and sturgeon and a special display on the life of the salmon.

La Grotte de Bara-Bahau✦✦ is a 100m-long cavern with drawings of horses, bison, deer and other animals scratched on the wall with flint and believed to be more than 17,000 years old. There are also scratchings made by the claws of a huge prehistoric bear.

If claustrophobia grips as you negotiate the tunnel leading into the **Gouffre de Proumeyssac✦✦** spare a thought for tourists of the past,

ary through the year, but
un–Aug 0900–1900, with late
ight opening to 2400 on Sat
n Jul–Aug.

a Grotte de Bara-Bahau
€€ Just west of Le Bugue, off
he D703; tel: 05 53 07 27
7; http://france-publicite.com/
4/bara-bahau. Open daily all
ear except Jan. Jul–Aug
900–1900, rest of year
000–1700.

Gouffre de Proumeyssac
€€ On D31, 3 km south of
e Bugue; tel: 05 53 07 27
7; e-mail:

who until 1952 entered the cave in a basket raised and lowered 52m by a mule-operated winch. No paintings or drawings this time, but the cave is rich in coloured stalagmites and beautiful crystalline formations.

Jardins d'Arborie⁺ (€€ tel: 05 53 08 42 74. Open mid-Jun–mid-Sept daily 1000–1900; rest of year daily 1000–1200 and 1430–1800) is a botanical park illustrating Périgord in miniature. There are 7000 rare species of plants, including bonsai, succulents and cacti.

The **Maison de la Vie Sauvage**⁺ (€€ 9 r. de la République; tel: 05 53 08 28 10. Open daily all year, Apr–Sept 1000–1300 and 1500–1900; Oct–Mar Sun 1400–1800) concentrates on birds, their habits, habitats, techniques for survival and hunting and their migratory patterns. There is a collection of stuffed birds and the palaeontology section houses a collection of more than 3000 samples of ammonites, gastropods, trilobites, etc.

proumeyssac@perigord.com; www.perigord.com/ proumeyssac/visit.htm. Open daily all year (except Jan) Jun–Aug 0900–1900; rest of year times vary. Guided tour of the abyss takes 45mins.

Farm-life of a century ago is demonstrated at the reconstructed **Village du Bournat** ✦✦ (€€€ *tel: 05 53 08 41 99; e-mail: le-bournat@ sitesenperigord.com; www.sites-en-perigord.com/le-bournat/default.htm. Open Mar–Dec daily 1000–1900*), where scenes involving groups of figures in different buildings show country folk at work and play. There are collections of agricultural machinery and tools.

Les Eyzies-de-Tayac ✦✦✦

Les Eyzies-de-Tayac 19 r. de la Préhistoire; tel: 05 53 06 97 05; e-mail: contact@leseyzies.com; www.ot-leseyzies.fr. Open all year.

Abri du Cap-Blanc €€ On the D48 in the Beune Valley, 6km east of les Eyzies; tel: 05 53 59 21 74. Open for guided tours (30 mins) daily Apr–Jun & Sept–Nov 1000–1200, 1400–1800; Jul–Aug 1000–1900.

Abri du Poisson €€ on the D47, 2km northeast of les Eyzies; tel: 05 53 06 86 00. Visits by booking at Grotte de Font-de-Gaume.

Grotte de Font-de-Gaume €€ On the D47 1km east of les Eyzies; tel: 05 53 06 86 00. Open (45-min guided tours, booking essential) mid-May–mid-Sept 0930–1730; rest of year 0930–1200, 1400–1730. Closed 1 Jan, 1 May, 1 and 11 Nov, 25 Dec.

Whichever way you approach it, les Eyzies comes as a surprise. From all directions you reach the village through charmingly rustic scenery: rolling hills dotted with woodland and farms and crossed by tumbling streams. Then, where the Vézère and Beune rivers meet, you come to this long thin village, hardly more than a single street, totally dominated by the massive, pale limestone cliff that has caused les Eyzies to style itself the World's Capital of Prehistory. This claim is certainly underscored by the concentration of other prehistoric sites in the surrounding area. The cliff is riddled with caves and shelters cut into the rock – used as homes and sanctuaries for thousands of years. Some families were still living in caves as recently as the 1950s, the last in a line of human habitation that stretched from the Stone Age to the brink of the Space Age.

Abri du Cap-Blanc ✦✦ one of a number of rock shelters in the area, contains a carved frieze of two bison and horses beneath which a human grave was discovered when the shelter was excavated in 1909. It is now a UNESCO world heritage site.

Abri Pataud ✦✦ is a large cavity in which evidence has been uncovered of civilisations from as far back as 35,000 BC. Sections of rock reveal flints, bones, the remains of fireplaces and a carved female figure. Other remains and artefacts uncovered during excavations in the shelter are displayed in an adjoining museum.

Abri du Poisson ✦ is so called because the figure of a salmon more than a metre long is carved into the roof. It dates from around 20,000 BC and is one of the oldest cave sculptures found so far. Delicate carvings and paintings of mammoths and other animals, created about 15,000 years ago, are spread over 100m of wall in the **Grotte de Bernifal** ✦.

The nearby **Grotte des Combarelles** ✦✦, discovered in 1901, has some 300 engravings of bears, bison, horses, reindeer and mammoths, also dating from around 15,000 years ago. Some of the animals are depicted in full gallop. The works, some superimposed on others, cover 130m of wall.

Grotte de Font-de-Gaume ✦✦ rivals the famed Lascaux cave, further up the Vézère Valley, in the number and quality of its prehistoric paintings, although some have suffered from vandalism since the cave's discovery

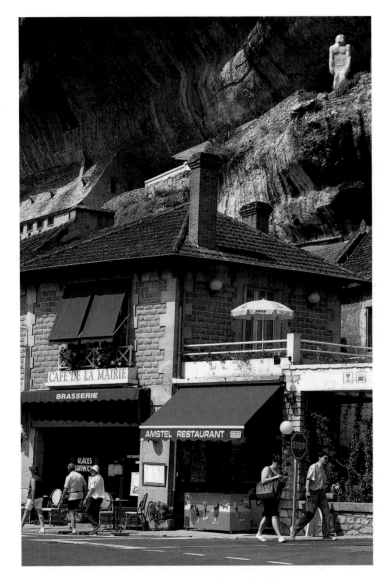

Abri Pataud €€ *Les Eyzies; tel: 05 53 06 92 46. Open early Feb–Mar and mid-Oct–mid-Nov Tue–Sun 1400–1700; Apr–Jun and early Sept–mid-Oct Tue–Sun 1000–1230 and 1400–1800; Jul–early Sept daily 1000–1900.*

Grotte de Bernifal €€ *On the D47 4.5km east of les Eyzies; tel: 05 53 29 66 39. Open for 1-hour guided tours Jun–Sept 0930–1230 and 1430–1830 (no lunch break in Jul–Aug); rest of the year by appointment.*

Grotte des Combarelles €€ *On the D47 3km east of les Eyzies; tel: 05 53 06 86 00. Open (45-min guided tours, booking at Grotte de Font-de-Gaume essential) 0930–1730. Closed Sat, 1 Jan, 1 May, 11 Nov and 25 Dec.*

in the 18th century. Among the many remarkable works is a stunning frieze of bison painted on white calcite. The contours of the rock face have been skilfully utilised to give the animals a three-dimensional form. The threat of environmental damage to the fragile paintings by humidity and carbon dioxide introduced by visitors may mean the cave has to be closed and replaced by a reproduction, as at Lascaux.

Right
Les Eyzies

Grotte du Grand Roc €€ *On the D47 2.5km northwest of les Eyzies; tel: 05 53 06 92 70; e-mail: grandroc@perigord.com; www.grandroc.com. Open for guided tours (30 mins) in English or French Feb–Nov 0930–1900 in summer season, 1000–1800 out of season. Not accessible for visitors with disabilities.*

Musée National de la Préhistoire €€ *Les Eyzies; tel: 05 53 06 45 45; e-mail: mnp.eyzies@culture.gouv.fr; www.musee-antiquitesnationales.fr. Open all year, for 1 hour visit Jul–Aug 0930–1830, Sept–Jun 0930–1200, 1400–1730.*

For a change of style, try the **Grotte du Grand Roc***, which has an amazing display of stalactites, stalagmites and other formations. There is also an excellent view of the Vézère Valley from the cave's entrance. An exhibition centre at **Habitats Préhistoriques de Laugerie-Basse** (€€ *on the D47 3km northwest of les Eyzies; tel: 05 53 06 92 70. Open all year except Jan; Jul–Aug 0930–1900, rest of year 1000–1800. Disabled access. Reduced price tickets available for visits combined with the caves of Grand Roc*) displays reproductions of prehistoric artefacts and bones discovered on the site beside the Vézère, just upstream of les Eyzies. The originals have been scattered among different museums and private collections.

For an overview of the area's prehistory (and, literally, its countryside) climb up to the **Musée National de la Préhistoire****, housed in the recently enlarged and considerably restored 13th-century château poised halfway up the cliff above the village. The museum is a cornucopia of wall paintings, rock carvings and prehistoric artefacts uncovered in the area in the 20th century. For a glimpse into the world of cave exploration, visit **Musée de la Spéléologie*** (€€ *les Eyzies; tel: 05 53 35 43 77. Open Jul–Aug daily 1100–1800*), where the history of the pursuit, caving equipment, and studies of geological formations and subterranean animal and plant life are exhibited in chambers carved out of the living rock.

MONTIGNAC***

Lascaux II €€€ *Off the D704 (well signposted from all directions) 1km south of Montignac; tel: 05 53 35 50 10. Open (45-min guided tours) Jul–Aug daily 0930–1900; Apr–Jun Tue–Sun 0900–1900; late-Jan–Mar and Sept–Dec 1000–1200 and 1400–1730. Closed 25 Dec and first three weeks of Jan. There is a daily limit of 2000 tickets, which is soon reached in the peak season. No disabled access.*

Left
Montignac

Here is a case of the attraction diminishing the town, for just outside Montignac, a pleasant riverside community on the Vézère, lie **les Grottes de Lascaux**, probably the most important and certainly the most famous prehistoric site in Europe.

The original cave consists of four galleries with more than 1500 coloured paintings and engravings of animals superbly executed up to 17,000 years ago. It was discovered in 1940 by four schoolboys searching for a dog that had fallen into a hole. The cave was officially opened to the public eight years later and in the next 15 years attracted more than a million visitors, but the carbon dioxide and humidity they introduced began to damage the priceless works of prehistoric art. There was only one way to preserve the works – and that was to close the cave.

To avert public disappointment, it was decided to build a replica and **Lascaux II***** opened in 1983. The 'copy-cat' cave, about 200m from the original, is the result of painstaking research and exceptionally detailed reconstruction. The cave paintings themselves were carefully photographed and the artist Monique Peytral copied

🅷 **Régourdou** €€
Adjacent to Lascaux
site; tel: 05 53 51 81 23.
Open Jul–Aug daily
0900–1800; May–Jun
0900–1200 and
1400–1830; Sept–Apr
1000–1200 and
1400–1800. Advance
booking (14 days) essential.

the photographs, utilising the techniques and materials used by the original painters. Lascaux II is a reconstruction of the two major galleries – the Bulls' Hall and the Axial Gallery – which contain the finest examples, and there are displays showing how the original masterpieces were created and telling the history of the cave.

A kilometre east of Lascaux II is **Régourdou**✶, a prehistoric site where the 70,000-year-old skeleton of a man, together with other bones and artefacts, were unearthed in 1954. 'Régourdou Man' now rests in the Périgord Museum in Périgueux, but a cast of his jawbone and a number of tools and bones found on the site are displayed in a small museum.

LA ROQUE ST-CHRISTOPHE✶✶

🅷 **La Roque St-Christophe** €€
Peyzac-le-Moustier, off the
D706, 3.5km from Tursac;
tel: 05 53 50 70 45; e-mail:
contact@roque-st-christophe.
com; www.roque-st-
christophe.com/indexgb.html.
Open all year, Jul–Aug
1000–1900; Nov–Feb
1100–1700; Mar–Jun and
Sept–Oct 1000–1830.

Nearly a kilometre in length and rising 80m above the Vézère Valley between the villages of Tursac and Peyzac-le-Moustier, this imposing cliff is like a prehistoric high-rise apartment block with about 100 caves hollowed out on five levels. Archaeological findings unearthed there suggest that the cliff dwellings were in use from up to 35,000 years ago. Fireplaces, stairways and carved-out passages, as well as post holes, drainage channels and water tanks provide evidence of continuous human habitation over the millennia.

ST-AMAND-DE-COLY✶

🅷 **St-Amand-de-Coly Presbytery** €€ Tel:
05 53 51 67 50. Open
Jul–Aug Mon–Fri 1030–
1230 and 1530–1900; rest
of year weekends and public
holidays 1500–1800.

Roofed with slabs of limestone, the old houses of this small village (pop. 300) are totally dominated by the fortress-like church that gives the place its name. It is one of Périgord's best-fortified churches – so well protected, indeed, that in the 15th and 16th centuries it was known as the St-Amand Fort. From a chamber above the main door, defenders were able to rain rocks and boiling oil down on to attackers, and in 1575 Protestants occupying the church were able to withstand a six-day siege by 20,000 soldiers backed up with heavy artillery.

In contrast to its militaristic exterior, the church's interior displays the simple, spacious beauty typical of Augustinian architecture – before the Hundred Years' War it was part of an Augustinian abbey. An audio-visual presentation on the church and its history is shown in the former presbytery.

ST-LEON-SUR-VEZERE✶✶✶

Right
St-Amand-de-Coly

Charmingly sited on a loop in the river, the village has much to offer, including one of the loveliest Romanesque churches in Périgord. The

Le Conquil €€ *Off the D66 across the bridge from St-Léon-sur-Vézère; tel: 05 53 51 29 03. Open May–Sept 1000–1900; rest of year 1000–1800.*

Château de Losse €€
Off the D706 2km north of Thonac; tel: 05 53 50 80 08; e-mail: chateaudelosse24@ yahoo.fr; www.uehha.org/fr/ Aquitaine/losse_en.htm. Open for guided tours (in English) Apr, May, Sept 1000–1230, 1330–1730; Jun–Aug 1000–1900. Disabled access over most of the house.

Espace Cro-Magnon €€ *le Thot; tel: 05 53 35 50 40. Open Apr–Sept 1000–1900; rest of year 1000–1230 and 1400–1730. Closed Mon out of season. Combined ticket with Lascaux II available.*

church's elegantly arcaded bell tower stands over the smoothly rounded apse and chapels like a mother hen guarding her chicks Inside are sections of Romanesque frescoes. Originally part of a 12th century Benedictine priory, the church was built on the site of a Gallo Roman villa, of which some remains may still be seen.

The village has two castles: Château de la Salle, on the square, with a 14th-century keep, and Château de Clérans, dating from the 15th and 16th centuries, overlooking the river. **Le Conquil**✦✦, in woodland on the opposite bank of the Vézère, is a limestone cliff into which dwellings were cut in prehistoric times. Visitors can gain an insight into such prehistoric skills as archery, flint knapping and rock painting. They can also enjoy a superb view of the valley.

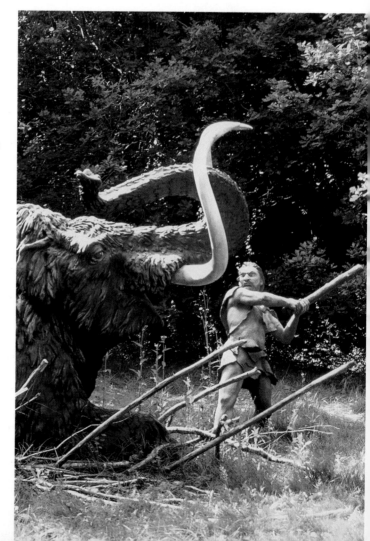

Right
Tursac's Préhistoparc

Visitors may tour the interior of the elegant **Château de Losse**✦✦, 4km upstream of St-Léon. Set high above the river and built in the 16th century, the château is superbly furnished with 16th-century cupboards and chests from Italy and Louis XIII furniture. For an exciting experience of prehistoric life, travel another couple of kilometres upstream to le Thot, where **Espace Cro-Magnon**✦✦✦ uses modern technology to re-create the distant past and serves as an introduction to the area's best-known cave sites, especially Lascaux.

Species of animals that have survived from the time of Cro-Magnon man, up to 35,000 years ago – such as bison and Przewalski's horses – roam the surrounding park while animatronics of such extinct animals as the mammoth and woolly rhinoceros give an extra touch of authenticity. The centre's innovative museum includes exhibits on prehistoric art and there are reproductions of paintings and engravings found in remote parts of Lascaux.

SERGEAC✦✦

Castel-Merle €€
Near Sergeac; tel: 05 53 50 79 70. Open for 1-hour guided tours daily Jul–Aug 1000–1900; rest of year closed Sat; Apr–Jun 1000–1200 and 1400–1800; Sept–Oct closes 1730. Nov–Dec groups by appointment only. Disabled access.

Sergeac is a pleasant riverside village with a restored Romanesque church, but its chief attraction, 1km to the west, is **Castel-Merle**✦✦, a prehistoric site that until recently was open only to professional archaeologists. A museum near the site displays necklaces and other artefacts from 150,000 years ago to the Gallo-Roman period. Some of the *abris* (shelters) in the area, including one with wall sculptures of animals, can be visited.

TURSAC✦✦

Tursac Préhistoparc €€
Tel: 05 53 50 73 19; e-mail: contact@prehistoparc.com; www.prehistoparc.fr. Open Mar–Nov 1000–1800, Jul–Aug 0930–1930; rest of year for groups by appointment.

The village provides another opportunity for a close-up look at prehistoric life. **Tursac Préhistoparc**✦✦ located in a small, steep valley, consists of a discovery trail leading to 20 or so reconstructions of aspects of daily life for Neanderthal and Cro-Magnon people, including cave painting, hunting and food preparation.

Accommodation and food

Château de Puy-Robert €€€ *route de Valojoux, Montignac; tel: 05 53 51 92 13. Open May–mid-Oct.* A 15-minute walk from Lascaux, the hotel–restaurant has 38 en suite rooms, a swimming pool and a well-deserved reputation. Imaginative cuisine is served in elegant surroundings.

Hôtel Cro-Magnon €€€ *les Eyzies-de-Tayac; tel: 05 53 06 97 06. Open May–mid-Oct.* Standing in parkland, this elegant country hotel has

22 rooms, en suite rooms and four apartments. Meals may be taken in the garden or in the rustic dining rooms. Private parking.

Domaine de la Barde €€€ *route de Périgueux, Le Bugue; tel: 05 53 07 16 54; www.domainedelabarde.com. Open all year.* The 14-room hotel is a restored, elegant 18th-century manor house set in formal gardens. Rooms have television and direct-dial telephones. Amenities include swimming pool, sauna and tennis. In the evening the restaurant is reserved for hotel guests.

La Faisandiére € *la Baronnie, close to Gouffre de Proumeyssac, le Bugue; tel: 05 53 07 24 17.* This farm–*auberge* has three double rooms and a 45-seat restaurant (**€€–€€€**) where home-made regional specialities are served.

Hôtel de France €€–€€€ *r. du Musée National, les Eyzies-de-Tayac; tel: 05 53 06 97 23. Open all year.* In a quiet location in the centre of the village, the hotel has 25 en suite rooms with direct-dial telephones and television, a swimming pool, garden and private parking. Its restaurant, Auberge du Musée (**€€–€€€**), specialises in Périgord cuisine.

Camping La Linotte, *le Bugue; tel: 05 53 07 17 61; www. campinglalinotte.com. Open Apr–late-Oct.* The campsite has 88 pitches; mobile homes and chalets are available for hire.

Les Marroniers € *pl. de la Gare, le Bugue; tel: 05 53 07 22 54.* This hotel–bar–restaurant has seven rooms for overnight guests and seating for up to 35 diners. Each room has television. The restaurant serves regional specialities.

Below
The River Vézère

Hôtel de Paris €–€€ *14 r. de Paris, le Bugue; tel: 05 53 07 28 16; e-mail: ehotpa@aol.com. Open all year.* Each of the hotel's 22 rooms has a direct-dial telephone, and there is a television room for guests.

La Roseraie €€–€€€ *pl. d'Armes, Montignac; tel: 05 53 50 53 92. Open Apr–Oct.* A charming hotel–restaurant at the heart of medieval Montignac. It has 14 well-appointed rooms and offers swimming, mini-golf, horse riding and tennis. Gastronomic meals are served in the garden-restaurant.

Hôtel Royal-Vézère €€–€€€ *pl. de l'Hôtel-de-Ville, le Bugue; tel: 05 53 07 20 01.* The riverside hotel has 53 en suite rooms with direct-dial telephones, television and balconies. A terrace where meals may be taken overlooks the river. Private parking. Rooftop swimming pool.

Camping Le Val de la Marquise, *le Bugue; tel: 05 53 54 74 10; www.val-marquise.com. Open Easter–mid-Oct.* Bungalows, caravans, mobile homes and chalets may be rented at this 104-pitch campground.

L'Abreuvoir €–€€ *31 Grand-Rue, le Bugue; tel: 05 53 03 45 45.* 'Food that looks good, smells good and tastes good' is the boast in this centrally located restaurant. As well as a 50-seat dining-room, there is space for 30 more diners on the terrace.

Le Chateaubriant €–€€€ *29 av. de la Préhistoire, les Eyzies; tel: 05 53 35 06 11; e-mail: info@leseyzies.com. Closed Jan.* Traditional dishes based

ⓘ Château de Lacypierre € *Tel: 05 53 29 39 28. Open by appointment (seven days' notice required) Easter–All Saints Day for guided visits.*

Château de Salignac-Eyvignes €€ *Tel: 05 53 28 80 06. Open (guided tours) Jun–Sept Wed–Mon 1030–1200 and 1400–1800. Last two weeks of Jun and first two weeks of Sept 1400–1800.*

on fresh regional produce are served in two large air-conditioned dining rooms and on a pleasant terrace in the tree-shaded garden.

De Laugerie Basse €–€€ *near the Grotte du Grand Roc, les Eyzies-de-Tayac; tel: 05 53 06 97 91; www.bugerie.basse.com.* Traditional cuisine dominates the menu in this restaurant where the dining terrace overlooks the Vézère Valley.

La Pergola €–€€ *16 av. de la Libération, le Bugue; tel: 05 53 54 18 05.* Pizzas, Italian cuisine and traditional Périgord dishes are on the menu. The dining room seats 60, the terrace 100. In the evening there is a pub bar and there is space for those who wish to play *pétanque*.

Les Trois As €€–€€€ *pl. de la Gendarmerie, le Bugue; tel: 05 53 08 41 57; e-mail: les3as@wanadoo.fr. Closed Feb.* Two locations for this sophisticated restaurant: the first can serve up to 200 on a terrace overlooking the river, the second seats 40.

Suggested tour

Total distance: The main route covers 127km and the detour 42.5km.

Time: Allow 3 hours' driving time and a full day (or even two, with an overnight stop) for sightseeing.

Links: At le Bugue you are only 10km north of the D29, part of the route west to Bergerac (*see pages 66–8*). From les Eyzies, the D47 heads southeast for 21km to Sarlat-la-Canéda (*see pages 132–5*). From Terrasson-la-Villedieu the N89 goes east for 10km to Brive-la-Gaillarde (*see pages 152–3*) and west towards Périgueux (*see pages 86–97*) 54km away.

Route: From **LE BUGUE ❶** follow the D703 for 4km to Campagne, then take the D706 northeast for 7km to **LES EYZIES-DE-TAYAC ❷**. Next, head east on the D47 and after 4km, in which you will pass the entrances to **Grottes de Font-de-Gaume** and **des Combarelles**, bear left on to the D48, which takes you by **Abri du Cap Blanc**. After 19km you'll reach **St-Geniès**, just east of the D704. This attractive village of yellow limestone houses has a 15th-century castle, the Gothic Chapelle du Cheylard, with 14th-century frescoes and a church with a 16th-century fortified porch.

Detour: From St-Geniès head southeast on the D61 and after 4km turn right on to the D60, which reaches St-Crépin-et-Carlucet in 2km. Here, the turreted **Château de Lacypierre⁺** may be visited by appointment. Take the D60 west for 4km, then head south on the D704 for 9km to Sarlat-la-Canéda (*see pages 132–5*). Follow the D47 for 8.5km to **Ste-Nathalène**, where you may visit the 16th-century Moulin-de-la-Tour for a free demonstration of the traditional production of walnut and hazelnut oils. Continue on the D47 for 5km and at la Font turn left on to the D61 to reach **Salignac-Eyvignes⁺⁺** in

10km. The village has pleasant streets, a square with a 13th-century convent and an attractive **medieval château**✦✦ with Renaissance and Louis XIII furnishings.

Back on the main route, leave St-Geniès on the D61 to reach Salignac-Eyvignes in 7km, then continue north on the D60 for 16km to Chavagnac, where you should bear left on to the D63, which leads through walnut orchards and vineyards to **Terrasson-la-Villedieu**, a lively riverside market town, in 10km. Cross the 12th-century bridge over the Vézère and head west for 7km to le Lardin-St-Lazare, where you cross back to the south side of the river and follow the D62 for 6km to Coly, where a lane on the right leads to **ST-AMAND-DE-COLY** ❸ in 3km.

Continue through the village to meet the D704 in a further 3km and turn right, reaching **MONTIGNAC** ❹ after 6km. From Montignac take the D706 for 9.5km and at **ST-LEON-SUR-VEZERE** ❺ cross the river on the D66 and after 5.5km reach **LA ROQUE ST-CHRISTOPHE** ❻, where it rejoins the D706 to continue through **TURSAC** ❼ and reach les Eyzies in 9km. From there head north on the D47 for 4km to Manaurie, a section that takes you near some important prehistoric sites, including **Grotte du Grand Roc**. At Manaurie turn left on to the D31, a winding lane that returns you to le Bugue in 11km.

Sarlat–Souillac

Ratings

Architecture	●●●●●
Walks	●●●●●
History	●●●●
Markets	●●●●
Restaurants	●●●●
Children	●●●
Food and drink	●●●○○
Museums	●●●○○

E ast of Sarlat-la-Canéda the Dordogne Valley presents a landscape of slumbering villages and rolling countryside basking in history. The river also moves at a gentle pace, its meanders becoming less extreme above the grand curve of the Cingle de Montfort. Sarlat, lauded by many as the handsomest town in Périgord, has a riverside ambience but is actually some 10km from the Dordogne. Souillac, right on the river, is just across the border in Quercy, in the Lot *département*. The two places have many similarities – both are dissected by major roads that obscure their true charm and both appeal to those who love to potter in narrow alleyways and lanes, perhaps finding a gem of a family-run restaurant or bar. Sarlat is an attraction in itself – its streets a living museum of architecture. Souillac is perhaps more workaday but still has much to offer.

SARLAT-LA-CANEDA✦✦✦

ⓘ **Sarlat-la-Canéda**
Office de Tourisme,
Ancien Evêché, r. Tourny; tel:
05 53 31 45 45; e-mail:
bestofperigord@perigord.com
or tourisme@sarlat.com;
www.sarlat-tourisme.com.
Open all year 0900–1200
and 1400–1900; summer
season 0900–2000. Guided
tours arranged. Tourist office
also on av. du Général de
Gaulle open Jul–Aug only.

Sarlat (as it's more generally known) is a wanderer's town, a place where you can follow your feet along narrow alleyways full of atmosphere, into streets and squares lined with ancient houses – so many, in fact, that the town is in effect a museum of architecture, protected by law since 1962. It's only fair to point out, however, that those streets and squares can become rather crowded at the height of the holiday season, for Sarlat is popular with tourists. But the plus side of this is that there are plenty of cafés, restaurants and bars and no shortage of accommodation and the town is positively jolly on Wednesdays and Saturdays when a massive market is set up around pl. des Oies (Goose Square). Geese, *foie gras* and fruit and vegetables aside, there is plenty to see in Sarlat.

Ancien Evêche✦, adjoining the cathedral in pl. du Peyrou, is the old Bishop's Palace, now converted into a theatre. One of its occupants was the Italian Bishop Nicolo Goddi, a friend of Catherine de Medici.

Place de la
Petite Rigaudie

0   100m

0   100 yards

Boulevard Eugène Le Rc

Hôtel
de Gisson

Boulevard Nessmann

Place
de la
Bouquerie

Hôtel
Plamon
Ste Marie

Place
des
Oies

Hôtel
de Vassal

Hôtel
de Génis

Rue Victor Hugo

Place
de la
Liberté

Rue Fénelon

Hotel
de Ville

Rue du Présidial

Rue Jean-Jacques Rousseau

Rue de la République

Rue Albéric Canuet

Hôtel
de Grézel

Rue de la Lib

Rue de la
Salamandre

Rue d'Albusse

La Présidial

Boulevard Henri Arlet

Hôtel
de Maleville

Maison de
la Boétie

Place
de Peyou

Musée

Cathédrale St-Sacerdos

Rue M   gne

Rue Sylvain
Cavaillez

Lanterne
des Morts

Cours
des
Fontaines

Cours
des
Chanoines

Rue du Siège

Boulevard Voltaire

Rue Tourny

Rue Jean-Joseph Escande

Ancien
Evêché

Place de la
Grande Rigaudie

Boulevard Henri Arlet

Place du
14 Juillet

Sarlat-la-Canéda

The building has an interesting mixture of architectural styles, with Gothic and Renaissance windows on the first and second floors respectively.

The **Cathédrale St-Sacerdos** was built mainly during the 16th and 17th centuries on the site of a church built in the 12th century. The original church was knocked down by an ambitious bishop who wanted a cathedral. The **Chapelle des Pénitents Blancs**, on the quieter, west side of the town, was completed in 1626 as part of the Pères Récollets religious foundation.

Sarlat is noted for its medieval *hôtels* – town houses built mainly during the second half of the 15th century when the place began to prosper again after the deprivations of the Hundred Years' War. **Hôtel de Génis**, next to the Présidial, the seat of pre-Revolutionary magistrates, is a big building with seven stone corbels supporting its overhanging upper storey. **Hôtel de Grézel**, near the town hall, is a more sophisticated building, easier on the eye with a tower and a half-timbered façade. But two buildings that best exemplify Sarlat's architectural heritage are the **Hôtel de Maleville** and the **Hôtel Plamon**. Hôtel de Maleville, pl. de la Liberté, was built by a 16th-century equivalent of a Yuppie, Jean de Vienne, a man of humble birth who rose to become Henri IV's financial secretary. The house was later sold to the Maleville family, who combined it with two other existing buildings to create a splendid mansion with stone reliefs of Henri IV and Marie de Medici grandly decorating the main entrance. Hôtel Plamon also carries a sculpted declaration above the front door – the shield of the Selves de Plamon family, prominent members of the cloth merchants' guild. It, too, combines buildings from different periods and so shows the development of the town's architecture. The narrow **Plamon Tower**, next door to the house, on r. des Consuls, isn't as tall as it looks: the windows have been made smaller the higher they get.

In a garden off r. Sylvain Cavaillez, behind the cathedral, is Sarlat's mysterious **Lanterne des Morts**, dating from the end of the 12th century. The cylindrical tower has a coned roof and two rooms. The

Musée-Aquarium
€€ av. Gambetta,
Sarlat-la-Canéda; tel: 05 53
59 44 58. Open Jul–Aug
daily 1000–1900; Apr–Jun
and Sept–mid-Nov
1000–1200 and
1400–1800.

**Musée Automobile de
Sarlat** €€ 17 av. Thiers,
Sarlat-la-Canéda; tel: 05 53
31 62 81. Open Nov–Mar;
weekend and public holidays
1400–1830; Apr–Jun and
mid-Aug–Oct daily
1400–1830; Jul–mid-Aug
1000–1900 (and at night
2030–2330 Tue, Wed).

Cabanes du Breuil €€
Off the D47 at Allas, 10km
west of Sarlat (signposted);
tel: 05 53 29 67 15; e-mail:
info@cabanes-du-breuil.com;
www.cabanes-du-breuil.com.
Open all year, Jun–Sept
1000–1900; Mar–May and
Oct–mid-Nov 1000–1200
and 1400–1800; mid-
Nov–Feb Sat–Sun
1000–1200 and 1400–1700.

Château de Puymartin
€€ Off the D47, 9km west
of Sarlat; tel: 05 53 59 29
97; e-mail: Xavierde-
MONTBRON.PUYMARTIN@
wanadoo.fr; www.best-of-
perigord.tm.fr. Open Jul–Aug
daily 1000–1200 and
1400–1830; Apr–Jun and
Sept–mid-Nov 1000–1200
and 1400–1800.

ground floor room has pointed arches and domed vaulting, but the room in the roof is inaccessible. Popular belief says the tower is a lantern of the dead – towers built to provide light and comfort for souls of the departed at night – but the room that would have been lit is sealed. Another theory is that the tower was built to commemorate a visit by St Bernard in 1147.

Right
Sarlat-la-Canéda

The town's best-known building, both historically and architecturally, is **Maison de la Boétie** on r. de la Liberté. Built in 1525, it has two archways at ground level, and the two upper floors have large mullioned windows with carved decorations on the stone frames. A richly decorated dormer window is in the steep gabled roof. The house was the birthplace in 1530 of Etienne de la Boétie, writer, magistrate and close friend of Michel de Montaigne, who was with him when he died in 1563. La Boétie's passionate plea for liberty, *Contr'un*, is said to have been an inspiration to Jean-Jacques Rousseau.

The past, present and future of the Dordogne river are explored at the **Musée-Aquarium**❖❖, where some 30 species of freshwater fish can be viewed at close quarters, as can such ocean species as Atlantic salmon, shad and lamprey. Exhibits show the development of fishing methods over thousands of years and there are sections on river craft, navigation, dams and modern management.

Aficionados of veteran and vintage cars will be in their element at the **Musée Automobile**❖, where a *concours d'élégance* of some 60 vehicles is ready for inspection. The oldest car in the collection is a Panhard-Levassor, built in the early 1890s, and another honourable exhibit is one of the few survivors of the 600 'Marne Taxis', which took 6000 troops from Paris to the Marne battlefield in 1914. Other *marques* represented include Bentley, Bugatti, de Dion-Bouton, Ferrari, Hispano-Suiza and Rolls-Royce.

Out-of-town places worth visiting are the **Cabanes du Breuil**❖❖ and **Château de Puymartin**❖❖. The *cabanes* are a group of ancient dry stone huts known as *bories* in Périgord. Soundly constructed, with conical roofs, the buildings are of uncertain age and their original function is a mystery. Built in the 15th and 16th centuries, the château stands on top of a steep hill and consists of several buildings linked by walls and towers. Inside, there are Aubusson tapestries, decorative panelling, paintings and period furnishings.

SOUILLAC❖❖

Souillac *blvd Louis-Jean Malvy; tel: 05 65 37 81 56; e-mail: souillac@ wanadoo.fr. Guided tours available. Open all year including Sun in high season.*

Standing on the borders of Périgord and Quercy, Souillac (pop. 3500) is a lively commercial town made busier by the fact that it is dissected by the N20. Move away from the centre, however, and you can find pockets of tranquillity among pleasant streets and squares.

The town has a history of turmoil. During the Hundred Years' War its abbey was repeatedly sacked by the English, but rebuilt in the 17th century only to be closed during the Revolution. Today, most of its buildings are used as a tobacco warehouse. In 1562 the monastery was pillaged by Huguenots and a decade later its buildings were set on fire; only the church was saved. The **Eglise Ste-Marie**❖, built in the 12th century, has three domes above the nave and transept and a half dome over the chancel. The best-known feature of the church,

🄼 **Musée des Attelages de la Belle Epoque** €€ *r. Paul Chambert, Souillac; tel: 05 65 37 05 75. Open Jul–Aug daily 1000–1200 and 1500–1900; Apr–Jun and Sept–Oct 1430–1830.*

Musée National de l'Automate et de la Robotique €€ *r. Morlet, Souillac; tel: 05 65 37 07 07; e-mail: musee.automate@ souillac.net; www.souillac.net/ musee.automate. Open Jul–Aug daily 1000–1900; Jun and Sept 1000–1200 and 1500–1800; Apr–May and Oct Tue–Sun 1000–1200 and 1500–1800; Nov–Mar Wed–Sun 1400–1700.*

though, is the west doorway, which was rebuilt inside out during restoration in the 17th century. Richly carved reliefs relate the story of the monk Theophilus who was extricated by the Virgin from a pact he had made with the devil.

The **Musée des Attelages de la Belle Epoque**✧ houses 60 19th-century horse-drawn carriages, with harnesses and stable gear displayed in a tack room. If you are travelling with children, you certainly won't want to miss the **Musée National de l'Automate et de la Robotique**✧✧, a collection of some 3000 mechanical toys, working models and robots. The core of the collection is a thousand automata donated by the family of Jean Roullet, who created spectacular Christmas window displays for the Bon Marché department store in Paris. Appropriately, the museum and the movements of figures in the collection are controlled by computer.

Accommodation and food

Camping les Acacias *Sarlat; tel: 05 53 31 08 50. Open May–Sept.* Sites for motor homes are among the 89 pitches on this campground, which has a restaurant and bar, takeaway food, launderette and a swimming pool.

Hôtel Altica € *av. de la Dordogne, Sarlat; tel: 05 53 28 18 00. Open all year.* A 'new generation' hotel offering simple but comfortable accommodation in modern surroundings at a budget price. Each of its 46 en suite rooms can accommodate up to three persons. No restaurant, but breakfast is available.

Auberge du Puits €–€€ *5 pl. Puits, Souillac; tel: 05 65 37 80 32; e-mail: aubpuits@souillac.net. Closed Dec–Jan.* The hotel has 19 rooms with television and direct-dial telephones. Wine by the glass is available in the restaurant €€–€€€.

Camping le Caminel *Sarlat; tel: 05 53 59 37 16. Open Mar–mid-Nov.* The campground has 100 pitches, with tents, mobile homes and chalets for hire. Full facilities for motor homes; restaurant; grocery store; takeaway meals; bar; launderette. Swimming pool.

La Couleuvrine €–€€ *1 pl. de la Bouquerie, Sarlat; tel: 05 53 59 27 80; e-mail: lacouleuvrine@wanadoo.fr. Closed second half Jan.* The hotel–restaurant is in a listed building with a tower that was once part of the city's ancient ramparts. Its 25 en suite rooms are individually decorated and furnishings are antiques. There are direct-dial telephones and television. The restaurant (€€) specialises in regional cuisine based on regional produce obtained locally.

Grand Hôtel €€–€€€ *1 allée Verninac, Souillac; tel: 05 65 32 78 30. Closed Dec–Mar.* Barely 50m from blvd Louis-Jean Malvy (the N20), the hotel has 42 en suite rooms with air conditioning, television and

Opposite
Souillac's abbey church

direct-dial telephones. There is a terraced dining area and wine is served by the glass in the restaurant (€€–€€€).

Hôtel de la Madeleine €€–€€€ *1 pl. de la Petite Rigaudie, Sarlat; tel: 05 53 59 10 41; e-mail: hotel.madeleine@wanadoo.fr. Closed Jan–early Feb.* Situated on the edge of the medieval city, the hotel has 39 en suite rooms each with air conditioning, soundproofing, television, direct-dial telephone and mini-bar. The restaurant (€€–€€€) specialises in regional dishes with the personal touch of the chef-proprietor.

Hôtel la Pagézie €€–€€€ *Temniac, Sarlat; tel: 05 53 59 31 73; e-mail: hotel-pagezie@wanadoo.fr. Closed Jan–mid-Mar.* This small (nine en suite rooms) hotel has a superb position in the hills 1.5km north of Sarlat and there are lovely panoramic views from the terrace. There is a swimming pool in the garden. The restaurant serves regional cuisine.

Camping les Perières *Sarlat; tel: 05 53 59 05 84. Open Apr–Sept.* The ground's 100 pitches include sites for motor homes and there are mobile homes and chalets for hire. Restaurant and bar; takeaway food; grocery store and launderette. Swimming pool.

Hôtel des Recollets €–€€ *4 r. J-J Rousseau, Sarlat; tel: 05 53 31 36 00; e-mail: contact@hotel-recollets-sarlat.com; www.hotel-recollets-sarlat.com.* Built around the cloisters of a 17th-century convent, with an attractive

Below
Souillac's abbey church

courtyard, the hotel has 18 rooms. There is secure parking for cycles and excursions are organised from the hotel.

Relais de Moussidière €€€ *Sarlat; tel: 05 53 28 28 74. Closed mid-Nov–Mar.* Located in a country park with a lake, five minutes from the centre of Sarlat, this hotel of great character has 29 en suite rooms, pool, bar and a gastronomic restaurant. Tennis, golf and horse riding nearby.

Camping Le Rivaux *Sarlat; tel: 05 53 59 04 41. Open Apr–Sept.* 100 pitches; simple facilities. Tents and caravans for hire.

Hôtel la Salamandre €€–€€€ *2 r. de l'Abbé Surgier, Sarlat; tel: 05 53 59 35 98. Open all year.* Close to the medieval part of the city, the hotel is a former distillery now equipped with 30 en suite rooms and five apartments. No restaurant, but breakfast is available.

Hostellerie-Restaurant la Verperie €€–€€€ *allée des Acacias, Sarlat; tel: 05 53 59 00 20; e-mail: hotellaverperie@wanadoo.fr; www.laverperie.com. Open mid-Mar–mid-Nov.* Just five minutes from the centre of town, the hotel is in a quiet setting. It has 25 en suite rooms and offers free, private parking. A large swimming pool is in the grounds. The restaurant (**€€–€€€**) serves generous portions of home-cooked fare.

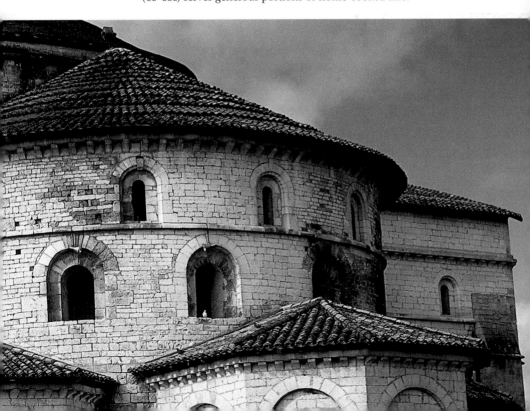

Vieille Auberge €€–€€€ *1 r. Recège, Souillac; tel: 05 65 32 79 43; www.la-vieille-auberge.com. Open all year.* With 19 en suite, air conditioned rooms, each with television and direct-dial telephone, the hotel also has private parking, exercise facilities, an indoor pool and a restaurant **€€–€€€**.

Suggested walk

Total distance: This is a gentle stroll around Sarlat of 1km.

Time: Without sightseeing stops, you could easily cover the route in 30 minutes. Why not allow yourself a couple of hours to see the sights and enjoy a sidewalk refreshment stop?

Route: Sarlat is very much a town of two halves, split more or less down the middle in the 19th century by the r. de la République, the main north–south thoroughfare. Most of the town's best-known sights lie to the east of the Traverse, as the main street is popularly known, though the quieter western sector has some interesting features. Among these are the Chapelle des Pénitents Blancs, a couple of medieval watchtowers – one sinisterly named Tour du Bourreau (Executioner's Tower) – and r. Jean-Jacques Rousseau, which has a number of attractive old buildings. However, you can save the western area for another time. On this tour we'll be concentrating on the eastern side.

Below
Sarlat by night

Start at pl. de la Grande Rigaudie, where there is a public car park, and take r. Tourny. After 50m turn right, crossing cour des Fontaines and cours des Chanoines to reach the Chapelle des Pénitents Bleus. Continue towards the back of the **Cathedrale St-Sacerdos ❶** and after another 50m turn right on to r. Sylvain Cavaillez to visit the **Lanterne des Morts ❷**. From a small park near the lantern there is a good view of the cathedral and its precincts.

Follow the cathedral end of the park round to r. Montaigne, turn left, then right on to r. d'Albusse to reach the Présidial and **Hôtel de Génis ❸**. About 25m beyond the Présidial follow r. du Présidial to the right and continue to the junction with r. Fénelon. Across the road, the building with the Renaissance façade is the 16th-century Manoir d'Aillac, which in 1640 became a convent for nuns of the Mirepoise order: during the French Revolution the convent was closed and the sisters executed. Turn left and follow r. Fénelon for 100m into pl. de la Liberté. Facing the square to your left is the Hôtel de Ville. A few metres beyond the town hall, on r. de la Salamandre, is the **Hôtel de Grézel ❹**.

Cross pl. de la Liberté and pass in front of Eglise Ste-Marie to enter pl. des Oies, scene of the town's very busy Wednesday and Saturday markets. On the right-hand side of the square are two more fine examples of medieval town houses – hôtels **de Gisson ❺** and **de Vassal ❻**. At the far end of pl. des Oies is **Hôtel Plamon ❼**, with the Fontaine Ste-Marie in front of it.

Return to pl. de la Liberté, passing the **tourist office ❽** and **Hôtel de Maleville ❾** on the right. Take the street on the right immediately after Hôtel de Maleville and follow it to **Maison de la Boétie ❿**, passing through the archway under the house to reach pl. de Peyou in front of the cathedral. Pass **Ancien Evêche ⓫** to your right and in 100m return to the starting point at pl. de la Grande Rigaudie.

The Bastides

Ratings

Mushrooms	●●●●●
Arcades	●●●●○
Archaeology	●●●●○
History	●●●●○
Markets	●●●●○
Scenery	●●●●○
Châteaux	●●●○○
Walking	●●●○○

By the time you have visited three or four of the smaller *bastides* you may be aware of some sense of *déjà vu*. Visit a few more and you'll appreciate the diversity in their configuration relating to the site, the geographical relief, history and landscape. Those who look closely at a *bastide* will be rewarded by a surprising number of clues about its human, cultural and economic history. *Bastides* were the new towns of the 13th and 14th centuries, making their mark particularly on Southwest France. They were built by the English and the French and were early – and in their time advanced – examples of town planning, with their characteristic grid layout, the central square for the market surrounded by the covered arcade. The creation of the *bastides* reflected a democratic expansion period in Europe. All had different economic, political, financial or military interests.

BEAUMONT*

ⓘ Office de Tourisme
pl. Centrale; tel: 05 53 22 39 12; e-mail: ot.beaumont@wanadoo.fr; www.pays-des-bastides.com. Open all year.

The *bastide* was founded by Edward I, King of England, in 1272. Most of its fortifications have gone, but a bit of the ramparts' remains can be seen. Many of the 13th- and 14th-century houses still exist. The fortified **Eglise St-Front***, in Gothic style, is distinguished by its four large towers. It was built after the rest of the village was completed. In one of the towers, which houses the bells, is the vast arch stone of the chancel vault, weighing nearly 450kg.

BELVES**

ⓘ Office de Tourisme
1 rue de Filhols; tel: 05 53 29 10 20; www.perigord.com/belves. Open mid-Jun–mid-Sept daily 1000–1300, 1500–1900; mid-Sept–mid-Jun Mon–Sat 1000–1230, 1500–1830.

This is not a *bastide*, but it is a small medieval town of great interest – and knows it, obligingly displaying plaques on its special attractions for the edification of its visitors. The initial pleasure is to approach from the D710 or D52 for an overview of the town spilling over its limestone enclave. No geometric streets here: houses and buildings are strewn around the castle and the church.

Musée de la Préhistoire €€

Belvès; tel: 05 53 29 10 93. Open all year, admission by appointment.

The Saturday market is a lively affair, with fresh butter and honey among its wares. The covered market, dating from the 15th century, has well-preserved supports of wood and stone. This and the old bell tower are in pl. d'Armes.

Belvès has a **Musée de la Préhistoire***, exhibiting items excavated in the area. The village is in a clearing of the great forest of Bessède, between the Lot and Dordogne rivers. Chestnuts and mushrooms are in abundant supply in autumn.

BESSE✤

Here is another forest village. It has a château from the 16th and 17th centuries and a **Romanesque church✤✤**. Detailed carvings on the west front doorway, believed to be from the 11th century, are of special interest, representing some of the Bible's more lurid scenes, and original sin and damnation.

CADOUIN✤✤✤

L'Abbaye du Cadouin and Musée de Suaire €€ Tel: 05 53 35 50 10; e-mail: semitour@ perigord.tm.fr; www.cister.net/viewabbey/72. 45-min guided tours Jul and Aug daily 1000–1900; shorter hours rest of year. Closed Jan.

Musée du Pèlerinage €€ Cadouin; tel: 05 53 61 46 53 (phone for information).

Musée de Vélocipède €€ Ancient Couvent de l'Abbaye, Cadouin; tel: 05 53 63 46 60. Open all year 1000–1900.

The town's market and old houses grew up around the famous **Cistercian abbey✤✤** in the Bessède Forest, though the village itself remained small. The abbey dates from the 12th century. Mention Cadouin and people think of the Cadouin Holy Shroud, which brought pilgrims to the abbey for centuries, and is still something people go to see. The embroidered linen cloth was believed to have been used to wrap Christ's head and to have been brought to Cadouin, probably by 1214, by a priest from Périgord. During times of danger, as in the Hundred Years' War, it was sent to places of safety to be looked after by monks. It was not until the late 15th century that it was returned to Cadouin.

A scientific study of the shroud in the 1930s suggested a connection with a caliph who had ruled in Egypt in the 11th century, and a 1982 study virtually confirmed the date, proving that it could not have enshrouded Christ's head. The shroud is exhibited in the abbey today in the **Musée de Suaire**. The abbey, in golden stone, is very beautiful, with many points of interest, notably the carved capitals in the cloisters, with four galleries, built in Flamboyant Gothic style in the 15th and 16th centuries.

Cadouin has a **Musée de Pèlerinage✤** (Pilgrimage) and a **Musée de Vélocipède✤** (Bicycle). The bicycle museum claims to be the biggest in France, with more than 100 cycles on show, from penny-farthings to a bicycle that took part in the first Tour de France in 1901 and another that competed in a race from Paris to Brest and back in 1893.

CHATEAU DE BIRON✤✤

Château de Biron €€ near Monpazier; tel: 05 53 63 13 39. Guided tours. Open Jul–Aug daily 1000–1900; rest of year closed Mon, times vary.

This massive structure – one of the biggest châteaux in the Périgord region – commands a great view from its lofty seat. It is about 7km southwest of Monpazier. They say pride comes before a fall, and Charles de Gontaut, a member of the Biron family in the time of Henri IV, provides a good illustration of this: it was his head that fell. As a so-called friend of the king, he received one exalted office after another and, in the late 16th century, the Barony of Biron was created. Charles was made a duke, and before long Governor of Burgundy. Showing no gratitude at all, he plotted to overthrow the

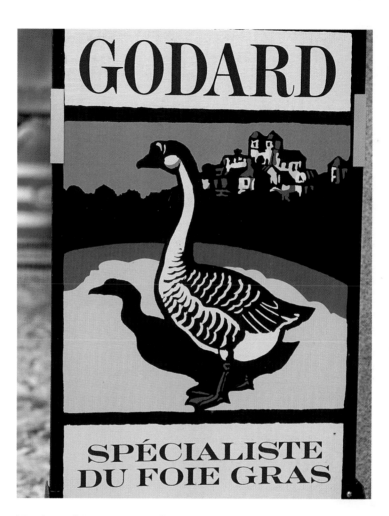

GODARD

SPÉCIALISTE
DU FOIE GRAS

Right
A regional speciality

kingdom of France. He was found out, and inconceivably forgiven by Henri. But he soon resumed his plotting. This time Henri was still prepared to forgive him on condition that he confessed. Charles was too proud to confess, so his head was cut off.

The castle was built over a period of several centuries by successive generations of the Gontaut-Biron family, starting with a 12th-century fortress. The result is a whole complex of buildings in different styles. It was rebuilt after Simon de Montfort knocked it down in the 13th century, and for years it bounced back and forth between the English and French. When maintenance costs became prohibitive for private owners more than 20 years ago, the Dordogne *département* bought it and carried out extensive restoration work.

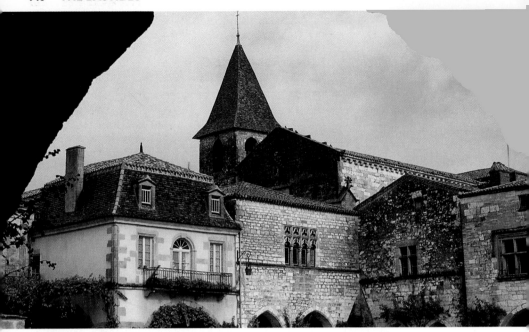

LALINDE

Château de Lanquais €€ *Tel: 05 53 61 24 24. Open daily Jul–Aug 1000–1900; rest of year closed Tue.*

Hôtel le Château *€€–€€€ 1 r. de la Tour; tel: 05 53 61 01 82; www.jpmoser.com/ lechateau.html. A small well-equipped 3-star hotel with restaurant (€€–€€€) and swimming pool. The seven guestrooms are en suite. Closed Jan.*

Lalinde, by the Dordogne to the east of Bergerac, was one of the first of the royal English *bastides*, having been founded by King Henry Plantagenet III in 1267. Even though the town has been quite heavily industrialised it still shows its *bastide* beginnings.

Near Lalinde, south of the river, is the **Château de Lanquais**✦✦, most of which was built in the 14th and 15th centuries, an addition to the fortification being built during the Wars of Religion. Two of the fireplaces are decorated with fine carvings. Visitors can tour the kitchens, laid out and equipped as in medieval times, and frequently filmed for TV programmes and the movies. If you are in Lalinde on a Thursday morning you may like to buy some wine, cheese, fruit and vegetables from the market. In the season (November to March) you can buy fresh truffles there.

MOLIERES✦

Maison de la Noix *Tel: 05 53 73 90 33. Open Jul–Aug 1000–1300 and 1430–1900; rest of year by appointment.*

Molières is a *bastide* whose population has shrunk over the centuries from about 1200 to 300. But it still has its central square and the nucleus of its grid-system streets. It also has its **Maison de la Noix**✦ or House of Nuts, which is a place where you can learn about how nut oil is made and about the cultivation, harvesting and use of the nuts. The fortress built to protect Molières still stands. Part of it is a dungeon.

MONPAZIER✦✦✦

ⓘ **Office de Tourisme**
*pl. de Comieres,
Monpazier; tel: 05 53
22 68 59; e-mail:
ot.monpazier@perigord.tm.fr;
www.pays-des-bastides.com*

Opposite
Monpazier

Here is a showpiece *bastide* that people want to revisit and persuade their friends to visit. Founded in 1284, it was declared a listed national monument in 1991. It is the archetypal village that time left untouched, yet is gratifyingly lacking in self-consciousness. Perhaps it is because it is also a workaday place in which the locals go about their business, accepting tourism without rancour.

Its streets are of the classic grid pattern and the square has its medieval covered market with little arcaded shops around it. The *cèpes* (Boletus mushrooms) are piled up on the market stalls in autumn.

VILLEFRANCHE-DU-PERIGORD✦✦

Below
Villefranche-du-Périgord

This *bastide* ranks close to Monpazier for its well-preserved state. Also like Monpazier, it is a great centre for wild mushrooms – there is a mushroom nature trail – and for chestnuts harvested in the woodlands

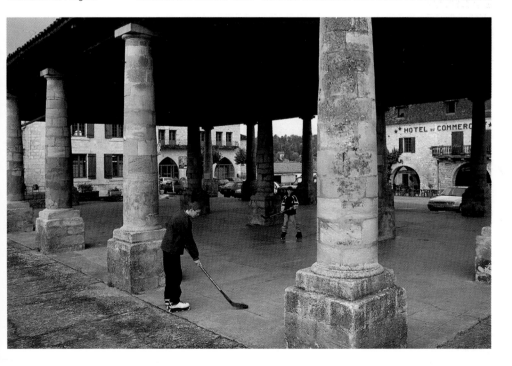

Syndicat d'Initiative *rue Notre Dame, Villefranche-du-Périgord; tel: 05 53 29 98 37; e-mail: ot.villefrancepgd@perigord.tm.fr*

in the area. The **Maison du Chataignier, Marrons et Champignons**** (*tel: 05 53 29 98 37*) presents exhibits on chestnuts, chestnut trees and mushrooms. Villefranche-du-Périgord was founded in 1261. It has a large covered market and some of its arcades remain.

Fortress villages

From a light aircraft flying over Aquitaine it's easy to pick out the *bastide* towns and villages by their 'noughts and crosses' streets and central squares. There are about 250 *bastides* in Aquitaine, a number of which are clustered in the southern part of the Dordogne.

During the 13th and 14th centuries, when the *bastides* were being built, the central focus of each became the village square instead of the church. The churches were built as strategically placed fortifications, and were used as a place of shelter for the people in times of invasion. From time to time some of the churches served as prisons.

Markets and trade fairs were held on the central square, and many medieval covered markets, with strong stone or stone and wood pillars, exist in fine condition today. Many still have the old grain measures in place. Around the square, buildings had arcaded fronts where tradesmen carried out their work.

The demographic growth of the time led to the regrouping of dispersed populations and according them franchises. For many decades the French and the English battled for supremacy, and founding the *bastides* was very effective from a military point of view – even more so from an economic angle. The citizens benefited from having the protection of their local seigneurs.

Among the founders of *bastides* during the two centuries were the counts of Toulouse, the royal dukes of Aquitaine, regional lords and the kings of France and the kings of England. As well as being centres of commerce, the squares had the civic and municipal buildings on their borders. The house of the seneschal or governor was always on the central square.

Accommodation and food

Auberge de la Salvetat €€ *route de Belvès, Cadouin; tel: 05 53 63 42 79. Open Feb–mid-Dec.* Twelve en suite rooms, a restaurant (€€) and swimming pool.

Camping la Bastide *route de Cahors, Villefranche-du-Périgord; tel: 05 53 28 94 57. Open Jun–mid-Sept.* 40 pitches (tents, caravans, mobile homes and chalets); motor homes accommodated. The site has restaurant, takeaway food, bar, launderette and pool.

Hôtel les Bruyères €–€€ *route de Cahors, Villefranche-du-Périgord; tel: 05 53 29 97 97. Closed two weeks in Feb.* The hotel has a swimming pool, 10 en suite rooms and a restaurant (€–€€).

Domaine de Fromengal *le Buisson de Cadouin; tel: 05 53 63 11 55. Open Apr–Oct.* This quality site has 98 pitches (tents, caravans, chalets, mobile homes); motor homes accommodated. It has a grocery store, takeaway food, bar, tennis and swimming pool.

Hôtel La Forge €€ *pl. Victor Hugo, Lalinde; tel: 05 53 24 92 24. Closed two weeks in Dec.* Fifteen en suite rooms and a restaurant (**€–€€**).

La Grande Veyiere *Molières; tel: 05 53 63 25 84. Open Apr–mid-Nov.* There are 64 pitches (tents, caravans, mobile homes, chalets); motor homes accommodated. Grocery store, takeaway, bar and laundry facilities on site.

Hôtel Manoir de Bellerive €€€ *route de Siorac, le Buisson de Cadouin; tel: 05 53 22 16 16; e-mail: manoir.bellevive@wanadoo.fr; www.bellerivehotel.com. Open Mar–mid-Dec.* The 12 rooms are en suite. The 3-star hotel offers tennis, swimming and a restaurant (**€€–€€€**).

Camping Moulin de la Guillou *route D703, Lalinde; tel: 05 53 61 02 91. Open May–Oct.* Waterside campground with 100 pitches with bar, swimming and tennis.

Le Moulin de la Pique *route D710, Belvès; tel: 05 53 29 01 15. Open May–mid-Sept.* Well-equipped waterside ground (tents, caravans, mobile homes, chalets), places for motor homes. Restaurant, grocery store, takeaway food, bar, swimming, tennis, launderette.

Camping Le Moulinal *Biron; tel: 05 53 40 84 60; e-mail: lemoulinal@perigord.com; www.lemoulinal.com/GB_welcome.htm. Open mid-Apr–mid-Sept.* Quality campground by the water with 250 pitches and just about every amenity – locations for tents, caravans, mobile homes, chalet, places for motor homes. On site are a restaurant, food store, takeaway, bar, disco, childcare, launderette, Internet café, swimming and tennis.

Camping Municipal Panoramique *le Buisson de Cadouin; tel: 05 53 63 46 43. Open June–Sept.* This is a basic site with 33 pitches.

Camping Les Nauves *Bos Rouge, Belvès; tel: 05 53 29 12 64. Open June–mid-Sept.* There are 100 pitches (tents, mobile homes, caravans, chalets). Amenities include restaurant, takeaway, bar, launderette, tennis and swimming.

Camping Le Parc *Sauveboeuf, Lalinde; tel: 05 53 61 02 30. Open Jun–mid-Sept.* Small site (27 pitches), with tents, caravans, mobile homes and chalets and places for motor homes. Bar and swimming pool.

Hôtel du Périgord €€ *pl. du 14 Juillet, Lalinde; tel: 05 53 61 19 86. Open all year.* All 20 rooms have private facilities and there's a restaurant (**€€**).

Hôtel La Petite Auberge €€ *Les Peyrouillines, St-Capraise-de-Lalinde; tel: 05 53 29 91 01. Closed two weeks in Nov and Feb.* The hotel has a restaurant (**€–€€**) and 10 en suite rooms.

Camping Du Pont de Vicq *le Buisson de Cadouin; tel: 05 53 22 06 70. Open mid-Apr–Sept.* Waterside site with 130 pitches (tents, caravans, mobile homes, chalets), space for motor homes. Bar, restaurant, food store and takeaway on site.

Hôtel Relais St-Jacques €€ *pl. d'Eglise, St-Capraise-de-Lalinde; tel: 05 53 63 47 54. Open year round.* Only five rooms, but all have private facilities. There is a restaurant (**€–€€**).

Suggested tour

Total distance: The route covers 117km.

Time: Driving time will be about 2½ hours, but give yourself a day for this fascinating trip through forests and ancient villages.

Links: At Lalinde, Bergerac (*see pages 66–8*) is only 19km to the west on the D660. From Belvès, travelling south, Villefranche-du-Périgord can be reached in 24km by way of the D710 and the D660.

Route: From **LALINDE ❶**, cross the Dordogne river, head west on the D703 for 3km to Couze-et-St-Front, then turn south on to the D660 for 6km, joining the D27 east, which reaches **MOLIERES ❷** in 9km and **CADOUIN ❸** 2km after that. Take the D54 southeast out of Cadouin, crossing the northern edge of the Forêt de la Bessède and arriving at **BELVES ❹** after 12km.

Next, follow the D52 southeast for 9km, passing through the village of St-Laurent-la-Vallée and continuing for a further 4.5km to **St-Pompont**, a village of typical Périgord houses. The English built a castle here in the 15th century, but now only a doorway remains. A cairn built on a hilltop on the western edge of the village is said to be a prehistoric burial mound. Take the D57 southwest for 9km to **BESSE ❺**, passing first through areas of scattered cultivation, then into an extensive forest of pines and chestnut trees. From Besse the road descends, twists and turns, then climbs again to reach **VILLEFRANCHE-DU-PERIGORD ❻** in 6km.

Leave Villefranche on the D660 west and in 3.5km take the D710 south for 9km and at St-Front-sur-Lémance turn right on to the D240. After 2km, at Sauveterre-la-Lémance, turn left on to the D426, reaching Lacapelle-Biron in 6.5km. From here, the D150 takes you to **BIRON ❼** and its imposing château. Continue north for 3km on the D53, turning right on to the D2 just beyond the small village of St-Cernin. The D2 leads to **MONPAZIER ❽** in 5km.

Continue north for 8.5km to St-Avit-Rivière. The river on which the village stands is the Couze, which joins the Dordogne after a very pretty run of some 18km. Turn left on to the D26 and in 2km arrive at **Montferrand-du-Périgord**, where there are stunning views to the south, looking over the river. The village itself is delightfully terraced and has a ruined château with a 12th-century keep. From the north bank of the Couze, follow the signs to **St-Avit-Sénieur** 4km north of Montferrand. The village name honours Avitus Senior, who served as a soldier in the army of the Visigoth king Alaric II, then became a hermit. A huge church and monastery buildings are the remains of an 11th-century Benedictine abbey.

Heading west, the D25 crosses a rustic landscape with some handsome manor houses and reaches **BEAUMONT** ❾ in 5km. From Beaumont the D660 travels north, staying close to the Couze and taking you back to Lalinde in 13.5km.

Around Brive and Rocamadour

Ratings

Caverns	●●●●●
Churches	●●●●○
History	●●●●○
Scenery	●●●●○
Walks	●●●●○
Architecture	●●●○○
Art	●●●○○
Children	●●○○○

For those spending their holiday touring the Dordogne and the Lot it's worth considering getting there by Motorail with the car on board. Brive is a main railway junction just over the Dordogne border in the Corrèze *département*. You could pause to see the museum in Brive's finest Renaissance town house, then leave the industrial conurbation for the pastoral expanses, green hills, lush valleys and walnut plantations of the region. Small medieval towns, the amazing pilgrimage destination of Rocamadour (teeming uncomfortably with visitors in summer), shops selling local foods and crafts, villages of rose-red stone – there's plenty to see. A 36-hectare lake for swimming and windsurfing, perhaps. A wildlife park. A monkey forest. Birds of prey demonstrating their soaring and nose-diving techniques at the Rock of Eagles. And aeons of nature's sculptures far beneath the ground in strange grottoes and gorges.

BRIVE✦

ⓘ **Brive** pl. 14-Juillet; tel: 05 55 24 08 80; e-mail: service-accueil@ brive-tourisme.com; www.brive-tourisme.com. Open all year 0900–1900, Sun 1000–1300; out of season. Closed Sun and public holidays.

Brive, or to use its full name, Brive-la-Gaillarde (the Bold), is not your typical tourist town, though if you dropped by parachute into its centre you could be forgiven for thinking so. Many of the 50,000 population work in the town's canning industry, but Brive's old heart beats with the gentle throb of past ages. Narrow twisting streets of well-restored tall buildings and new ones in gold sandstone live cheerfully together. You'll find good little cafés and interesting shops.

L'Eglise St-Martin✦, right in the city's heart, has a 14th-century nave and is believed to have developed from a monastery community 200 years earlier. The chancel was rebuilt in the 18th century, and the font has been dated as belonging to the 12th century. Archaeological excavations have suggested that previous places of worship on the site go back to the 5th century. Why Brive-the-Bold (or Brive-the-Brave)? Apparently the local people stood up gallantly to the many sieges they had to face.

Musée d'Art et d'Histoire €€ *Hôtel de Labenche, 26bis, bd. Jules Ferry, Brive; tel: 05 55 24 19 05. Open Apr–Oct 1000–1830; Nov–Mar 1000–1800. Closed Tue (90-minute guided tours available).*

Centre d'Études Edmond-Michelet € *4 r. Champanatier, Brive; tel: 05 55 74 06 08; www.centremichelet.org/inenglish.htm. Open all year Mon–Sat 1000–1200 and 1400–1800 except public holidays.*

The **Musée d'Art et d'Histoire**✦ is in the Hôtel de Labenche, a fine example of a Renaissance town house, and not only exhibits ancient items unearthed in the area but also reproduces some of the excavations that yielded them. The 17th-century Mortlake tapestries form a prized collection, showing rural scenes in rich colours.

In the **Centre d'Études Edmond-Michelet**✦, documents, photographs, maps and pictures relate to the work of the Resistance Movement locally and the camps to which local people were deported. Dachau gets special coverage as the prison camp where de Gaulle's minister, Michelet, was held.

BEAULIEU-SUR-DORDOGNE❖❖

ⓘ Beaulieu *6 pl.
Marbot; tel: 05 55 91
09 94; e-mail:
ot.beaulieu19@wanadoo.fr;
www.beaulieu-sur-dordogne.fr.
Open daily Apr–Sept; rest of
year closed Sun.*

**ⓗ Chapelle des
Pénitents €€**
*Beaulieu; tel: 05 55 91 11
31; e-mail:
chapelle.penitents.beaulieu@
wanadoo.fr; http://
perso.wanadoo.fr/chapelle.
penitents.beaulieu. Open
Jul–Aug daily 1000–1200
and 1500–1800; Sept
1030–1200 and
1500–1730; rest of year by
appointment (five days'
notice required).*

Below
Château de Castelnau

Apart from its natural beauty and narrow streets of thick-walled old buildings, Beaulieu has been put firmly on the tourist map by its 12th-century riverside church, with its marvellous Last Judgement sculpture and other points of interest: at **l'Eglise St-Pierre❖❖❖**, a conglomeration of rooftops of chapels, towers, the octagonal belfry and accoutrements gives the church distinction. Even as you approach the porch you discover why this Romanesque church, once part of a Benedictine abbey, gets special attention.

The sculpture depicting a vision of the Last Judgement at the south doorway provides much to absorb: Christ with trumpet-blowing angels and others bearing the Cross, Crown of Thorns and nails. Apostles, then the dead rising from their graves and a veritable chamber of medieval horrors. The well-preserved sculpture dates from the 1120s and was part of the work of some of the sculptors who carved the south doorway at Moissac (*see pages 212–21*). The interior has much to interest the connoisseur, and there is also a Trésor, a locked room containing such treasures as a 12th-century Virgin and ancient items of value from the 10th to 14th centuries. To view the Trésor you will need to make a special application to the tourist office. Downstream of l'Eglise St-Pierre is another much-photographed **Chapelle des Penitents❖**, now a small museum of local history.

BRETENOUX❖❖

ⓘ Bretenoux *av. de la
Liberation; tel: 05 65
38 59 53; e-mail:
ot.bretenoux@wanadoo.fr;
www.quercy-tourisme.com/
bretenoux. Open all year
0900–1200 and 1400–
1800, Sun high season
1000–1300; rest of year
closed Sun and holidays.*

**ⓗ Château de
Castelnau-
Bretenoux €€** *Tel: 05 65
10 98 00; www. monum.fr/
index.dml?new=1. Guided
tours Jul–Aug daily 0930–
1845; Apr–Jun and Sept
0930–1215 and 1400–
1815; Oct–Mar Wed–Mon
1000–1215 and 1400–
1715. Ticket office closes
45 min before closing times.*

The *bastide* village founded in the 13th century still has its square, covered arcades and parts of the ramparts. The big landmark near here – and big's the word – is the **Château de Castelnau❖**. Its red stone bulk fills the sky above the little community of Prudhomat, and is the second largest fortification in southern France. The keep dates from the 13th century, additions being made during the Hundred Years' War. Visitors on the guided tour learn about the Castelnau family who occupied the castle in medieval times.

Collonges-la-Rouge**❖❖**

All the stonework in this much-visited village blushes deep red. Collonges gets so busy in summer that cars are banned from its streets. A large parking area for cars and coaches is provided. People go to see the large, ornate houses, spiky with turrets and architectural whims, built mainly in the 16th century.

Gramat**❖❖**

ℹ️ Gramat *pl. de la République; tel: 05 65 38 73 60; e-mail: gramat@wanadoo.fr. Open all year, Apr–Sept 0930–1230 and 1400–1900, Oct–Mar closes 1800.*

🏛️ Police Dog Training Centre € *Le Ségala Gramat; tel: 05 65 38 71 59. Open house every Thur mid-Jun–mid-Sept 1530–1730.*

Parc Animalier de Gramat €€ *Tel: 05 65 38 81 22; www.gramat-parc-animalier.com. Open Easter–Sept daily 0900–1900; rest of year 1400–1800.*

This is a commercial centre of some 4000 people and the main town of the Gramat Causse, the limestone plateau that extends from the Dordogne Valley in the north to the Lot and Célé valleys in the south. The town has a sports centre, swimming pool and tennis courts. Horse races are held at a festival in early August. Local specialities in the shops include pewter and wrought-iron items, goose liver and truffles.

If you are in Gramat on a Thursday afternoon in summer you may like to watch a demonstration of **police dog handling❖**. Creatures of European origin, some species known from prehistoric times, can be seen in their natural habitat at the **Parc Animalier de Gramat❖❖**: ibex, bison, wild oxen, an ancient breed of horse and domestic poultry, pigs and other farmyard animals are among the species roaming the 36-hectare park. Trees, shrubs and plant specimens of the Gramat Causse are also on show.

Grottoes and Gorges**❖❖❖**

🏛️ Gouffre de Padirac €€€ *Gramat; tel: 05 65 33 64 56; www.gouffre-de-padirac.com. Open (guided tours) Apr–Nov 0900–1800 (1700 in Oct, Nov) daily.*

For experiences of sheer wonder, visit some of the grottoes and gorges of the region. Three of the most spectacular are worth deviating for. At **Gouffre (gorge) de Padirac❖❖❖** in the limestone Causse de Gramat, you take a boat ride along a river 103m underground to see the Lac de la Pluie (Lake of the Rain) and the vast stalactites hanging eerily above it. You go on to see another lake at a higher level and a vaulted chamber 94m high. You follow a path around the chamber's nooks and crannies, and get a good view of the lake and river, then return by boat through a series of galleries before disembarking. The bad news is that it's a climb of 455 steps to the surface; the good news is that you can take the lift if you prefer.

Visiting the beautiful **Grottes de Lacave❖❖❖** near Souillac involves a ride in a little open-top electric train and a lift to 12 caves with lakes, mirages and weird formations. Technology makes a bid to out-do

Les Grottes de Lacave €€ *near Souillac; tel: 05 65 37 87 03; www.grottes-de-lacave.com. Open daily (guided tour by electric train) Mar–Oct; Mar 1000–1200 and 1400–1700; Apr–Jun 0930–1200 and 1400–1800; Jul 0930–1230 and 1330–1800; Aug 0930–1800; Sept, Oct 1000–1200 and 1400–1700.*

Grotte de Presque €€ *Saint Médard de Presque; tel: 05 65 38 07 44; www.grottesdepresque.com. Open (guided tours 40 mins) Jul–Aug daily 0900–1900; Mar–Jun and Sept–mid-Oct 0900–1200 and 1400–1800; mid-Oct–Nov 1000–1200 and 1400–1700.*

nature in a 2000m² cave. Visual effects provide 'black light' and present a curious phosphorescent quality. A little imagination brings strange figures and scenes to visitors' minds in the sometimes grotesque, sometimes beautiful formations.

Stalagmite columns up to 10m high in various colours can be seen in several chambers at the **Grotte de Presque****, 5km from St-Céré. The walls are thick with fascinating shapes and folds – a veritable wonderland.

Right
Rocamadour

MARTEL**

ⓘ **Martel** *Palais de Raymondie; tel: 05 65 37 43 44; e-mail: martel2@wanadoo.fr; www.martel.fr/indexIE.php*

ⓜ **Musée de l'Hôtel de la Raymondie** €€ *Martel; tel: 05 65 37 30 03. Open Jul–Aug daily 1000–1200 and 1500–1800.*

Reptiland €€ *N140, Martel; tel: 05 65 37 41 00; www.reptiland.fr. Open Jul–Aug daily 1000–1800; rest of year 1000–1200 and 1400–1800. Closed Mon Nov–Mar.*

This place is close to paradise for the student of medieval architecture. It is a lovely little town, capital of the 11th-century Viscounty of Turenne and known as the Town of Seven Towers. Parts of the 12th-century ramparts may be seen. Architectural treasures include the 13th-century **Hôtel de la Raymondie**, built as a fortress and converted to a residential mansion in the 14th century. It now houses the town hall and a small museum displaying Roman items excavated at a site near the town.

Most of the streets have ancient buildings – a 12th-century tower here, a Renaissance doorway there. The 13th-century turreted Hôtel de la Monnai was where coins were minted. The Eglise St-Maur, built to double as a fortification, dating from the 13th and 14th centuries, has some fine 16th-century stained glass. A covered market at the pl. des Consuls belongs to the 18th century.

Reptiland*, on the N140 at Martel, presents nearly 90 reptile species, including snakes, crocodiles and lizards, with some scorpions and spiders.

ROCAMADOUR***

ⓘ **L'Hospitalier,** *Rocamadour; tel: 05 65 33 22 00; e-mail: rocamadour@wanadoo.fr; www.rocamadour.com. Open daily all year except 25 Dec and 1 Jan.*

ⓒ **Hôtel-Restaurant Ste-Marie** €€ *Rocamadour; tel: 05 65 33 63 07; e-mail: yves.lebastar@ free.fr.* One of a dozen 2-star hotels in Rocamadour, most with restaurants, the Ste-Marie has 23 rooms (17 en suite).

It is an incredible sight as you approach from Hospitalet or the Colzou road and see Rocamadour hanging on the cliffside, all red roofs and pale amber walls, with a castle on top. This is one of the great centres of pilgrimage of the Middle Ages and the most famous site in the Lot, poised on its perch in a narrow valley of the River Alzou. There is a great deal to see in Rocamadour, and in summer a continuous congestion of people trying to see it. Try to visit out of peak season when it should be less jam-packed.

Another downside: the souvenir shops. Most have shelf upon shelf of crudely fashioned pottery figures and so-called crafts, which detract from the reason that put the town on the map more than 700 years ago. This was the discovery of the mummified body of St-Amadour in a niche in the limestone in 1166.

Rocamadour's narrow streets are lined with buildings from the 12th to 15th centuries. The long sweep of the Pilgrims' Staircase is dramatic, with its slow procession of people, the most devout on their hands and knees, making their way towards the Chapelle de la Vièrge Noir. It contains the small statuette believed to be from the 12th century, and the Basilica St-Sauveur, where the body of the hermit saint was found, since which momentous discovery, miracles are said to have occurred. There are seven chapels in all, and they can be visited only with a guide. Unless you are a true pilgrim ask yourself how eager you are to take the tour, because in summer it can mean a lot of waiting about.

🅵 Forêt des Singes
€€ l'Hospitalet,
Rocamadour; tel: 05 65 33
62 72; e-mail: info@la-foret-
des-singes.com; www.la-foret-
des-singes.com. Open daily
Apr–Oct and some days in
Nov; Jul–Aug 1000–1830;
rest of year times vary.

Le Rocher des Aigles
€€ Rocamadour; tel: 05 65
33 65 45;
e-mail: rocherdesaigles@
rocamadour.com;
www.rocamadour.com/fr/
Curiosites/Aigles. Open daily
Apr–Aug afternoons only.

La Féérie du Rail €€
l'Hospitalet, Rocamadour;
tel: 05 65 33 71 06;
e-mail: contact@la-feerie.com;
www.la-feerie.com/
voyage_an.html. Open daily
Apr–mid-Nov. Demonstration
shows at various times from
1100–1800 (1630
Sept–Nov).

L'Aquarium €€
l'Hospitalet, Place de
l'Europe; tel: 05 65 33 73
61. Open Jun and Sept
1000–1200 and
1400–1800; Jul–Aug
1000–1900.

The most amazing sight in Rocamadour for many is the view of it hanging on to its cliff. With such great crowds drawn by Rocamadour, it is obvious that other diversions and entertainments will have been introduced. If you have children with you (and if you don't), this is where the fun starts. About 150 Barbary macaques live freely in 10 hectares of trees and open spaces of the **Forêt de Singes****. People can mingle with the monkeys, study them, take their photographs and feed them with popcorn sold at the entrance. **Le Rocher des Aigles****, near the Château de Rocamadour presents the big stars of the sky – eagles, vultures, owls and other birds of prey – flying freely to great heights and returning to their handlers' wrists. **La Féérie du Rail** is more than a model railway system. It has scenery, sound effects and all sorts of things moving in its midst, from the rise and fall of hot-air balloons to football matches. The **Old Toy Car Museum*** is a nostalgia trip among gleaming pedal cars made between 1910 and 1960 and a great collection of Dinky cars. **L'Aquarium*** showcases flora and fauna of cold continental waters, with fish and curious crustaceans.

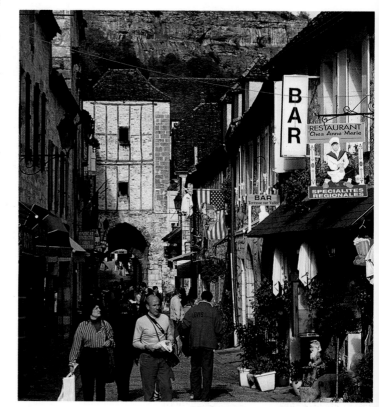

Right
Rocamadour's rue de la
Couronnerie

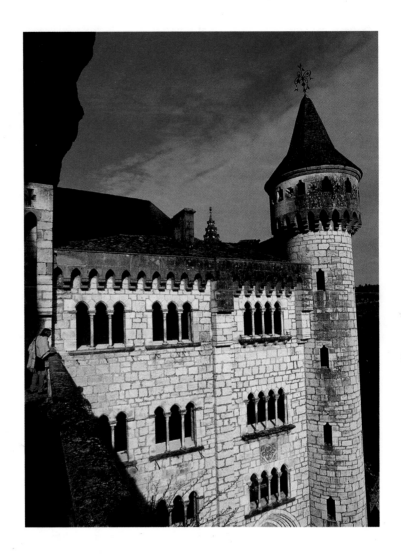

Right
Rocamadour's St-Sauveur

ST-CÉRÉ✦✦✦

ℹ **St-Céré** pl. de la
République; tel: 05 65
38 11 85; e-mail: saint-
cere@wanadoo.fr. Open daily
in high season 0900–1230
and 1400–1900, Sun and
public holidays 1000–1230;
rest of year 1000–1200 and
1400–1800. Closed Sun.

The centre of St-Céré has some venerable buildings in its little streets, having been lucky in surviving the Hundred Years' War with comparatively little plunder. Streets such as pl. du Mercadial and r. St-Cyr have houses from the Middle Ages to the 15th century. It was the hilltop fortification 2km north of St-Céré that defended the town from onslaught. Most of the castle has gone now, but two medieval towers – the Tours de St Laurent – can be seen long before you reach them.

Atelier Musée Jean Lurçat €€ *Tours de St-Laurent, St-Céré; tel: 05 65 38 28 21; e-mail: affaires-culturelles-sportive@cg.fr. Open mid-Jul–Sept daily 0930–1200, 1430–1830.*

Galerie du Casino € *av. Jean Mouliérat; tel: 05 65 38 19 60; e-mail: contact@le-casino.fr; www.le-casino.fr. Open daily 0900–1200 and 1400–1900. Closed Tue from Oct–Jun.*

This is where cubist artist Jean Lurçat made his home after World War II, having been introduced to the Lot region by his work in the Resistance Movement. He worked in several media, including ceramics and mosaics, and was responsible for restoring an interest in tapestries through his impact-making, sometimes strange, designs. Lurçat died in 1966, aged 74. His studio, examples of his work and some downstairs rooms of his home form a fascinating **museum**. In St-Céré, just off blvd Jean Lurçat, is the **Galerie du Casino***, exhibiting a large collection of Lurçat's imaginative tapestries. Temporary exhibitions are also held at the Casino.

Accommodation and food

Les Charmilles €€–€€€ *20 blvd St-Rodolphe de Turenne, Beaulieu-sur Dordogne; tel: 05 55 91 29 29; e-mail: contact@auberge-charmilles.com; www.auberge-charmilles.com/anglais/hotel.html.* Hotel with eight en suite guest rooms.

Chateau du Doux €€€ *Altillac, Corrèze; tel: 05 55 91 94 00; e-mail: lechateaududoux@wanadoo.fr; www.chateau-du-doux.com.* A castle renovated in 1995 providing 4-star accommodation in 19 rooms, and 11 apartments for up to six guests. Located directly north of Beaulieu and 50km from Brive. Courtesy car available.

Above
St-Céré

Château de Treyne €€–€€€ *Lacave; tel: 05 65 27 60 60. Closed mid-Nov–mid-Dec.* The 4-star hotel–restaurant is air conditioned and has 14 well-equipped rooms, swimming pool and tennis courts.

Hôtel Domaine de la Rhue €€–€€€ *Near Rocamadour; tel: 05 56 65 33 71 50; e-mail: domainedelarhue@wanadoo.fr; www.domainedelarhue.com.* The hotel is in a quiet location 6km on the road towards Brive. It has 14 rooms with direct-dial telephones.

La Segalières holiday village *route de Cajarc, Gramat; tel: 05 65 38 76 92. Open Jun–Sept.* Quality campsite with boulodrome, mini-golf, volley ball, tennis, swimming and a children's playground. 75 pitches.

Le Turenne €€–€€€ *1 blvd St-Rodolphe de Turenne, Beaulieu-sur-Dordogne; tel: 05 55 91 10 16. Closed mid-Dec–Jan.* A renowned restaurant in an old abbey. Also a comfortable place to stay (€€) with 15 rooms.

Suggested tour

Total distance: The main route covers 112km. The detour totals 25km.

Time: Much of the main route and the detour is over winding, very hilly roads, through picturesque and at times spectacular scenery, so allow 4 hours for driving time alone. Allow an hour for the detour.

Links: At Martel the N140 goes north for 33km to Brive-la-Gaillard and southeast for 58km to Figeac (*see pages 172–6*). The D703 heads west for 15km to Souillac (*see pages 135–6*).

Route: From **MARTEL** ❶ take the N140 south, crossing the Dordogne at Gluges, and after 5km head east on the D43 which reaches Carennac in a further 12.5km. **Carennac**, one of the most attractive villages along the river, was where François de Fénelon (*see Château de Fénelon, page 80*) spent 15 years as senior prior before becoming archbishop of Cambrai. The Maison de la Quercynoise is a museum featuring the Dordogne and the people who live along its course. The restored cloisters of the old priory and the 12th-century Eglise St-Pierre are also worth a visit.

At the eastern end of the village cross the river, then follow the D3 to Puybrun, a distance of 5km. Next take the D703 east for 5km to **BRETENOUX** ❷. From here head west again, this time on the D14, bearing south on to the D19 at Prudhomat, beneath the bulk of the **Château Castelnau-Bretenoux**, to reach **ST-CERE** ❸, then on to the D673 west, passing through Montal and near the **GROTTE DE PRESQUE** ❹.

At the hamlet of le Râtier, 12.5km from St-Céré, the D90 takes you for 2.5km to the **GOUFFRE DE PADIRAC** ❺. Return to le Râtier and follow the D60 south for 3km then turn right on to the D677 to reach **GRAMAT**, a busy agricultural centre, in 8km. From Gramat the most

spectacular way to **ROCAMADOUR** ❻ is by way of the D39 west and the D32 north, a distance of 17km. Leave Rocamadour on the D247 and travel north for 10km to reach **GROTTES DE LACAVE** ❼.

Detour: From Lacave take the D43 west to Belcastel, where a restored medieval castle is perched dramatically at the top of a sheer cliff overlooking the confluence of the Dordogne and Ouysse rivers. Pass the Château de la Treyne, another clifftop castle dating from the 14th century and now a hotel, to reach **SOUILLAC** ❽ (*see pages 135–6*) in a total of 10.5km. From Souillac head east on the D703 and after 7km turn right on to the D15, crossing the Dordogne from St-Sozy to reach Meyronne after a further 5.5km.

From Lacave the main route continues along the D23 through a striking terrain of rocks, cliffs and small fields to the lovely riverside village of Meyronne, one-time domain of the Bishops of Tulle, 7km away. Cross the river to Creysse, another very charming village of narrow streets and red-roofed housed. Next, after another 4.5km, comes Gluges, stunningly set at the foot of steep cliffs overlooking the river. From Gluges, Martel is 7km north along another scenic section of the D23.

Opposite
St-Céré

The Célé and Lot valleys

Ratings

Scenery	●●●●●
Caves	●●●●○
Villages	●●●●○
Architecture	●●●○○
Boating and canoeing	●●●○○
Castles	●●●○○
Walking	●●●○○
Children	●●○○○

The countryside embraced by the rivers Lot and Célé is among the most striking in the whole of Southwest France. It is very much a region of contrasts, though there is a common theme of rural tranquillity. There are mountainous areas, traversed by white-knuckle, corniche-style roads. There are sheer cliffs hanging over villages whose peaceful ambience draws a veil over centuries of bloodshed. There are delightful meadows and shady woodlands. And there are the two rivers, each quite different from the other. The Lot is the mightier – broad, fast-flowing and navigable – its power awesomely obvious as it plunges savagely over a weir. Here and there it is squeezed between cliffs and near its confluence with the Célé it provides an artistic touch to the towering village of St-Cirq-Lapopie. The Célé is the quiet one, gently tumbling over rocks and flowing serenely through ancient woods.

CABRERETS✦✦✦

🏛 Grotte du Pech Merle €€€ *Cabrerets; tel: 05 65 31 27 05; www.quercy.net/pechmerle/ visite_fr.html. Open daily Apr–Nov 0930–1200 and 1330–1700. Visitor numbers limited to 700 per day. Booking advised Jun–Sept.*

ℹ Office de Tourisme *Tel: 05 65 31 27 12; Open Apr–Sept; rest of year refer to office de tourisme, Saint-Cirq Lapopie; tel: 05 65 31 37 02.*

Cabrerets is in a stunning position, set against a background of rocky cliffs where the rivers Sagne and Célé meet. Nearby are the ruins of the Château du Diable, which is also known as the Castle of the English for it was from here during the Hundred Years' War that an English occupying force used to set out on raids. Also on the edge of the village is the massive Château Gontaut-Biron, built in the 14th and 15th centuries.

The real attraction here, however, is the **Grotte du Pech Merle✦✦✦**, discovered by two 14-year-old boys in 1922 and a close rival to Lascaux in the quality of its prehistoric paintings and engravings. More than a kilometre of chambers and galleries are open to the public. Among the works of art created more than 10,000 years ago is a frieze 7m long and 3m high with drawings of mammoths and bison. Elsewhere there are silhouettes of horses, with a pattern of dots, the engraving of a bear's head and handprints made by placing hands flat against the rock and tracing their shapes in various pigments. You can

Right
Cabrerets

🏛 Musée Amédée-Lémozi €€

Cabrerets; tel: 05 65 31 27 05; www.quercy.net/ pechmerle/musee.html. Open Palm Sunday to All Saints' Day daily 0930–1200 and 1330–1700. Combined entry ticket for cave and museum available.

also see the footprints of a prehistoric visitor to the cave, set forever as he trudged through what was then mud. One of the chambers contains the bones of bears that once sheltered there.

Adjoining the entrance to the cave is the **Musée Amédée-Lémozi**, named after the Abbé Lémozi, a local priest with a special interest in prehistory and speleology. It was his work that inspired the two youths who found the cave in 1922 and it was he who recognised its importance. The museum houses a display of works of art, tools, weapons and other artefacts from 160 prehistoric sites in France.

CAJARC✧

🏛 Maison des Arts Georges-Pompidou
€€ *route de Figeac, Cajarc; tel: 05 65 40 78 41 or 05 65 40 63 97. Open daily 1400–1800. Closed Tue.*

This small town, which has more of the ambience of places closer to the Mediterranean, has two special distinctions: it was the birthplace of the writer Françoise Sagan and is the former home of President Pompidou, and it is thanks to M. Pompidou that Cajarc has become an important centre of contemporary art. The works of leading European artists displayed in exhibitions are staged in the **Maison des Arts Georges-Pompidou✧**. Temporary exhibitions of contemporary art are also held in the gallery, **L'Acadie✧** (**€€** *pl. de l'Eglise, Cajarc; tel: 05 65 40 76 37. Open mid-Mar–Nov Tue–Sun 1000–1900*).

CAPDENAC✧

ℹ Office de Tourisme & Musée de Donjon
Cardenac-le-Haut *pl. Lucter; tel: 05 65 50 01 45; e-mail: ot-capdenac-lot@ wanadoo.fr; www.capdenac.net. Open Jul–Aug Mon–Sat 0930–1230 and 1430–1830, Sun 1430–1830; Sept–Jun Tue–Sat 1400–1800. Closed Sun, Mon.*

With ramparts dating from the 13th and 14th centuries, including ancient gateways and the bulk of a turreted square keep, the village has changed little over the centuries. Set on a promontory in a meander of the Lot, it gazes down on Capdenac-Gare, a busy rail junction on the opposite bank. The community's history, with the emphasis on Gallo-Roman and medieval times, is related in the **Musée de Donjon✧**, housed in the old keep, where you will also find the tourism office.

CENEVIERES✧✧

🏛 Château de Cénevières €€
Cénevières; tel: 05 65 31 27 33. Open (guided tours) Easter–Sept daily 1000–1200 and 1400–1800; Oct daily 1400–1700.

Overlooking the village and the River Lot is the imposing **Château de Cénevières✧**. The site, some 70m high, has held fortifications since the 7th century, but the present structure, considerably altered during the Renaissance period, dates from the 13th century. The oldest part is the keep and there are 15th-century wings connected by a Renaissance gallery with Tuscan columns. A beautiful painted ceiling dominates the drawing-room, which also contains Flemish tapestries. Visitors touring the castle are also taken into the kitchens, the keep and an alchemy room which has an alchemist's oven and 16th-century frescoes showing scenes from Greek mythology. The terrace affords superb views along the Lot Valley.

CUZALS✦✦✦

The big attraction in this village in the rocky hills above the valley is the entertaining and informative **Musée de Plein Air de Quercy✦✦✦**, which traces life in the region between the French Revolution and World War II. The open-air museum covers some 50 hectares and there are reconstructions of a milliner's shop, a bakery and a dentist's surgery of 1900. Examples of Quercy architecture are also on show and there is a collection of old agricultural equipment. In July and August some of the machinery, the mill and the baker's oven are operated by local people in period costume. There are ox-cart rides for children.

Musée de Plein Air de Quercy €€€
Cuzals; tel: 05 65 22 58 63; e-mail: museedepleinairduquercy@wanadoo.fr. Open Jul–Aug Sun–Fri 1000–1900; Jun 0930–1830; Apr–May and Sept–Oct 1400–1800.

LARROQUE-TOIRAC✦✦

One of a number of charming villages on the river's north bank, Larroque-Toirac has a major attraction in the form of the **Château de Larroque-Toirac✦✦**, which was rebuilt by Louis XI after being razed at the end of the 14th century. The castle was built by the powerful Cardaillac family in the 12th century and during the Hundred Years' War frequently changed hands between the English and the French forces. Inside, there are fine 15th-century fireplaces, 16th-century frescoes and furnishings from the early 17th century.

A child's footprint, left in clay some 4000 years ago, can be seen along with human skeletons in the **Grottes de Foissac✦✦**, near the village. Items found in the caves suggest that they were inhabited about 2700 years ago and were used as quarries and catacombs. They were rediscovered in 1959. There are 8km of galleries with beautiful rock formations and white stalactites. The roof of one gallery is covered with bulbous stalactites known as 'the onions'. The caves are drained by an underground stream that joins the Lot.

Château de Larroque-Toirac €€ Larroque-Toirac; tel: 05 65 34 78 12; e-mail: contact@chateautoirac.com; http://chateau.toirac.free.fr. Open (guided tours) mid-Jul–early Sept daily 1000–1200 and 1400–1800.

Grottes de Foissac €€€ Larroque-Toirac; tel: 05 65 64 77 04; e-mail: Grotte.de.Foissac@wanadoo.fr; www.aveyron.com/histoire/prehist.html. Open for guided tours Jun–Sept 1000–1800; Apr, May, Oct 1400–1900. Other times by appointment.

Above
Cuzals open-air museum

Marcilhac-sur-Cele❖❖

ⓘ Office de Tourisme
*Maison du Roy-Le
Bugue; tel: 05 65 40 68 44;
e-mail: figeac@wanadoo.fr;
www.tourisme.fr/office-de-
tourisme/figeac.htm*

Grotte de Bellevue
*46160 Marcilhac-sur-Célé;
tel: 05 65 31 28 77; e-mail:
contact@grotte-bellevue.com.
Open Jul–Aug.*

Set against a backdrop of cliffs, Marcilhac is an enchanting village collected around a ruined **Benedictine abbey**❖ founded in the 11th century. The abbey flourished until it was very badly damaged in raids by English and French troops during the Hundred Years' War. Although parts of the abbey today are roofless, there are some well-preserved medieval features, including some fine carvings in stone and wood and 15th-century frescoes.

Above the village, 1.5km to the northwest, is the **Grotte de Bellevue**❖❖, discovered in 1964. The cave contains an amazing range of stalactites, stalagmites, columns and 'streaky bacon' formations of ochre and white calcite. Slim, candle-like stalagmites stand in contrast to Hercules' Column, a pillar 4m high and 3.5m in circumference.

Right
Marcilhac-sur-Célé

St-Cirq-Lapopie❖❖❖

ⓘ St-Cirq-Lapopie *pl.
du Sombral; tel: 05 65
31 29 06; e-mail: saint-cirq-
lapopie@wanadoo.fr. Open
all year.*

One of the most beautiful villages in the region – some say in the whole of France, St-Cirq (pronounced 'San-sear') stands dizzyingly on a rocky escarpment that plunges vertically for 80m to the left bank of the Lot. It looks like an illustration in a book of fairy-tales, but has had more than its fair share of violence over the centuries. Occupied since Gallo-Roman times, the village is named after St-Cyr who was martyred along with his mother in Asia Minor during the reign of Diocletian. St-Amadour is said to have brought the martyr's relics to the area. The Lapopie part of the name comes from a family of local lords who occupied the castle at the top of the rock in the Middle Ages.

The castle attracted the attention of many invaders and was repeatedly besieged. Among those who tried and failed to seize it was Richard the Lionheart in 1198. It was demolished on the orders of Louis XI in 1471, but the ruins were still fought over during the Wars of Religion. Henri de Navarre put an end to the site's importance in 1580 when he had the remaining walls flattened. Today, the village is a delightful jumble of steep, narrow streets of cheerful red-roofed houses.

Until the 19th century the main industry was wood-turning and many craftsmen worked in small shops. An exhibition of the objects

Maison de la Fourdonne €€ *r. de la Fourdonne, St-Cirq-Lapopie; tel: 05 65 31 21 51. Open Tue–Sun 1400–1800. Guided tour 1500 daily. Closed Jan.*

Musée Rignault €€
Château de la Gardette, St-Cirq-Lapopie; tel: 05 65 31 23 22. Open Jun–Oct daily 1000–1230 and 1430–1800 (Jul–Aug 1900). Closed Tue.

they produced and the tools they used is in the **Maison de la Fourdonne***. A collection of antique furniture and *objets d'art* from Europe, Africa and China is housed in the **Musée Rignault***.

Accommodation and food

Auberge de la Sagne €€ *route Grotte de Pech Merle, Cabrerets; tel: 05 65 31 26 62. Open mid-May–Sept.* The hotel has 10 en suite rooms with direct-dial telephones. There is private parking, a pool and outdoor dining area. The small restaurant (€€) serves dinner only.

Auberge du Sombral €€–€€€ *St-Cirq-Lapopie; tel: 05 65 31 26 08. Open Apr–mid-Nov.* Primarily a restaurant, where you can get a budget lunch and dine outside, the establishment also has eight guest rooms (€€–€€€) with en suite facilities and direct-dial telephones.

Les Gabarres €€ *Tour-de-Faure, near St-Cirq-Lapopie; tel: 05 65 30 24 57. Open all year.* No restaurant, but 28 en suite rooms with direct-dial telephones. The hotel has private parking, a garden and swimming pool.

Hôtel des Grottes €–€€ *Cabrerets; tel: 05 65 31 27 02. Open Apr–Oct.* The main feature here is a riverside terrace. The hotel's 18 en suite rooms have direct-dial telephones and there is a swimming pool and private parking. The restaurant (€€) serves wine by the glass.

Camping de la Plage *St-Cirq-Lapopie; tel: 05 65 30 29 51; e-mail: camping-laplage@wanadoo.fr; www.campingplage.com. Open all year.* The campground has 120 pitches and caravans and mobile homes are available for hire. Activities include boating, canoeing, caving and horse riding.

Below
St-Cirq-Lapopie

Hôtel Ségalière €€ *380 av. F. Mitterand, Cajarc; tel: 05 65 40 65 35. Open mid-Mar–mid-Nov.* The hotel has 24 en suite rooms with direct-dial telephones and television and has a garden, swimming pool and private parking. The restaurant (**€–€€€**) serves wine by the glass, and a budget lunch is available. There is an outside dining terrace.

Camping la Truffière *route de Concots, St-Cirq-Lapopie; tel: 05 65 30 20 22; e-mail: contact@camping-truffiere.com; www.camping-truffiere.com. Open May–Sept.* The site has 96 pitches, with caravans and chalets for hire. Special events for children.

Suggested tour

Total distance: The route covers 100km.

Time: Driving time is around 2 hours, but allow a whole day for this absorbing trip.

Links: From Figeac the D922 south reaches Villefranche-de-Rouergue (*see page 177*) in 35km. From Conduché the D662 heads west for Vers in 14km, then the D653 continues for 15km to Cahors (*see pages 182–91*).

Route: From **Figeac** (*see pages 172–81*) follow the D13 (signposted Cahors) for 4km to the big railway viaduct, then take the D41 towards Boussac, which is reached in a further 5km. This first stretch is over a wide valley with wooded hills and the river clinging to the roadside. At Boussac the valley begins to close in and the road and river start to wind, running between cliffs from time to time.

Espagnac-Ste-Eulalie, 8km beyond Boussac, is a charming village of turreted houses set against cliffs and surrounding the Ancien Prieuré Notre-Dame, a convent founded in the 12th century, badly damaged during the Hundred Years' War and rebuilt in the 1400s. It now serves as a rural centre. Another attractive village, reached after 4km of pleasant countryside dotted with typical pigeon houses, is Brengues, where the D38 crosses the Célé.

Continue west on the D41 for 5.5km to St-Sulpice, lying at the foot of a cliff and guarded by a private castle, which has stood here since the 12th century. Another 3.5km and you reach **MARCILHAC-SUR-CELE** ❶, where the Grotte de Bellevue can be found 1.5km northwest of the village. After a further 6.5km the D41 passes through Sauliac-sur-Célé, huddled beneath a dramatic cliff riddled with caves in which the villagers took refuge in times of strife. At the hamlet of Liauzu, 3km beyond Sauliac, you turn away from the river at last, heading north on the D40 for 3km to **CUZALS** ❷.

Just north of Cuzals, turn left and travel 2km to Orniac, then head south on the D42, reaching **CABRERETS** ❸ in 5.5km. At Conduché, 4km south of Cabrerets, the Célé joins the River Lot. Take the D662 west for 1km then cross the Lot to **Bouziès**, where you can follow the GR36 footpath for 500m to visit a section of towpath carved out of solid rock when the river was a commercial waterway and now decorated with a relief of fish and crustaceans, the work of the contemporary sculptor, D. Monnier.

From Bouziès head east on the D40 and after 5km, climbing steadily all the way, stop at the viewpoint on the left – there is a car park – for a superb view of the confluence of the two rivers and, even more spectacular, **ST-CIRQ-LAPOPIE** ❹, towering over the Lot. The village is reached in a further 1.5km. At Crégols, 2km upstream, continue to follow the river on the D8, reaching **CENEVIERES** ❺ in 5km.

Cross the river at Calvignac, 4.5km upstream, then head east on the north bank, following the D662 for 6.5km to **CAJARC** ❻. The next village, Montbrun, 7km along the D662, overlooks the Lot from a rocky promontory and is itself dominated by a ruined castle that was once the home of a brother of Pope John XXII. Beyond Montbrun, the countryside softens into a patchwork of fields and the river and valley both widen. Within 6km you reach **LARROQUE-TOIRAC** ❼ and beyond there the D662 moves away from the river and reaches Figeac in 13km.

Ratings

Scenery	●●●●●
Architecure	●●●●○
Museums	●●●●○
Walks	●●●●○
Children	●●●○○
History	●●●○○
Outdoor activities	●●●○○
Villages	●●●○○

Figeac

What connection has a medieval French town with Ancient Egyptian art works and a replica of the Rosetta Stone? The answer is Jean François Champollion, born in Figeac in 1790, who devoted much of his life to deciphering Egyptian hieroglyphics. Situated on the River Célé, a tributary of the Lot, Figeac is a friendly little town set in a region of green heights, rugged limestone plateaux and tree-lined streams. The town's old quarter has narrow alleys twisting between tall, well-preserved sandstone houses from the 13th to 15th centuries. Figeac developed around a monastery in the 9th century; the abbot and seven consuls governed the town. Early in the 14th century the king intervened and Figeac was given a licence to print money – literally. The Mint Museum and the tourism office are in the same fine 13th-century building, the Hôtel de la Monnaie.

FIGEAC✧✧✧

ⓘ **Figeac** *Hôtel de la Monnaie, pl. Vival; tel:* 05 65 34 06 25; e-mail: figeac@wanadoo.fr; www.quercy-tourisme.com/ figeac. *Open daily Jul–Aug 1000–1930, Sept–Jun 1000–1200 and 1430–1800, closed Sun.* The office is in one of the town's finest 13th-century *soleilho* buildings, which also houses the Mint Museum.

Right
Figeac

History
Students of architecture will find much to catch their attention in this attractive little town (pop. about 10,000), which has known periods of considerable prosperity through the ages. There are carved façades, sculpted décors, a few octagonal stone chimneys, Renaissance doorways, and numerous half-timbered houses with decorative brickwork.

For the interested amateur and the specialist alike, the big appeal is the *soleilho*, fine examples of which can be seen in the old

Tourist train €€
Tel: 05 65 34 49 86.
For a fun way to tour the
old town and the waterside
area – and get a
commentary into the
bargain – climb aboard *Lou
Fijagal*, the tourist train, for
a 40-minute ride. *Runs
Jul–mid-Sept. Departures
from tourist office between
1000 and 1200 and 1500
and 1900. In peak season
there's a nocturnal tour at
2130.*

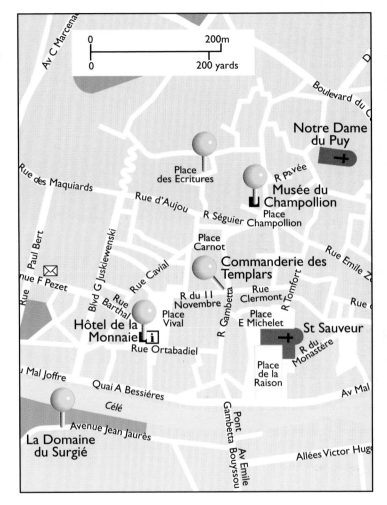

quarter. These are the tall houses of pale amber sandstone with open attics, typical of the 13th to 15th centuries. Goods would be stored at ground-floor level in workshops with open archways. The middle floor was the living quarters and the open attic – the *soleilho* – was where such items as vegetables and woollen cloth were stored. The roof was supported by pillars.

A stroll through the old quarter reveals much of Figeac's past, century by century, though the Hundred Years War' and the Wars of Religion took their toll. World War II was disastrous, too, with more than 500 Figeac people being deported by the Nazis. The River Célé, more intimate than the wide Lot or Dordogne, runs along the southern part of the town.

Commanderie des Templars €€
*41 r. Gambetta, Figeac.
Daily 1-hour guided tours
are held Jul–Sept between
1000 and 1300 and
1400–1930. There are also
Tue and Thur evening tours;
rest of year by appointment.*

The former abbey church of St-Sauveur was founded near the river in 838. Parts of the present building date from the 11th century. The font is supported by four Romanesque capitals from another part of the church. Because of the richness of its architectural heritage and its fine state of preservation, Figeac was declared a *Secteur Sauvegardé* (protected sector). In 1990 it became one of France's network of Cities of Art and History.

Sights

La Domaine du Surgié € *route de
Roussilhe, Figeac; tel: 05 65
34 59 00; e-mail:
surgie.camp.lois@
wanadoo.fr. Open Apr–Sept.
1100–2200 Jul–Aug,
1400–1900 Apr–Jun and
Sept in school holidays.*

Le Centre Nautique *tel:
05 65 34 18 76. Open
Jun–Sept. For canoe or kayak
hire contact Figeac Eaux
Vives (base at Domaine du
Siegle, Jul and Aug); tel: 05
65 50 05 48.*

Commanderie des Templars*
The Order of the Knights Templars was established in Figeac in the 1180s, when the Commanderie was built. The wooden staircase to the guardroom was put up in the 15th century.

La Domaine du Surgié***
This is Figeac's riverside leisure park and nautical centre. The leisure park has trampolines, inflatable animal models, an adventure course, *pétanque*, mini-golf, swimming pool, pedaloes and kayaks. The nautical centre provides a wavy pool, large swimming pool, water skiing and other water activities. The park has a bar-restaurant with brasserie, snackbar and a spacious terrace. Tourist accommodation and a campsite with 103 pitches, are in the northern part of the park.

Guided tours**
The tourist office runs general guided tours (€€) from Sunday to Friday in July and August at 1700. Themed tours are offered on designated dates in July and August. *Figeac Yesterday and Today, Merchants of Figeac in the Middle Ages* and *Medieval Art and Architecture* are among the themes. Trips to four historic villages near Figeac (one village

Above
Figeac's Rosetta Stone

**ⓘ Musée du
Champollion €€ r.**
*des Frères Champollion,
Figeac; tel: 05 65 50 31 08;
www.ville-figeac.fr/musee.
Open daily Jul and Aug
1000–1200 and
1430–1830, Mar–Jun and
Sept–Oct same hours but
closed Mon, Nov–Feb
Tue–Sun 1400–1800.
Closed 1 Jan, 1 May, 25
Dec. Guided visits are held
on Tue in school summer
holidays at 1030. Visits year
round in English can be
arranged for groups.*

**Musée de l'Hôtel de la
Monnaie €€** *pl. Vival,
Figeac; tel: 05 65 34 06 25.
Open daily Jul and Aug
1000–1300 and
1430–1900, May, Jun and
Sept 1000–1200 and
1430–1800, same hours in
Apr except closed Sun,
Oct–Mar 1100–1200 and
1430–1730.*

visited on each tour) are held on occasional Wednesdays, departing at 1030. There are also twice-monthly themed torchlight visits in Figeac.

Information about a children's programme of activities organised in July and August is available from the tourist office. From April to June and in September a *Discover Figeac* visit is arranged on occasional Saturdays at 1630, and there's a choice of three occasional themed tours. Throughout the year the tourist office organises visits and themed tours of the town for groups, by arrangement.

Musée du Champollion✦✦✦

The bookshop run by Jean François Champollion's father is now the Musée Champollion – three floors of Egyptian vases, jewellery, statuettes, documents, papyrus fragments, funeral objects including mummy wrappings, sarcophagi and other items, many bearing hieroglyphics.

Champollion, born in 1790, spoke six languages by the age of 14. He went on to develop some interpretative work on hieroglyphics by Thomas Young, an Englishman, and worked on deciphering the Rosetta Stone (*see Place des Ecritures, page 176*). During his expedition to Egypt he spent much time deciphering texts. He died, aged 42, a year after becoming curator at the Egyptology Museum, which he had founded at the Louvre in Paris.

Musée de l'Hôtel de la Monnaie (Mint Museum)✦

Housed in the same late 13th-century building as the tourist office, the museum displays old coins, Figeac town seals from more than 700 years ago, grain measures and sculpture work from local ancient buildings.

Museum village

A 12th-century fortification perched on rocks above the village of Cardaillac, 11km north of Figeac, may be visited: two towers remain, only one of which is open to the public. You climb a spiral staircase to the two-room tower, which has vaulted ceilings, and you are rewarded by a glorious view of the countryside and the River Drauzou running through it.

Much of Cardaillac itself is a museum, the Musée Eclat, which is spread over several sites. The two-hour guided tour is packed with interest. You find out about the craft of making winegrowers' baskets – once an important rural industry in the village – and see other local crafts. Other exhibits illustrate the part the school plays in local affairs and the general way of life in the village, and how day-to-day modern living fits in with Cardaillac's history.

Guided tours take place daily in July and August, 1500–1800. In September there is just one departure at 1500. Group visits the rest of the year are by arrangement (*place de la Tour, Cardaillac; tel: 05 65 40 10 63*). There is no set charge: you are asked to make a donation at the end of the tour.

Espace Patrimoine €
5 r. de Colomb, Figeac;
tel: 05 65 50 05 40. Open
daily Jul–Sept 1000–1230 and
1500–1900; Apr–Jun and mid-
Sept–Oct 1000–1800. Closed
Mon. Nov–Mar open on
request.

Place des Ecritures✦✦✦

(€ off pl. Carnot) This is a tranquil and shady haven moments from Figeac's busy streets – a greatly enlarged replica of the black granite Egyptian Rosetta Stone set into the floor of a courtyard enclosed by typical medieval architecture of the town. The setting, close to the Champollion Museum, was created by the American artist Joseph Kosuth, and unveiled in 1991. An adjacent small courtyard has a French translation of the hieroglyphics on the Rosetta Stone, engraved on the glass front of a vaulted cellar. Steps lead up to a terraced garden in which are growing papyri: the plant from which the Egyptians made 'paper'.

Portrait d'une Ville: Figeac✦

A permanent exposition offering lectures on Figeac and a summer programme of discovery visits and year round events for local people, students and those interested in learning about the town, one of a network of 120 Cities of Art and History in France.

NAJAC✦✦

Forteresse Royale €
Open daily. Guided visits
daily Jul and Aug 1000–1300
and 1500–1900, closes 1800
in Jun and 1700 in Apr, May,
Sept. Rest of year open by
appointment; contact tourist
office Villefranche-de-Rouergue,
tel: 05 65 45 13 18.

This medieval village sits loftily on the narrow ridge of a rocky promontory overlooking a bend in the River Aveyron. Its one street leads about 1km along the ridge to a wider part on which sits solidly the ruins of a 12th-century castle, the **Forteresse Royale**, of which the great circular keep is 33.5m high. Najac and its castle are an impressive sight from the river. Equally, to look down on the curved sweep of the Aveyron from the village is a scenic treat.

Right
Najac

VILLEFRANCHE-DE-ROUERGUE✣✣

Chartreuse St-Sauveur € Tel: 05 65 45 13 18. Open daily Jul–Sept 1000–1200 and 1400–1800.

This is a fine example of a *bastide* village, with its narrow streets in a grid pattern and its arcaded central square and marketplace. The square is dominated by the great hulk of l'Eglise Notre-Dame with its 55m belfry. The town, on the River Aveyron, was founded in 1252 by Alphonse de Poitiers, brother of King Louis IX. On the river just south of the town is the former **Chartreuse (charterhouse) St-Sauveur✣** and cloisters. The 15th-century Carthusian foundation, now a hospital, is claimed to be the only complete charterhouse open to the public in France.

VILLENEUVE✣

Anyone interested in medieval ecclesiastical art should make a point of looking at the frescoes in this *bastide* village south of Figeac. They depict 12th-century pilgrims on their way to Compostela beneath the figure of Christ. The picturesque village has neat and tidy streets of well-preserved old stone houses.

Right
Villeneuve

Accommodation and food

Hôtel des Bains €–€€€ *1 r. du Griffoul, Figeac; tel: 05 65 34 10 89.* The 16-room hotel has a range of amenities, including garage parking, bar and terrace.

Hôtel-Bar de Champollion €€ *3 pl. Champollion, Figeac; tel: 05 65 34 04 37.* A terrace, bar and cable TV are among the facilities at this centrally situated 10-room hotel.

Château du Viguier du Roy €€€ *r. Emile Zola (r. Droite), Figeac; tel: 05 65 50 05 05. Closed mid-Nov–late Mar.* This is Figeac's 4-star 20-room hotel, with restaurant (**€€–€€€**), bar, garden, swimming pool, jacuzzi, tennis and cable TV.

Chez Marcel Hôtel-Restaurant € *r. du 11 mai 1944, Cardaillac; tel: 05 65 40 11 16. Open mid-Feb–mid-Sept.* The five-room property 11km north of Figeac has a terrace for outdoor dining.

La Courtepaille Hôtel-Bar €€ *12 pl. Carnot, Figeac; tel: 05 65 34 21 83.* Only six rooms, but guests have the benefit of a brasserie and bar.

Camping à la Ferme *Chez Mme Therondel, 16 r. de Puits Ste Marie, Bagnac-sur-Célé (15km northeast of Figeac); tel: 05 65 34 25 40. Open 1 Jun–1 Sept.* This is a 'Welcome to the Farm' site with eight pitches for tents, caravans or motor homes.

Hôtel-Restaurant de la Gare €–€€ *Bagnac-sur-Célé (15km northeast of Figeac); tel: 05 65 34 92 47.* The hotel has 10 guest rooms with cable TV. It has a bar and a terrace.

L'Oustel del Barry €–€€ *pl. de Bourg, Najac; tel: 05 65 29 74 32. Open late Mar–late Oct. Closed Mon except Jul–Sept.* In a beautiful setting overlooking the River Aveyron, the hotel has 21 mainly small rooms, most with bath or shower, and a renowned restaurant.

Camping Les Rives du Célé *Domaine du Surgié, Figeac; tel: 05 65 34 59 00. Open Apr–Sept.* Tents, caravans, mobile homes and chalets to rent. There are 103 pitches on the partly shaded campground. Amenities include restaurant and takeaway food, grocery store, swimming pool, mini-golf and entertainment.

Le Terminus St-Jacques Hôtel-Restaurant €€ *27 av. George Clemenceau, Figeac; tel: 05 65 34 00 43. Closed four weeks in Oct–Nov.* South of the river, the hotel has 11 rooms with garden, cable TV and bar.

Le Toulouse Hôtel-Restaurant € *4 av. de Toulouse, Figeac; tel: 05 65 34 22 95. Open all year.* The eight-room hotel has a bar and parking for guests' cars.

Crêperie la Sarrasin €–€€ *6 r. Balène, Figeac; tel: 05 65 34 76 44. Closed Sun and Mon (Mon only in peak season).* Relaxing *crêperie*.

Le Dinée du Viguier €–€€ *4 r. Boutaric, Figeac; tel: 05 65 50 08 08.* Popular restaurant with seating for 100 inside or on the terrace. Accessible for wheelchairs.

Jackson Burger € *2 r. Cordeliers, Figeac; tel: 05 65 34 42 40. Open 1100–2400.* A good place for a quick bite.

Pizzaria del Portel € *9 r. Ortabadial, Figeac; tel: 05 65 34 53 60. Closed Mon all year, Sun lunchtime in winter.* As well as a satisfying pizza you may find some entertainment laid on here.

La Puce a l'Oreille €–€€ *5–7 r. St-Thomas, Figeac; tel: 05 65 34 33 08. Closed Sun evening and Mon except in high season.* Comfortable restaurant with terrace.

Le Sphinx Brasserie-Restaurant €–€€ *7 pl. Carnot, Figeac; tel: 05 65 50 07 36.* Good range of savoury dishes in pleasant atmosphere. There's a bar and a large terrace.

La Table de Marinette €–€€ *51 allée Victor Hugo, Figeac; tel: 05 65 50 06 07. From Oct–late May closed Sat and Sun.* Popular restaurant and bar with up to 50 covers indoors and terrace seating for another 100.

Suggested walk

Total distance: The walk covers a little over a kilometre. There is a fairly steep climb up to pl. du Puy.

Below
Villefranche-de-Rouergue

Time: Allow 1½ hours.

Route: The walk takes you through the narrow medieval streets of Figeac's old town. From the tourist office in pl. Vival head across the car park and follow r. du 11 Novembre to the right. Turn left into r. Gambetta, the main street of the old town, where the 12th-century **COMMANDERIE DES TEMPLARS** ❶ will be found on the left. Continue into pl. Carnot, which has a covered marketplace. Follow the square round to the left and turn right into r. Séguier then cross the street, turning into r. de la Monnaie, an alley leading into **PLACE DES ECRITURES** ❷, with the huge replica of the Rosetta Stone tucked away among a surrounding of medieval buildings. The archway on one side of the square leads into r. des Frères Champollion and the entrance to the **MUSEE DU CHAMPOLLION** ❸.

Follow the very narrow lane to the end, then turn left into r. de Colomb. Ruelle St-Jacques, a narrow street on the right, climbs to pl. du Puy, where there are views of the town. Here, too, is **Eglise Notre-Dame-du-Puy**, which was used as a Protestant fortress during the Wars of Religion. The church has a massive walnut altarpiece, carved in the 17th century. At the right-hand end of pl. du Puy take the steps down to r. Bantaric, which leads into pl. Champollion, dominated by an infirmary founded in the 14th century by the Knights Templars. The street running to the left out of the square is r. Emile Zola, the town's oldest thoroughfare with arcades and houses with fine Renaissance doorways.

Below
Figeac old town

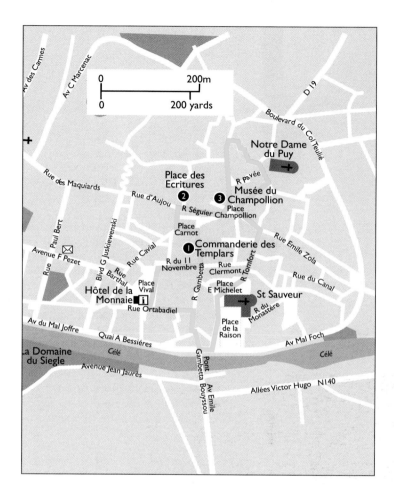

Less than 50m along r. Emile Zola turn right into r. Tomfort. This leads to pl. Edmond Michelet and the **Eglise St-Sauveur**, founded as an abbey church in the 11th century. The neighbouring church is **Notre-Dame-de-Pitié**, formerly a chapterhouse, which became a place of worship in 1623 when Protestants left the town. It contains fine examples of painted wooden panels, including one of the Infant Jesus foreseeing the Crucifixion. From pl. Edmond Michelet follow r. Capote into pl. aux Herbes and turn left into the lower section of r. Gambetta.

Almost at the river end of the street turn right into r. Balène, where the 14th-century **Château de Balène** is now a public hall and exhibition centre. Follow the street round to r. Ortabadial and cross the road to return to the tourist office.

Cahors

Ratings

Architecture	●●●●●
Food and wine	●●●●●
History	●●●●○
Scenery	●●●●○
Shopping	●●●●○
Art	●●●○○
Nightlife	●●●○○
Tours	●●●○○

Cahors is the chief town in the *département* of the Lot in the Midi-Pyrénées. Most of the city is within a great loop of the River Lot, which is crossed by the Pont de Valentre complete with its three towers and regarded as the best-preserved medieval bridge in France. Many buildings of the same period still stand. The earliest site, though not intact, is the Arc de Diane – remains of Gallo-Roman baths. St Etienne's Cathedral reflects periods between the 11th and 17th centuries. Modern history is recorded in the Resistance Museum. The celebrated 'black' Cahors wines spread the city's name around the world. A wine museum opens from July to September, and a number of local vineyards are open to the public. With its wide squares, its Old Quarter and its riverside gardens, Cahors is a place of charm and character.

History

ℹ️ Office de Tourisme Cahors, *pl. François Mitterrand, Cahors; tel: 05 65 53 20 65; e-mail: cahors@wanadoo.fr; www.mairie-cahors.fr. Open all year Mon–Sat (open Sun in Jul–Aug).*

Comité Départmental de Tourisme de Lot, *107 quai Cavaignac, Cahors; tel: 05 65 35 07 09; e-mail: le-lot@wanadoo.fr; www.tourisme-lot.com. Open all year.*

The city (pop. 20,000) owes its existence to a spring by the River Lot. The spring, fed by an underground well 20km away, is said to have been discovered by Carthusian monks and was used by the Gauls and later the Romans. The discovery in 1991 of hundreds of coins from the dawn of Christianity supports the theory that the spring was considered sacred. It is the source of Cahors's drinking water supply to this day.

The Pont Valentré, a magnificent and well-preserved bridge, is the city's top attraction for most visitors. Cahors honours its famous sons, notably Pope John XXII, whose papacy was from 1316 to 1334. He founded the University of Cahors and was the power behind the taming of the River Lot, having sluices and dams installed and the Pont Valentré built, giving new impetus to local commerce. A 34m tower serves as a monument to the Pope.

Cemetery

Rue de la Poudriere

Rue du Pape Jean XXII

Rue de la Barre

Ile de Cabessut

Rue de la Rivière

Quai Ludo Rolle

Rue Martin Baudel

Rue P M Cayrat

Rue J du Bellay

Rue Léon Blum

Rue Emile Zola

Rue de la Caserne

Musée de la Résistance

St Barthélémy

Rue St Barthélémy

Le Lot

Rue de la Croix

Rue P Mendès-France

Place Général De Gaulle

Avenue Charles de Freycinet

Rue des Thermes

Rue des Cadourques

Rue des Augustins

Rue Emile Zola

Boulevard Gambetta

Rue des Soubirous

Quai de Regourd

Rue Château du Roi

Railway Station

Parc A Tassart

Musée Henri Martin

Rue J Vidal

Pont Cabessut

Sacre Coeu

Rue des Jac

Rue Joachim Murat

Rue du Portail Alban

Quai Champollion

Quai Lagrive

Avenue Pierre Sémard

Avenue Anatole France

Rue de la Chartreuse

Rue Caviole

Rue du Marechal Foch

Rue Clément Marot

Cathédrale St-Etienne

Avenue Jean Jaurès

Rue F Suisse

Place Chapou

Rue St James

Rue St-Urcisse

Avenue André Breton

Les Halles

Place Galdemar

Rue Clemenceau

ont Valentré

Rue du Président Wilson

Place F Mitterrand

Rue de Lastie

Allées Fénelon

Theatre

Rue Blanqui

R Cel Delmas

Rue Donzelle

Espace Valentré

Rue G Sindou

Rue Saint Géry

Rue Etienna Brives

Quai Ségur D'Aguesseau

Fontaine des Chartreux

Allées des Soupirs

Rue Jules Michelet

Rue Victor Hugo

Rue Saint Maurille

Rue Hautesserre

Rue des Jardiniers

Rue des Hortes

Rue des Carmes

Boulevard Gambetta

Rue Victor Lafage

Rue du Pot Trinquat

Rue St Georges

Avenue Mermoz Collinot

Quai Eugène Cavaignac

Pont Louis-Philippe

Le Lot

↓ Panoramic view

0 ——————— 300m
0 ——————— 300 yards

A guide giving the addresses of more than 500 restaurants offering authentic local cooking in the Lot region, from village inns to prestigious establishments, is available from the Departmental Committee of Tourism (*see address page 182*). For a free publication giving information about the Association de Bon Tables du Lot – it lists 22 places of high reputation run by talented head chefs – contact the **Chambre de Commerce et Industrie du Lot-et-Garonne** *52 cours Gambetta, tel: 05 53 77 10 00. Their list of hotels and restaurants is also on a website, www.hotel-restaurant47.com/anglais/welcome.htm*

Cathédrale St-Etienne € *pl. Chapou, Cahors. Open daily.*
Chapelle St-Gausbert
€€ *Tel: 05 65 23 07 50; http://architecture.relig. free.fr/cahors.htm. Open daily in summer 1000–1200 and 1400–1800.*

The main thoroughfare in Cahors is the Boulevard Gambetta, home of the 19th-century Hôtel de Ville (City Hall) and the Palais de Justice (Palace of Justice). The street is named after Léon Gambetta, born in Cahors in 1838, who became a lawyer in Paris and a flamboyant republican prime minister. He died in 1882 at the age of 44.

In the Old Quarter of Cahors are narrow lanes, mansions, gates and the Henry IV house where the king once stayed. Today, visitors find much to enjoy, from medieval architecture to local food products and vineyard tours.

Right
Cahors Cathédrale St-Etienne

Guided tours €€
These are arranged all year for groups by the tourist office. For individuals, two themed guided tours of the medieval city are held at 1600 on Mon Jul–Sept, also in Jul and Aug at 1700 on Mon, Tue, Thur and 1030 Fri. They take in the Cathedral and parts of the old town dating back centuries. Tours last 2½hrs including a visit to the Mount Saint-Cyr military school which gives a panoramic view of the town; a shorter tour lasts 1½hrs and includes the medieval streets, the Cathedral, Maison Henri IV, the Ramparts, the Arc of Diane and the Pont Valentré. Tours begin at the Tourist Office, Place François Mitterrand. Booking and information from the tourist office.

Tourist Train, Le Petit Train de Cahors €€ Tel: 05 65 30 16 55; e-mail: le-petit-train-de-cahors@ wanadoo.fr. 40-min tours of the old town and its monuments daily 0930–1845, starting from allée des Soupirs (200m from Pont Valentré).

QuercyRail €€ pl de la Gare tel: 05 63 40 11 93; www.trains-fr.org/unecto/ quercyrail. Offers day or half-day trips in the Lot Valley using old rolling stock restored by a conservation group.

Discovery cruises €€ Tel: 05 65 23 94 72. 90-min boat trips depart from quai Pont de Valentré, Apr–Nov, and follow the loop in the river round the medieval town and through one of the locks. Commentary in English on request.

Historic foundations

Arc de Diane: The most ancient parts of Cahors are the remains of the Gallo-Roman thermal baths and the foundations of a theatre beneath the present Chambre d'Agriculture. The **Cathédrale St-Etienne** was built as a fortress in which people could find refuge from attackers. Work began in 1110, and by the 14th century ramparts had been built, turning the city into a virtual island. Parts of these are still visible: one of the surviving fortifications is a great tower at the western end of the city.

In the 1300s Cahors began to prosper greatly and expand: Lombard bankers, merchants and men of international business affairs moved in and the city became the finance centre of Europe. Houses and mansions were built of brick; stone was used for great arcades. It was in this period that Cahors-born Jacques Duèse became Pope John XXII. He endowed the University of Cahors and enhanced commerce by installing dams, sluices and mills along the River Lot. Building of the great **Pont Valentré** began as early as 1308. Much of the present-day city belongs to this era and the Renaissance period that followed, from the 1500s.

Sights

Cathédrale St-Etienne**

With a history of barbarian invasions of Cahors, safety and defence were uppermost in the minds of those building the cathedral, on the site of a 6th-century church, and they made a fortress of it. A number of periods covering some six centuries are represented, accentuated by 19th-century restoration work.

Within the cathedral precincts the **Chapelle St-Gausbert*** contains portraits of nearly 100 bishops from the 3rd to the 16th centuries, a fresco of the Last Judgement, and 16th-century ceiling paintings. A carving around the north doorway, dating from about 1135, depicts the Ascension. The cathedral's two great domes are 16m in diameter, rising above the 20m-wide nave. The fine cloisters were added in the early 16th century. Sculptures of a pilgrim – Cahors is near the route to Compostela – and a garland of sea shells may be seen here.

City tours**

You can take a guided tour of the Old Quarter or get a general introduction to Cahors by taking a half-hour narrated trip on the **Tourist Train****. Because the River Lot flows around three sides of the city, you can see many of the sights from the deck of a trip boat. For an excursion into the picturesque Lot Valley, take a break from the car and let **QuercyRail****escort you.

🅑 **Musée de Vin** r. de la Chartrerie; tel: 05 65 23 97 32. Open daily Jul–Aug 1000–1200 and 1500–1900. Closed Tue. Free entry.

🅐 **Le Bowling** (10 rinks), Belle Croix; tel: 05 65 35 71 46. Open Wed, Sat, Sun 1600–0200, Tue, Thur, Fri 1900–0200.

Discos are **La Palmerai**, Fontanes, Lalbenque, near Cahors; tel: 05 65 21 86 64. Open Fri and Sat 2230–0500 and **Le Look**, route de Paris, Cahors; tel: 05 65 22 57 19. Check opening hours.

Nightlife At least three Cahors music bars stay open until the early hours: **Biscot 'O' Rock** (r. St James; tel: 05 65 53 18 26. Open Mon–Fri 1900–0200, Sat 1700–0200); **Le Duplex** (r. Gustave Larroumet; tel: 05 65 22 14 56. Open daily to 0100 and to 0200 in summer); and **The Irish Pub** (pl. des Consuls; tel: 05 65 53 15 15. Open Mon–Sat 1800–0200).

The city has two cinemas – the **ABC** (r. des Augustins) and **Le Quercy** (r. Emile Zola), a couple of discos and a late-night bowling alley.

Galleries of Art*

Paintings of the French landscape and other works of art from the 19th and 20th centuries are displayed in the **Musée Henri Martin***. Temporary exhibitions are staged at the **Tourist Office Gallery*** and at **La Chartrerie*** (35 r. de la Chartrerie; tel: 05 65 37 11 03) in the **Musée de Vin***, which is also a cultural centre. Exhibitions of paintings and sculptures by contemporary artists are held at the **Compagnie des Arts*** (44 r. St André; tel: 05 65 22 57 41. Open Tue–Sat 1500–1900).

Museums and markets

Musée Henri Martin* €€ r. Emile Zola, Cahors. Tel: 05 65 20 88 66. Open Jun–Oct daily except Tue 1100–1800 (Sun 1400–1800); e-mail: museehenrimartin@free.fr; www.mairie-cahors.fr/musee. Landscapes and modern art.

Tourist Office Gallery* € pl. F. Mitterrand; tel: 05 65 53 20 65. Open daily except Sun and public holidays, Dec–Mar 0930–1230 and 1330–1800, Apr–mid-Jun and mid-Sept–Nov, 0900–1230 and 1330–1830, mid-Jun–mid-Sept 0900–1900. Free entry to temporary exhibitions.

Maison Henry IV* €€ r. St-Urcisse, Cahors; tel: 05 65 35 04 35. Open Easter–Sept 1000–1200 and 1400–1730; to 1800 in Aug.

Henry de Navarre, later to become Henry IV, stayed in this 16th-century private house, which is a listed monument. It has furniture from the 15th to 18th centuries, and stone fireplaces.

Les Halles* pl. Galdemer. Open Tue–Sat 0800–1230 and 1500–1900, Sun 0900–1200.

Every day except Monday is market day in Cahors. Traders offer regional wines and food products, fruit, vegetables, fish, shellfish, bread, conserves, nuts, pizzas, foie gras and meat and dairy products.

Musée de la Résistance* € pl. Bessières; tel: 05 65 22 14 25; e-mail: cahors.musee-de-la-resistance@libertysurf.fr. Open daily all year, except 25 Dec, 1 Jan, 1 May.

An illuminating insight into the perilous work of the Resistance Movement in the wild, often remote, terrain of the Lot département in World War II. Each of five rooms is devoted to a different aspect of the movement's work.

Musée de Vin*/de la Chartrerie***

Housed in the cultural centre, one of Cahors's principal monuments, the museum presents information on the history, culture, tradition and production of the region's celebrated wines, with displays of the final product.

Musée d'Art religieux*

Access from the Cathedral cloister. A collection of religious artefacts in the St Gausbert chapel, with beautifully preserved 15th-century murals. One curiosity is a piece of cloth displayed in a reliquary and claimed to be the linen cap that covered Christ's head in the tomb. It was brought from the Holy Land by a 12th-century bishop and was instrumental in Cahors being granted the status of a cathedral city.

Opposite
Cahors Pont Valentré

Pont Valentré €€
Tel: 05 65 53 20 65.
Pedestrian bridge.
*Exhibitions open daily Jul and
Aug 1000–1230 and
1430–1830.*

A devil of a job

The long time that it took to build the Pont Valentré is blamed on the devil. According to legend, the bridge's architect, exasperated by the demands on his time, decided to sell his soul to the devil in return for speeding up progress. Presumably the devil did his bit, as matters improved. But as the work neared completion, the architect got cold feet, fearing for his eternal future. So he asked the devil to fetch water in a sieve. The devil made some gallant attempts but couldn't oblige, and took his revenge by breaking off the topmost stone of the central tower. Every time it was replaced he knocked it off again. The tower is still known as the Devil's Tower. During bridge restoration work in 1879, the top stone was firmly fixed once and for all, and a carved figure of the devil trying to dislodge it was added.

Panoramic view of Cahors *
Take a 7-km drive from Cahors leaving by the Louis Philippe Bridge to Mont St-Cyr: from a viewing platform here you get a bird's-eye view of the city, with blvd Gambetta forming a clear dividing line between medieval and modern Cahors.

Pont Valentré***
It took nearly 70 years for the bridge to be completed (1308–1370s). It was an impressive and beautiful structure, and still is today, although it has undergone considerable alteration through the centuries. The bridge has six arches and three towers, and is a prime example of medieval defence architecture in Europe. Exhibitions and displays depicting the bridge's history are presented in summer in the central tower.

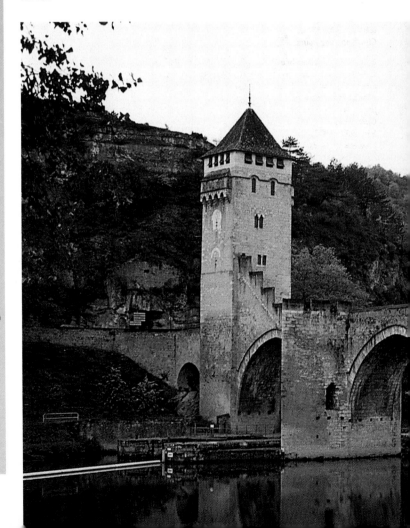

Buying local products

A map showing 600 growers throughout the region producing *les grand vins de Cahors* is available free from tourist offices, hotels and other outlets. The tourist office can supply a list of nearly 50 vineyards and châteaux with their appellations that welcome visitors. Food products of the area can be bought direct from specialists in the villages and countryside of the region, and in Cahors itself. Some concentrate mainly on one item, such as truffles, offered fresh in season (Nov–Mar) and conserves, sold in Cahors at *66 r. Frederic Suisse; tel: 05 65 22 24 80*. Others offer a veritable Aladdin's Cave of delights: *foie gras* of goose and duck, goose and duck *confit*, pâté, juniper berry liqueur, nut oil, cassoulet, mushrooms, smoked duck breast, conserves and an assortment of apéritifs, liqueurs and the wines of Cahors and the Southwest.

Among those in Cahors with varied gastronomic fare are **La Cedre Valentrée**, *32 av. A. Breton; tel: 05 65 22 66 16* and **Franche Lippée**, *22 r. de la Préfecture; tel: 05 65 35 56 79*.

Accommodation and food

Auberge de Jeunesse de Cahors (Youth Hostel) € *espace Frédéric Suisse, 20 r. Frédéric Suisse; tel: 05 65 35 64 71. Open 24 hours a day.* In an old convent building, the hostel, 500m from the station, has rooms ranging from two beds up to 11 beds. There is a restaurant service as well as a kitchen for guests' use. The hostel has a bicycle garage.

La Bourse € *7 pl. Rousseau, Cahors; tel: 05 65 35 17 78. Closed Sun.* A small hotel with eight guest rooms, a restaurant and a terrace.

Château de Mercuès €€€ *Mercuès; tel: 05 65 20 05 72. Open Easter–end Oct, closed Wed except in Jul and Aug.* The 4-star château in its own extensive grounds is about 5km from Cahors in the direction of Villeneuve-sur-Lot. There are 30 rooms, a restaurant, tennis courts and a pool, and access for disabled guests.

A l'Escargot € *5 blvd Gambetta, Cahors; tel: 05 65 35 07 66. Closed Sun evening and Mon.* Facing pl. Général de Gaulle, the 2-star hotel has eight rooms with TV and telephone.

Hôtel Gril-Campanile €€ *Rond Point de Regourd Sud, RN20 Cahors; tel: 05 65 22 20 21.* The 49-room, 2-star hotel has lifts, access for travellers with disabilities and a restaurant.

Le Melchior € *pl. de la Gare, Cahors; tel: 05 65 35 03 38.* 20 rooms with TV and telephone, and a restaurant in this 2-star property.

Camping Municipal St-Georges *St-Georges, Cahors; tel: 05 65 35 04 64. Open mid-Apr–Oct.* Basic site. Events held. 45 pitches.

Camping: Rivière de Cabessut *r. de la Rivière, Cahors; tel: 05 65 30 06 30. Open Apr–Oct.* Amenities at this site north of the city include a bar, food, mini-golf, swimming pool and events. 103 pitches.

Hôtel Terminus €€–€€€ *5 av. Charles de Freycinet, Cahors; tel: 05 65 53 22 00.* This 3-star hotel has lifts, wheelchair access, garage parking and a restaurant. The 22 rooms have TV and phone.

Auberge du Vieux Cahors €–€€ *144 r. St-Urcisse, Cahors; tel: 05 65 35 06 05. Closed Tue evening and Wed except in high season.* Regional cuisine, fish and *fruits de mer* are the specialities of this restaurant in the south of the city.

Le Bistrot de Cahors € *46 r. Daurade; tel: 05 65 53 10 55.* Popular small bistro serving good regional food.

Crêperie au Coeur de Lot € *71 r. du Chateau du Roi, Cahors; tel: 05 65 22 30 67. Crêpes* and salads, à la carte.

Le Grill de Archipel €–€€ *Ile de Cabessut, quai Ludo-Rolles; tel: 05 65 35 95 64. Closed Sun evening and Mon except in peak season.* On an island in the Lot on the eastern side of the city, the restaurant offers an interesting Mediterranean cuisine.

Le Soleil Ho € *36 r. Mordaigne, Cahors; tel: 05 65 22 02 52. Closed Mon.* Chinese food, modestly priced.

La Taverne €–€€€ *pl. Escorbiac, Cahors; tel: 05 65 35 28 66. Closed weekends except in season.* Proprietor-chef Jean-Luc Ratier serves regional food and gastronomic specialities in his restaurant near the tourist office.

A la Tentation €–€€ *34 pl. Chapou; tel: 05 65 35 31 44. Closed Mon and all Jan and Feb.* Traditional and regional fare at this popular spot opposite the cathedral.

Suggested tour

Total distance: The route covers just over 102km.

Time: Allow 2½ hours for driving – say a good half day for sightseeing and drinking in the scenery.

Links: The D911 at the start of the route, continues from Rostassac for 50km to Villeneuve-sur-Lot (*see page 197*). The N20 connects Cahors and Souillac (*see pages 135–6*). From Vers you can travel to Figeac (*see pages 172–6*) by way of the D653 or the Lot and Célé valleys (*see pages 164–71*).

ⓘ Musée Zadkine €€
les Arques; tel: 05 65 22 83 37. Open daily 1000–1300 and 1400–1900. Closed 25 Dec, 1 Jan, 1 May, 1 Nov. The key to **Chapelle-St-André** *is held at the museum.*

Eglise St-Laurent €
les Arques; No tel. Open Jun–Sept daily 1000–1900; rest of year 1400–1700.

Musée Murat €€
Labastide-Murat; tel: 05 65 21 19 23. Open Jul–Sept daily 1000–1200 and 1400–1800.

Below
Cahors vineyards

Route: Leave **CAHORS ❶** on the D911 and head for **Mercuès ❷**, 5km northwest, where the Hôtel Château de Mercuès is exactly that – the town's old castle, built in 1212, enlarged 200 years later and the scene of numerous conflicts during the Hundred Years' War and the Wars of Religion. Continue on the D911 for a further 10.5km to Rostassac, then take the D660 for 4.5km to **les Junies ❸**, which has a 15th-century castle with round towers and a massive 14th-century church.

Turn right on to the D37 and in 3km reach **Lherm ❹**, an attractive village of limestone buildings. Its church, in woodland just outside the village, has a Romanesque apse and a carved altarpiece decorated with gold. Another 4km along the D37 you reach **les Arques ❺**, a tiny village (pop. 160) with a **museum✦** celebrating the work of the internationally acclaimed sculptor, Ossip Zadkine (1890–1967). The Russian-born Cubist lived in les Arques from 1934. Two of his most important pieces – *Christ* and *Pietà* – can be found inside the 11th-century **Eglise St-Laurent✦** in the centre of the village. The nearby **Chapelle St-André-des-Arques✦** contains a series of 15th-century frescoes discovered by Zadkine in 1954.

From les Arques take the D46 west for 4km, then turn right on to the D673 to reach Montcléra in another 2km. **Château de Montcléra ❻** has a 15th-century gate, a square keep and round towers with machicolations. The *bastide* village of **Cazals ❼**, built by the English, comes after a further 3km. **Salviac ❽**, another 7km along the D673, has a Gothic church with attractive stained-glass windows. Leave Salviac on the D2 east and after 2km turn right on to the D6 at Dégagnac; after another 2km, head east on the D2 again for 9.5km to St-Chamarand, where the D2 crosses the N20. 3km beyond the N20 turn right on the D17 to reach **Labastide-Murat ❾** in 7km.

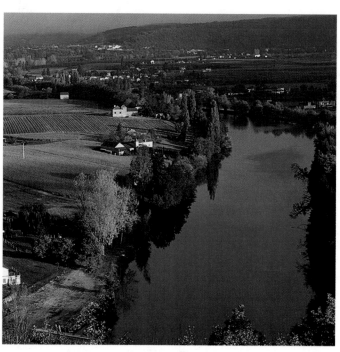

Standing at more than 400m, Labastide-Murat is on one of the highest points on the Gramat-Causse. The town's name honours Joachim Murat, who was born here in 1767.

The son of an innkeeper, he became a soldier whose heroism brought him to the attention of Napoléon. Later he became the Emperor's brother-in-law and the king of Naples. He was shot in 1815 when the Bourbons returned to Naples. His story is told in the house where he was born, now the **Musée Murat***.

From Labastide-Murat head south on the D32, which merges with the D653 after 13.5km. For the next 7.5km the roads descends, scenically following the River Vers to its confluence with the Lot at the village of Vers. From here the D653 continues west, affording some very pleasant views of the Lot, which it follows for 15km, returning you to Cahors.

Cahors–Villeneuve-sur-Lot

Ratings

Botanic gardens	●●●●●
Dolmens	●●●●○
History	●●●●○
Scenery	●●●●○
Walks	●●●●○
Wine	●●●●○
Art	●●○○○
Children	●●○○○

There are serene places to be found in this part of the winding River Lot, even in high summer. You can stroll around old villages unsullied by crowds and climb hills high above the river for wonderful views. From a hilltop at Luzech you can survey just about the entire town and the meander of the Lot that almost encloses it. Take a walk from the wine centre of Prayssac, a cheerful town, to prehistoric dolmens. Your camera will probably be put to good use in most of the small towns and villages interspersed with vineyards and orchards on the banks of the Lot. Picturesque Puy-l'Evêque has houses built into the steep river bank. When you've had your fill of long-past history visit Villeneuve-sur-Lot. It retains a few ancient features but it's mostly modern, and it's the biggest metropolis between Cahors and Agen.

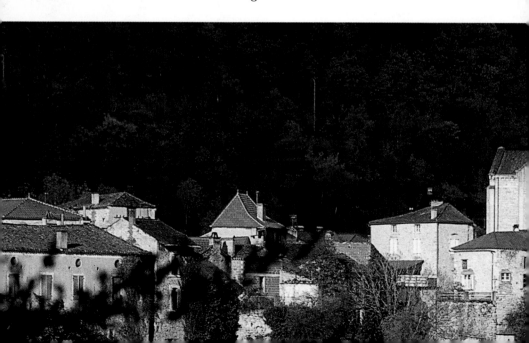

0 10km

Monflanquin

Cuzorn

D124

Monsempron-Libos

D710

Puy-l'Évêque

D673

Fumel

D911

D660

Catus

Francoulè

N2

D911

Prayssac

Castelfranc

Mercuès

E09

Pradine

Montayral

Lot

St-Vite

Albas

Luzech

Douelle

Cahors

D911

Trentels

D102

Mauroux

Villeneuve-sur-Lot

Lot

D656

Sauzet

D653

Penne-d'Agenais

D661

Tournon-d'Agenais

St-Pantaléon

D653

L'Hospitalet

Grottes de Lestournelle

St-Antoine-de-Ficalba

D103

D656

Montaigu-de-Quercy

Montcuq

Q U E R C

D212

Hautfage-la-Tour

St-Cyprien

tirou

D110

Frespech

Roquecor

D953

D2

Castelnau-Montratier

N21

Laroque-Timbaut

Beauville

Touffailles

Bourg-de-Visa

Lauzerte

Montpezat-de-Querc

D656

Pont-du-Casse

Cazes-Mondenard

N113

D957

Mirabe

Layrac

Caudecoste

D953

Barguelonne

D927

Lafrançaise

L'Honor-de-Cos

ALBAS*

Previous page
Albas

This beautiful old village in a neat hillside setting above the Lot's south bank sits amid dense woodland. The narrow streets, old houses and the remains of the bishops' castle are all well worth exploring, for the views and the timeless atmosphere.

CASTELFRANC*

This is a *bastide* village. It had a lucky escape in the early 1500s when the plague had been rampant but stopped short of the town walls. A small chapel commemorates the fact.

DOUELLE*

This village is about 15km from Cahors. If you want to stretch your legs in pleasant surroundings, take a look at the giant mural by Didier Chamizot on the river bank.

LUZECH**

ⓘ **Luzech** *Office de Tourisme Maison des Consuls, r. de la Ville, tel: 05 65 20 17 27; e-mail: office.de.tourisme.de.luzech @wanadoo.fr; www.ville-luzech.fr*

ⓒ **Boat trips** *including a wine-tasting are organised by Cie Navilot, Caix Boating Centre; tel: 05 65 20 18 19. Cruises 1630–1830 daily mid-Apr–Oct. Alternatively, canoes and kayaks can be hired by the hour or day or longer from Safaraid, Albas. Tel: 05 65 30 74 47; e-mail: safaraid@aol.com*

This is the first town of any size on the Lot west of Cahors. Like Cahors it was built within a horseshoe formed by a large river meander, making it almost an island. Luzech originally had two castles; the 12th-century square keep of one still exists.

Go to the top of Impernal Hill if you want an excellent view of Luzech. The hill formed a naturally defended site, which was first exploited by the area's neolithic inhabitants. Later the Gauls built strong defences there. Wander around the old quarter of Luzech among little alleys and the quays and buildings that survive from the Middle Ages. The Penitents' Chapel is from the 12th century.

Luzech's **Musée Archeologique Armand-Viré**** is housed in a vaulted cellar at the Maison des Consuls, rue de la Ville, an atmospheric home for articles excavated in the area. They include tools and artefacts from the palaeolithic era through to Gallo-Roman times. If you have time, enjoy a two-hour **boat trip**** on the Lot.

PRAYSSAC*

ⓘ **Office de Tourisme** *pl. d'Istrie Prayssac; tel: 05 65 22 40 57.*

This is another place where you can walk to some dolmens. The little town always seems busy – it is a noted centre for the wine trade.

Several châteaux offer guided tours. Prayssac has a farmers' market on Sundays at pl. de la Liberté, from 0800 to 1300.

PUJOLS❖❖

ⓘ Office de Tourisme *Le Bourg; tel: 05 53 36 78 69; e-mail: contact@otpujols47.info; www.mairiedepujols.free.fr*

Barely 1km from the southwest gate of Villeneuve is this medieval walled town. From its elevated position you can get a good view of Villeneuve's *bastide* qualities. Pujols's church of St Foy le Jeune, which has some 15th-century frescoes, is used for art exhibitions. After all the medieval churches seen in this part of France, it is a change to come across one that has no ancient origins at all. The Eglise Ste-Catherine was consecrated in 1937, having been erected on the site of a previous church from which some notable stained glass was conserved for use in its successor. The 17th-century Chapelle des Penitents contains a large collection of processional staffs and some fine glassware.

Below
Puy l'Evêque

PUY-L'EVEQUE❖

ⓘ Puy l'Evêque *Office de Tourisme, pl. de la Truffière; tel: 05 65 21 37 63; e-mail: office.de.tourisme. puy.l.eveque@wanadoo.fr. Open all year.*

A pretty little town in a pretty cliff-side location, capped by the church and the remains of the castle. The 14th-century fortified church is known for its great belfry porch and the ancient tombs in the churchyard. The castle keep still shelters the houses below it. Near Puy l'Evêque is St-Martin-le-Redon, known for its spring water, which is said to be beneficial for those with skin problems.

Into the action

The Cahors area, with the Lot Valley, is a useful centre if you enjoy sporting activities. Whether you fancy a half-day bicycle ride or a parachute jump, it's easy to organise in this region. If you have the time for a long-distance ride on horseback or mountain bike, or a canoe exploration along the River Lot, you can try a new category of accommodation introduced in the Lot *département* – the Rando-Etape.

Rando-Etapes are stopping points specially for the non-motorised. Rando is short for *randonnée* – a long-distance walk or ride – and *étape* means stage. Rando-Etapes may be a *gite d'étape*, *chambre d'hôte* (bed and breakfast) or other type of lodging. It has to be open from Easter to the end of October and to accommodate at least 10 people. A bike shelter and enclosure for horses are required. 'Tourisme Equestre' approved places have to provide stalls or horseboxes. Meals may be provided or there may be a kitchen for self-catering.

Long-distance accompanied horse rides from two to seven days are provided by a Cahors establishment that also offers rides by the hour. Lessons for novices are available. Contact the **Association Departmentale de Tourisme Equestre de Lot** *Cahors; tel: 05 65 35 07 09; e-mail: le-lot@wanadoo.fr*

Footpath walks up to 175km and shorter circular walks of a few hours are suggested throughout the Lot region by the **Comité Départemental du Lot** (*107 quai Cavaignac, Cahors; tel: 05 65 35 07 09; www.tourisme-lot.com*). More than 150 shorter walks are outlined in a collection entitled *Promenades and Randonnée*, on sale at tourist offices.

Mountain bike rides by the day, or for between four and 12 days, are organised by **Cap Liberté** *Conduché, St-Cirq-Lapopie; tel: 05 65 24 21 02; e-mail: vtt@cap-liberté.fr; www.cap-liberte.fr (in French only)*. The company also has mountain bikes for hire. For details of all-road cycling and mountain biking, contact the **Comité Départemental de Cyclotourisme** *du Lot, Résidence Souihol, Saint Céré; tel: 05 65 10 98 90; e-mail: randocyclovtt46@wanadoo.fr; http://perso.wanadoo.fr/randocyclovtt46*

Canoes may be hired by the day, half day or hour from **Lot Navigation Nicols** *Le Bourg, Bouziès; tel: 05 65 24 32 20; e-mail: lotnavigation@aol.com; www.lotnavigation.com*. Two-person canoes and one-person kayaks are available from **Club Canoe-Kayak MJC**, who run day-long accompanied descents and longer trips (*Base Canoe Kayak, 1 pl. Chico Mendes, Cahors; tel: 05 65 22 62 62*). The season covers about seven weeks in July and August. For a list of canoeing clubs and/or a list of activities, contact the **Comité Départemental de Canoe-Kayak** *at pl. Chico Mendes, Cahors; tel: 05 65 35 91 59, e-mail: cdck46@9online.fr*

Water-skiing is another option. Contact **Cahors Sport Nautique** *Base Nautique de Regourd, Cahors; tel: 05 65 30 08 02*, open every afternoon in July and August, Monday, Wednesday and Saturday afternoons in June and September, weekends and public holidays in May and October.

VILLENEUVE-SUR-LOT❖❖

---

❶ Villeneuve-sur-Lot
47 rue de Paris; tel: 05 53 36 17 30; e-mail: tourisme@ville-villeneuve-sur-lot.fr; www.ville-villeneuve-sur-lot.fr. Open 0900–1200 and 1400–1800; Jul–Aug 0900–1900. Closed Sun.

❶ Aquatic Garden
(Latour Marliac) €€ Etablissement Botanique, le Temple-sur-Lot; tel: 05 53 01 08 05; e-mail: LM1875@aol.com; www.latour-marliac.fr. Open daily May–Sept 1000–1700. Shop opens Mar–Sept 1000–1800.

Musée de Gajac €
2 r. des Jardins; tel: 05 53 40 48 00. Open daily except Tue 1000–1200 and 1400–1800, Sat, Sun afternoon only. Closed public holidays.

The River Lot sees no point in taking the shortest route from A to B. It likes to wriggle along creating delightful views and making big loops, which were ideal for the establishment of communities.

A popular overnight stop for visitors and a lively, mainly modern, town, though it was founded in 1264 and was considered one of the most important *bastide* towns in the Southwest. The town has managed to retain many of the little streets of half-timbered and brick houses of past centuries. Pl. de la Fayette is a good example of this preservation. Stone houses from the 18th and 19th centuries mingle comfortably with modern developments. In the shelter of hills around the town are orchards and vineyards. Villeneuve is known for its regional market and the sweet, plump plums used to make Agen's famous plum brandy.

The Villeneuve area claims to be the birthplace of the water lily. Whether or not this is so, the **Latour Marliac Aquatic Garden❖❖❖** is a marvellous place to visit. The ornamental lake dates back to 1870. A lake fed by a natural spring contains France's national collection of water lilies, and there is a waterfall. A greenhouse contains tropical plants and some amazing giant water lilies from the Amazon.

Villeneuve's original fortifications have disappeared except for two brick and stone gates in the ramparts, the Porte de Pujols (southwest) and the Porte de Paris (northeast).

Château de la Sylvestrie❖ is one of France's rare medieval courts, dating from the 12th to 15th centuries. In the romantic setting of an old riverside windmill, a municipal museum the **Musée de Gajac**, has recently opened, exhibiting archaeological items, displays relating to the Lot's history, the *bastide* of Villeneuve and a collection of art works mainly of the 18th to 20th centuries.

Accommodation and food

Aquitaine Hôtel €–€€ *29 av. Lazare Carnot, Villeneuve-sur-Lot; tel: 05 53 49 00 50.* The hotel has 22 en suite rooms and a restaurant (**€–€€**).

La Carriere €€ *Albas; tel: 05 65 36 74 98; e-mail: bookings@lotfrance.com; www.lotfrance.com. Open all year.* Bed & breakfast and gîtes in the village of Albas, run by an English couple. Sleeps up to 10 guests.

Club de Vacances Duravel *route de Vire; tel: 05 65 24 65 06; www.clubdevacances.nl. Open late Apr–end Sept.* This site takes caravans and mobile homes and provides swimming, tennis and entertainment. 237 pitches.

Camping de l'Ecluse *Le Payras, Douelle; tel: 05 65 30 98 09. Open Apr–mid-Sept.* On the river, with canoes and kayaks, the site has a restaurant, tennis and entertainment. 17 pitches.

Les Gardes €–€€ *Prayssac; tel: 05 65 22 41 98. Open Apr–Oct.* Gîte offering various sports and games and swimming. There is a garden and parking. Wheelchair accessible.

Hôtel le Glacier €–€€ *11–13 blvd G. Leygues Villeneuve-sur-Lot; tel: 05 53 70 70 14.* Bath or shower in 19 of the 28 rooms.

Camping Municipal le Rooy *N21, Villeneuve-sur-Lot; tel: 05 53 70 24 18. Open mid-Apr–Sept.* The basic campground has 63 pitches.

Hôtel des Platanes €–€€ *40 bd. de la Marine, Villeneuve-sur-Lot; tel: 05 53 40 11 40. Closed the last week in Aug.* Small family hotel in a quiet residential area close to the town centre. 20 rooms.

Hôtel des Ramparts € *1 r. Etienne Marcel, Villeneuve-sur-Lot; tel: 05 53 70 71 63.* Nine-room hotel, five en suite.

Hôtel la Résidence €–€€ *17 av. Carnot, Villeneuve-sur-Lot; tel: 05 53 40 17 03.* Of the 18 rooms, five are en suite.

Hôtel-Restaurant Henry € *Puy l'Evêque; tel: 05 65 21 32 24.* The restaurant (€–€€) seats 120 and there are 75 places on the terrace. The hotel has 19 rooms.

Below
Villeneuve-sur-Lot

Hôtel Terminus €–€€ *2 av. Mal Foch, Villeneuve-sur-Lot; tel: 05 53 70 94 36.* The hotel has a restaurant (**€–€€**) and 12 guest rooms, each with bath or shower.

La Truffière €€ *Puy l'Eveque; tel: 05 65 21 34 54. Closed on Sun evenings except in the season. Open all year.* The 10-room hotel has a restaurant (**€–€€**) and terrace.

L'Auberge Imhotep €–€€ *Albas; tel: 05 65 30 70 91.* This country restaurant specialises in the traditional fare of the region.

Auberge du Vieux Duelle €–€€ *Le Bourg, Douelle; tel: 05 65 20 02 03. Closed two weeks in Dec–Jan.* The restaurant (**€–€€**) seats 30, with seating for 60 more on the terrace. There are 17 guest rooms with TV and phone. There's a swimming pool and children's playground.

Ferme Auberge La Roseraie € *Duravel; tel: 05 65 24 63 82. Closed Mon and Thur lunchtimes. Open late Jun–early Sept.* Traditional regional cuisine is served here in the 50-cover restaurant or on the terrace, which seats 60.

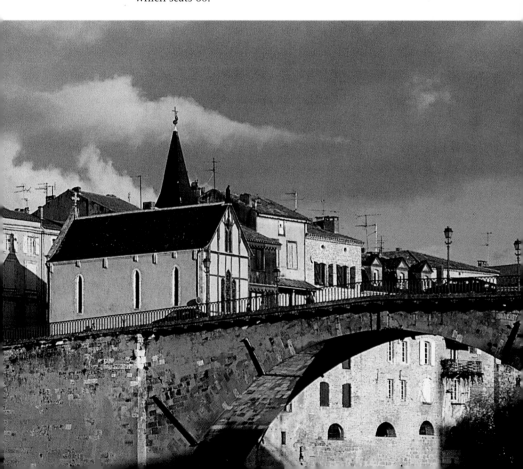

Pilgrims' bridge

In the 16th century the crews of three boats were planning to sail down the River Lot at Villeneuve, but for some inexplicable reason they could make no headway. Some mysterious force seemed to prevent them from moving forward. Utterly perplexed, one of the sailors dived over the side to try and locate the problem. Eventually he emerged with a statuette of the Virgin Our Lady of All Joy. Presumably the boats were then able to make progress, because the men vowed to build a chapel at the spot where the incident occurred. That is why one of the places of worship in Villeneuve-sur-Lot is la Chapelle du Bout du Pont (the chapel at the end of the bridge). It became a place of pilgrimage for the boatmen on the Lot, and is still there. The bridge is the Pont Vieux, or Pont de Cieutats, built by the English in the 13th century. Its three defence towers were destroyed in the 17th century.

ℹ Along the Lot are a number of vineyards and wine cellars open to visitors: a list of these is available from the tourist office in Cahors: *pl. François Mitterrand; tel: 05 65 53 20 65.*

Suggested tour

Total distance: The route covers 57km.

Time: Some of the roads are steep and narrow. Allow 2½ hours for driving and at least half a day to include sightseeing.

Route: From **VILLENEUVE-SUR-LOT** ❶ follow the D661 east for 10km to **Penne-d'Agenais** ❷, a popular riverside destination for tourists and pilgrims paying homage to the Virgin. Originally an English possession, it was involved in many conflicts and suffered badly during the Wars of Religion. It was so badly battered over the years that it was largely in ruins by the 20th century. Restored in recent years it is now a great place for strolling around. Notre-Dame-de-Peyragude is a modern Romanesque-Byzantine sanctuary where pilgrimages are held. It is built on a hilltop where there is a wonderful panoramic view of the Lot Valley from Villeneuve to Fumel in the east. A number of splendidly restored half-timbered houses are to be seen in r. de Ferracap and adjoining streets. Porte de Ricard is named after Richard the Lionheart who ordered the building of the town's first defences.

Leave Penne by the D103, climbing steadily into the region known as les Serres du Bas-Quercy, where peaceful, fertile valleys lie between chains of steep limestone hills. After 9km the road reaches **Hautefage-la-Tour** ❸. The tower that gives the village its name is an elegant hexagonal belfry, part of Notre-Dame-de-Hautefage, a Gothic-style church. The village square, shaded by plane trees, contains an ancient wash house and a pilgrims' fountain.

At the southern end of the village turn left and follow the unclassified road that winds down steeply for 5km to reach the delightful small village of **Frespech** ❹, where some of the houses date from the 11th century, as do the surrounding defensive walls and the Romanesque church. Head south out of Frespech, descending to join the D656 after 3km. Turn right and travel on the D656 for 5km, where another right turn, this time on to the D110, leads in 2km to **Laroque-Timbaut** ❺, a picturesque village with a covered market and ancient houses huddled against the remains of castle walls.

Grottes de Fontirou and Parc Préhistorique €€ *Off the N21 at Castella; tel: 05 53 40 15 29; www.grottes-fontirou.com. Open for guided tours Apr–Jun and first half Sept 1400–1730; Jul–Aug 1000–1230 and 1400–1800.*

Grottes de Lestournelles €€ *Ste-Colobie de Villeneuve; tel: 05 53 40 08 09. Open mid-Jun–mid-Sept daily 1000–1200 and 1400–1900; rest of year Sun 1400–1900.*

Continue north on the D110, climbing again for 5km to join the N21, just beyond Bayle. Turn right on to the N21 and after 2km, at St-Antoine-de-Ficalba, follow the signs to **Grottes de Fontirou** and **Parc Préhistorique de Fontirou** . The caves have white stalagmites strikingly set against the ochre and grey walls of the galleries. The park leads visitors on a woodland tour through some 4.5 billion years and there are scenes showing dinosaurs and other extinct animals, birds and reptiles. A neolithic village gives an insight into life at the dawn of human history. Turn right on leaving the park, then take the D212 then D220 north for 6km to the **Grottes de Lestournelles** , where seven chambers with stalactites and huge pillars are open to visitors.

Head north on the D220 and after 2km turn right on to the D118, then in 6km arrive at **PUJOLS** , a village with Renaissance and timber-framed houses surrounded by the remains of 13th-century ramparts. Continue on the D118, returning to Villeneuve in 2km.

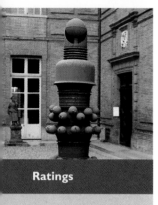

Montauban

Ratings

Art	●●●●●
Markets	●●●●●
Food specialities	●●●●○
Museums	●●●●○
Architecture	●●●○○
Historical sites	●●●○○
Scenery	●●●○○
Children	●●○○○

Montauban's pinkish-red brick buildings and beautiful old arcades represent much history. The *bastide* town was founded in 1144. The Pont Vieux, grandly spanning the wide River Tarn, was built nearly 700 years ago. The Musée Ingres displays the works of Jean-Auguste-Dominique Ingres (1780–1867), born in Montauban, and other artists. The town was handed to the English in the Hundred Years' War, later to be re-conquered by the French. During England's regime the Black Prince built on the ruins of a château (now the Ingres Museum). The cellar contains the Black Prince's room, where instruments of torture and other items are now displayed. The Musée de la Résistance poignantly displays Montauban's World War II history. Two acacia trees in the town were used by the Reich to hang martyrs of the Resistance. The big and boisterous Saturday market draws people from the surrounding fruit-growing country.

History

ⓘ Montauban Office de Tourisme *pl. Prax-Paris; tel: 05 63 63 60 60; e-mail: officetourisme@montauban.com; officetourisme.montauban.com. Open Mon–Sat 0930–1230 and 1400–1830; Jul–Aug Mon–Sat 0900–1900, Sun 1000–1200 and 1500–1800. Guided tours of the town daily 1000 and 1600 (not public holidays).*

Fortified towns and villages known as *bastides*, developed in Southwest France in the Middle Ages, are regarded as the earliest examples of urban planning. Each had a covered market and the streets were laid out symmetrically. Montauban, founded in 1144, is considered to be the prototype for later *bastides*. The Old Town, with the pl. Nationale at its core, has 17th-century covered walkways or arcades of timber, providing welcome shade in the heat of summer.

Once a centre of the weaving industry, Montauban has been the principal town of the Tarn-et-Garonne region since 1808. The local economy is based on agriculture and fruit production, supported by a diversity of other industries. Prior to its 1144 charter – by which Alphonse Jourdain, Count of Toulouse, created Montauban – a small farming community existed near the River Tarn. Major building work took place in periods of prosperity. These included **l'Eglise St-Jacques**,

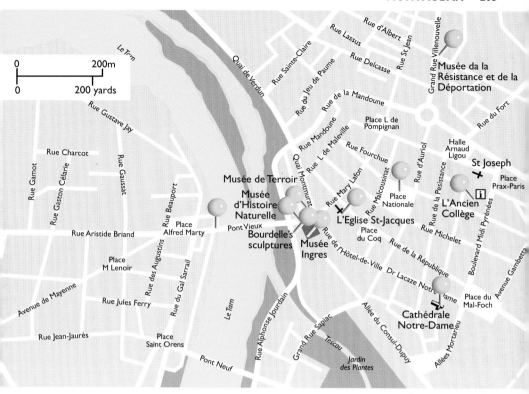

ⓘ Le Comité départemental de tourisme de Tarn-et-Garonne (for information on the region), *2 blvd de Midi-Pyrénées Montauban; tel: 05 63 63 31 40.*

Reservations *Service départemental de réservations, Loisirs Accueil Tarn-et-Garonne, 2 blvd de Midi-Pyrénées, Montauban; tel: 05 63 66 04 42; e-mail: loisirs.accueil82@wanadoo.fr*

Office de Tourisme *2 rue du College, Ancien College, Montauban; tel: 05 63 63 60 60; e-mail: webmaster@ville-montauban.fr; www.montauban.com*

begun in 1230, and the great bridge over the River Tarn, begun in 1311, both still existing.

The Hundred Years' War, the plague and a great famine took their toll, and it was not until the 15th and early 16th centuries that Montauban got back on its feet. Building, commerce, agriculture and artistic culture revived and flourished. In the 16th century Montauban emerged as a Protestant stronghold from a series of religious wars between 1562 and 1598. The 18th-century **Cathédrale Notre-Dame** contains an Ingres masterpiece, *Louis XIII's Pledge.*

Sights

Bourdelle's sculptures❖❖

Six years before the death of the acclaimed local artist Dominique Ingres, the gifted sculptor Emile-Antoine Bourdelle (1861–1929) was born in Montauban. His works can be seen around the town, notably the *Dying Centaur* in bronze, adjacent to the Natural History Museum, and a dramatic battlefield scene – a memorial to the 1870 war – near the Ingres museum and pl. Bourdelle.

🅘 **Cathédrale Notre-Dame** € r. Notre-Dame. Open daily (donations welcome).

L'Eglise St-Jacques € r. de la République, Montauban (donations welcome).

Farm visits €€ la Tome du Ramier, le Ramier, near Montauban; tel: 05 63 03 14 49. Open all year. Advance booking advised.

L'Ancien Collège In Montauban tourist office complex. For opening times contact tourist office.

Musée Ingres €€ Palais Episcopal, 19, rue de l'hôtel de Ville, Montauban; tel: 05 63 22 12 91; www. montauban.com/tourisme/ ingres.asp. Open Jul–Aug daily 0930–1200 and 1330–1800; rest of year 1000–1200 and 1400–1800, but closed Tue and Sun am.

Cathédrale Notre-Dame⁺

Built to celebrate the triumph of the Catholic religion in a Protestant city, following the Revocation of the Edict of Nantes, the classical-style cathedral was designed by noted architects of the day, François d'Orbay and Robert de Cotte. It was constructed in pale stone and inaugurated in 1739. In the left side of the transept is the Ingres painting, *Louis XIII's Pledge*.

L'Eglise St-Jacques⁺⁺

Dating from 1230, the church, with its distinctive octagonal bell tower, was partially destroyed and rebuilt in the first half of the 18th century. Marks of cannonballs, relics of the 1621 siege, may be seen at the bottom of the bell tower. One of the three chapels off the nave contains an altar and a sculpture by Joseph Ingres, father of Dominique. The cost of the original building was raised partly by donations and also by fines imposed on well-to-do individuals who were considered to be too finely dressed.

Farm visits⁺

A 'Welcome to the Farm' agricultural tourism booklet is available from the tourist office. Fruit farms, wine estates, honey farms, goat herds and specialists producing flowers, escargots, *foie gras* and traditionally made breads and cheeses may be visited in the Tarn-et-Garonne region. At la Tome du Ramier, 3km from Montauban, you can see how milk from 160 cows is transformed into hundreds of maturing cheeses. The farm routine and the rearing and care of the cows and heifers are outlined.

L'Ancien Collège⁺

You will see the former Jesuits' College if you call at Montauban tourist office – it is housed there. Originally a private house, the brick-built structure was bought by the Jesuits who founded their college there at the end of the 17th century. It has been put to several uses since, including a cannon foundry and, more recently, a primary school. There was talk of demolishing the building when a fire caused considerable damage in 1961, but eventually it was restored and re-opened as a cultural centre. The tourist office occupies a spacious hall.

Musée Ingres⁺⁺⁺

Built on the site of a 12th-century castle owned by the counts of Toulouse, the impressive red-brick edifice that houses the Ingres Museum was developed as the Bishop's Palace (begun in 1664), following three centuries of neglect. Before this long period of decay the Black Prince, son of the king of England, began to build on the old castle ruins in 1342. Part of the cellar was the Black Prince's guardroom. Today instruments of torture and various artefacts and relics from the distant past are displayed in the room. Art works by Jean-Auguste-Dominique Ingres (1780–1867) and other artists are exhibited on five floors.

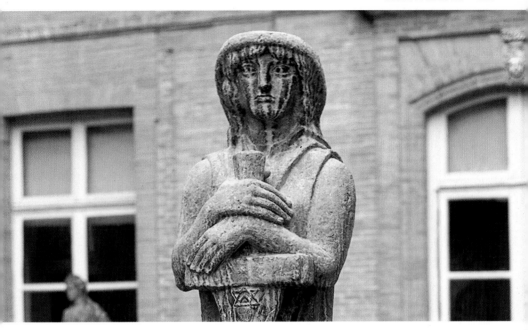

The devotee will want to spend a good two to three hours here, although improvements to lighting and labelling would be appreciated. Ingres and other Montauban-born artists, and some who painted local landscapes, are represented on the ground floor. Bronzes by Montauban resident Antoine Bourdelle (1861–1929) are exhibited. On the top floor are drawings and paintings by Ingres and some of his pupils. There's a reconstruction of the room where Ingres relaxed with his violin, with the instrument in pride of place.

Among the artist's best-known paintings on display are *Jesus Among the Doctors*, *Ossian's Dream*, *Portrait of Madame Gonse* and the nude *Angelique*. Ingres bequeathed many paintings and 4000 drawings and made generous donations to the museum, which opened in 1843. Separate areas in the museum are devoted to the French, Spanish and Flemish schools of the 17th and 18th centuries. In the museum's courtyard are terracotta figures by Joseph Ingres, father of Dominique.

Musée d'Histoire Naturelle*
Four thousand birds, mammals (including primates), reptiles and fish reflect the taxidermist's art. Palaeontology and mineral collections are housed in the museum, established in the mid-19th century.

Musée de Terroir*
Below the Natural History Museum, this 'museum of the soil' presents one man's collection over a period of 40 years of artefacts, implements and household items relating to the lives of peasants in the region in days gone by.

Above
Musée Ingres

Musée de la Résistance et de la Déportation €€ *33 Grand Rue, Villenouvelle, Montauban; tel: 05 63 66 03 11. Open Tue–Sat 0900–1200 and 1400–1800. Closed Aug.*

Pont Vieux €€ For a change of perspective on the town, hire an electric boat on the River Tarn. *Boats are moored near the Pont Vieux, and are available daily from mid-Jun to mid-Sept.*

Musée de la Résistance et de la Déportation✦✦✦

This new museum provides a moving insight into the dedication of the Resistance Movement in this region of France in World War II during the German occupation and the supreme sacrifice made by many local people. Photographs, documents, letters, reports and other exhibits ensure that the memory of the Resistance workers' courage lives on.

Place Nationale✦✦

A centre of urban life since the 12th century, this is the heart of Old Montauban, a forerunner of *bastide* towns and villages, with an early 'grid system' of streets at right angles to one another, leaving a large open square in the middle – pl. Nationale. Fire destroyed two of the adjoining timber arcades in 1614 and the other two in 1649, but all were rebuilt to the original design and survive today. Wednesday and Saturday markets are held there in winter and theatrical performances take place there in summer.

Pont Vieux✦✦

A bridge – the enduring Pont Vieux crossed by countless vehicles daily – was built between 1311 and 1335 over the River Tarn. Originally it had three towers: one at either end and a triangular central one that contained an altar dedicated to Ste Catherine. Opposite the central tower was a balance that operated a metal cage. Blasphemers were put into this cage and dipped three times in the river as a punishment.

Below
Montauban and the banks of the Tarn

Pigeon houses

Les pigeonniers are a
feature of the landscape
in Southwest France
generally and Tarn-et-
Garonne in particular.
They come in many
styles of architecture
and were introduced
centuries ago not so
much as a food source
but for the pigeon
manure, which was used
for fertilising the land.

The bridge is 205m long. Above the bridge's seven arches are small arches through which water can pass when the river is in spate, lowering the risk of flooding.

Accommodation and food

Hôtel Campanile €€ *r. Louis Lepine, Parc Albasud, Montauban; tel: 05 63 23 00 02; e-mail: mtb61@wanadoo.fr.* Some of the 46 rooms are non-smoking. The 2-star hotel, open all year, has a restaurant and enclosed parking.

Hôtel Climat de France €€ *Aussonne (RN20), Montauban; tel: 05 63 66 51 61.* Quiet 38-room, 2-star hotel with restaurant and bar handy for the autoroute A20 north of the town.

Hôtel du Commerce €–€€ *19 pl. Franklin Roosevelt, Montauban; tel: 05 63 66 31 32.* There are 28 tastefully decorated rooms in this 1-star hotel near the Cathedral. Bar, garage parking.

Hôtel Ibis €€ *Pont de Chaume, Rocade Est, av. de Montclar, Montauban; tel: 05 63 20 20 88.* The largest of the town's hotels, the Ibis has 62 comfortable air conditioned rooms, swimming pool, tennis court and garden, restaurant and bar. Easy access to the RN20.

Camping du Lac € *Vallée des Loisirs, Lafrançaise; tel: 05 63 67 33 22.* Approximately halfway between Montauban and Moissac, 17km

Fairs and markets

In spring the countryside around Montauban turns pink and white with fruit tree blossom. The Saturday market teems with townspeople and the farming community from surrounding villages has stalls piled high with local walnuts, cheeses, live chickens, flowers, herbs, pickles, jams and salad crops. In spring bunches of young asparagus are a big attraction, then the first of the strawberries arrive. Apples, peaches, nectarines, dessert grapes, plums, greengages and mushrooms vie for space on the stalls; geese, ducks, *foie gras* and the new crop of walnuts, hazelnuts and chestnuts make an appearance in autumn.

Montauban goes in for markets. As well as the all-day Saturday market there's one on Wednesday mornings at pl. Lalaque, another on Tuesday afternoons and evening markets in July and August. An agricultural show takes place in the first weekend in October. Fairs are held in every season – in March, July, October and December, and in mid-November there's a honey fair.

northeast of Montauban on the D927, this 3-star, 33-pitch campground offers tennis, a swimming pool, showers, restaurant and bar among its facilities.

Hôtel du Lion d'Or €–€€ *22 av. de Mayenne, Montauban; tel: 05 63 20 04 04.* The 21-room hotel, close to the railway station, has a bar and restaurant and parking for guests' cars.

Camping Municipal d'Ardus-Plage € *Lamothe-Capdeville; tel: 05 63 31 32 29.* The shady campground 8km north of Montauban has a restaurant and bar, grocery store, electricity, showers and telephone. There are 33 pitches.

Hôtel d'Orsay €€ *31 r. Salengro, Montauban; tel: 05 63 66 06 66. Closed for the two middle weeks in August.* Opposite the railway station, the hotel has 20 sound-proofed rooms with air conditioning. There is a restaurant of high repute and a bar. Secure parking.

L'Agora € *9 pl. Nationale, Montauban; tel: 05 63 63 05 74.* A snack bar handy for shoppers and stallholders in the market.

Café des Brasseurs € *22 pl. Nationale, Montauban; tel: 05 63 63 54 56.* Good beer and a modestly priced menu.

Café Flamand €–€€ *8 r. de la Republique, Montauban; tel: 05 63 66 12 20. Open daily until 0200.* Call here for the beer – they specialise in Belgian, German and English brews.

Le Comedy-Bar €–€€ *2 r. de la Résistance, Montauban; tel: 05 63 63 24 72.* Good choice of hot and cold food served promptly and with a smile. Pricey bottled beer. As still happens in France, women from

Planning a picnic? Call at **Tartabelle**, *9 r. de la Comédie, Montauban; tel: 05 63 91 10 74.* They have good quiches, pizzas, vegetarian tarts, sandwiches and other savouries.

abroad may find the toilet arrangements disconcerting – they have to go by men in the urinal to reach their toilet.

Cuisine d'Alain €€–€€€ *29 av. Roger Salengro, Montauban; tel: 05 63 66 06 66.* This is the restaurant at the Hotel d'Orsay, of which Alain Blanc and his wife are the proprietors. Fresh home-grown herbs are used in his innovative dishes. Most of the ingredients are produced locally. Desserts are artistic: if not rushed off his feet your waiter may create a design on your plate with sauces and cream, such as a seahorse, bird or flower. Alain's cuisine has a devout following – best to book.

Suggested tour

Abbaye de Beaulieu €€ *Ginals; tel: 05 63 24 50 10.* Phone for opening times.

Total distance: The main route covers 123km. The detour adds 30km.

Time: Driving time for the main route is about 3 hours, with an extra hour if the detour is followed. Give yourself a full day's outing, however, to get the most out of the varied scenery, towns and villages along the way.

Links: From Caylus the D926 heads northeast to Villefranche-de-Rouergue, from where the D922 travels due north to Villeneuve and Figeac (*see pages 172–6*). At Caussade you can head north to Cahors (*see pages 182–91*) on the N20 or the faster A20, the autoroute that opened in the summer of 1998. From Lafrançaise the D927 takes you west to Moissac (*see pages 212–21*), where the N113 continues to Agen.

Route: From **MONTAUBAN ❶** follow the D115 east. At first the countryside is fairly bland, but at Montricoux, after 20km, the road begins to run alongside the Aveyron river, which is soon twisting and turning through the famed Gorges de l'Aveyron. The road also twists and turns as the terrain becomes more rugged, the river on one side and forested hills on the other. **St-Antonin-Noble-Val ❷**, 26km from Montricoux, is a lovely old riverside town sustaining a medieval ambience. Its town hall, built in 1125, is the oldest civic building in France. Visitors can enjoy canoeing, caving, climbing, cycling, horse riding, rambling, swimming and tennis. The town is named after an early evangelist who brought Christianity to the area.

Detour: Leaving St-Antonin on the undulating D75 brings you in 13km to the D33, where a left turn leads within 2km to the **Abbaye de Beaulieu****, founded in 1144, now restored and housing a collection of modern art. Continue north on the D33 for 8km to reach **Parisot**. Standing 375m above sea level, the village offers a superb panorama of the northeast Quercy and Rouergue. It has a lovely 16th-century covered market. Join the D926, turning left to reach Caylus in 9km.

From St-Antonin, continue on the main route by following the D19 for 12km north to **Caylus ❸**, a small, ancient town with a fortified

ℹ **Caussade** 11 r. de la
Republique; tel: 05 63
26 04 04; e-mail:
caussade.tourisme@free.fr.
Open daily.

Montpezat-de-Quercy
blvd des Fossés; tel: 05 63
02 05 55. Open daily
(Apr–Oct).

Gothic church and a covered market dating from the 14th century and other medieval buildings. The large village of **Septfonds** ❹, 15km west of Caylus on the D926, has a number of prehistoric standing stones and dolmens. **Caussade** ❺, 7km further on, is a hat-making town: everything from beach caps to creations for the couturiers of Paris, as well as traditional straw boaters. It also has a wealth of 16th- and 17th-century architecture.

Leave Caussade on the N20 north. After 6km head west on the D38 to reach **Montpezat-de-Quercy** ❻ in a further 6km. Highlights here are the 16th-century Flemish tapestries in the Collegiale St-Martin, and the 17th-century cloisters in the old Convent des Ursulines, now a school. Continue on the D20 for 12km to **Molières** ❼, a 13th-century *bastide*, and a further 15km to Lafrançaise, where a left turn on to the D927 will take you over the confluence of the rivers Aveyron and Tarn to return to Montauban in 17km.

Also worth exploring

From St-Antonin you can continue to follow the Aveyron upstream by taking the D115 east to **Féneyrols**, a village whose remedial mineral waters have been renowned since Roman times, **Varen**, which has an 11th-century church and a 15th-century château, and **Laguépie**, an attractive village standing on a bend in the river. 25km in total.

Below
St-Antonin

Castelnau-
Montratier

Montpezat-
de-Quercy

Belfort-du-Quercy

Puylaroque

Parisot

s-
denard

6

14

A20

E9

D17

11

Lère

13

23

3 Caylus

**Ancienne Abbeye
de Beaulieu-
en-Rouergue**

Sèye

7

Molières

D926

Monteils

9

4

Septfonds

11

Verfeil

Caussade **5**

24

Mirabel

L'Honor-
de-Cos

Lafrançaise

N20

Réalville

14

Albias

D95

2

St-Antonin-
Noble-Val

l'Aveyron

Aveyron

12

D115

D600

10

Cazals

Forêt   de   de la   Grésigne

△
520

21

uzac

Aveyron

D927

15

D115

Montricoux

Gorges

18

D115

Penne

Vaour

Nègrepelisse

5

Bruniquel

Vaïssac

58

24

11

1 Montauban

Montbeton

14

0   10km

12

D964

31

Monclar-de-Quercy

Castelnau-de-
Montmiral

Cahuzac-
sur-Vèr

22

Ratings

Ecclesiastical art	●●●●○
History	●●●●●
Arts and crafts	●●●●○
Food	●●●●○
Scenery	●●●●○
Walks	●●●●○
Children	●●●○○
Sport	●●●○○

Moissac

For many people on a history and culture tour of Southwest France, Moissac is the ultimate site. They marvel at the sheer beauty of the 76 decoratively carved capitals of the cloisters of St-Pierre. This wealth of Romanesque art from the 12th century has a powerful emotional impact. The abbey church's great south doorway is a masterpiece of the same period. Intricately carved in stone are the figures of Christ, St John and figures from the Book of Revelations. Set in fruit-growing country, Moissac is a small town through which the Canal Latéral à la Garonne runs. Nearby is the confluence of the rivers Tarn and Garonne. The area is famous for the golden *Chasselas de Moissac* – the sweet grape served as a dessert. Painters, potters, glass-blowers, stained-glass makers, *objets d'art* restorers and other artists and craftspeople have studios and workshops in r. Jean Moura.

History

ℹ **Moissac Office de Tourisme** *6 pl. Durand de Bredon, tel: 05 63 04 01 85; e-mail: office.moissac@wanadoo.fr; www.frenchcom.com/moissac. Open Oct–Mar daily 1000–1200 and 1400–1700; Apr–May 0900–1230 and 1400–1800; Jun and Sept 0900–1800; Jul–Aug 0900–1900. Closed 1 Jan and 25 Dec. Guided walks are organised by the tourist office daily and Fri evenings in Jul and Aug, and by reservation the rest of the year.*

Moissac✦✦✦ is an attractive little town by any standards, but, as its inhabitants will tell you, it has three things that give it special appeal to the tourist: stone, water and fruit. The first refers to the Romanesque carvings in the abbey cloisters and around the south portal. There is a 10-minute film about the carvings and history of the 76 individually carved capitals of the cloisters available to watch in the video theatre of the town's tourist office, which is conveniently placed within the abbey complex.

The water is in the River Tarn, and its port at Moissac, which joins the Garonne nearby, and the Canal Latéral à la Garonne, which brings boating visitors to the town and flows beneath flower-bedecked bridges. An aqueduct carries the canal over the river.

The fruit has grown in the wide acreages in the surrounding countryside since Roman times. Today, 200,000 tonnes of fruit a year are produced – peaches, pears, nectarines, cherries, plums, greengages, melons, kiwi fruit and soft fruits. Adding another 15,000 tonnes to this figure is the supreme sweet *Chasselas* table grape. Moissac is also known for its arts and crafts shops. Local people and visitors promenade by the Canal Latéral à la Garonne on summer evenings, admiring the moored boats, or walk in the meadows by the River Tarn.

Sights

L'Abbaye de St-Pierre €€ *pl. Durand de Bredon; tel: 05 63 04 01 85; cloisters; tel: 05 63 04 05 73. Open daily 0800–1800, services Mon–Fri 1830, Sat 1930, Sun 1030.*

L'Abbaye de St-Pierre✦✦✦

The Abbey was founded in the 7th century but was subject to a series of attacks by Normans, Arabs and others. The present building was consecrated in 1063. Pilgrims on their way to Compostela stopped in the church.

The south door is a venerated work of art: a Romanesque sculpture illustrating the Apocalypse recorded by St John in the Book of Revelations. The carved stone, said to date between 1100 and 1130, shows Christ sitting in judgement; Matthew, Mark, Luke and John are represented; the Elders sit in a long row, each with individual and expressive faces. A guided tour reveals much of the detail.

ⓘ Centre d'Art Roman € *blvd Leon-Cladel, Moissac; tel: 05 63 04 41 79; e-mail: art.roman.moissac@wanadoo.fr*

Musée St-Jacques €€ *r. de l'Inondation, Moissac; tel: 05 63 04 10 34. Open all year 1400–1800 winter; 1500–1900 summer.*

Musée du Vieux Moissac € *in l'Abbaye de St-Pierre; tel: 05 63 04 03 08. Open daily except Mon.*

Below
The 11th-century Cloisters of the Abbaye de St-Pierre

Part of the Abbey is Gothic, built of brick, and part is Romanesque. The Cloisters, nearly 1000 years old, cannot fail to impress. Forming archways along each of the four sides of a grassy square, the 76 columns, alternately single and double, present a symphony of light and shade. The capitals and their sculpted marble panels are amazing sculptures, both because of the detail – each one is different – and because of their incredibly fine state of preservation. Many relate to the sculptor; others show birds, flowers, palm leaves and embellishments. At one time there were plans to build a railway line through the site, but sanity prevailed and an act of official vandalism was averted. Four groups of polychrome sculptures are among the restored wall decorations in the church.

A unique collection of 2000 reproduction illuminated manuscripts in the **Centre d'Art Roman** (Romanesque Art Research Centre) in the former seminary is available to researchers and is sometimes on public display.

Musée St-Jacques**

A permanent exhibition of religious art is staged in the former Eglise St-Jacques. Old Moissac and the railway are also featured. Temporary exhibitions are held regularly.

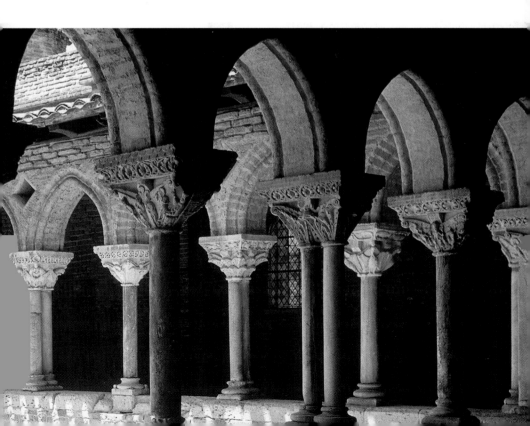

L'Espace Montauriol Galerie du Cloître € *pl. Durand de Bredon, Moissac; tel: 05 63 04 40 00. Open all year.*

Souffleurs de Verre (glass-blowers) € *9 r. Jean Moura, Moissac; tel: 05 63 04 21 46. Open to the public Tue–Sun 1000–1230 and 1500–1830.*

Le Petit Train de Moissac provides a useful introduction to the town (€€ *tel: 05 63 04 01 85. Open May–Sept daily*).

Musée du Vieux Moissac✧✧

Housed in 17th-century abbey lodgings, the museum displays important regional collections of furniture, pottery, earthenware, head dresses and religious art.

Pont Napoléon✧

Planned by Napoléon I on his return from Spain and inaugurated by Napoléon II, the bridge, of brick and stone, crosses the Tarn and links r. du Pont and av. Marcel Cugat.

La Rue des Arts✧✧✧

Spend a few fascinating hours among the art and craft outlets and workshops, the antique and bric-à-brac shops. Rue Jean Moura is the main 'street of arts' but some artists are located in adjacent town-centre streets. There are art and porcelain restoration people, specialists in lace, painters, stained-glass artists, potters, glass-blowers, woodcarvers, jewellers, antique dealers and second-hand dealers. For more information contact the Association Rue des Arts (*9 r. Jean Moura, Moissac; tel: 05 63 04 21 46*).

Ceramics, paintings, sculptures and other works by artists living in the region are exhibited at **L'Espace Montauriol Galerie du Cloître.**

Activities

Children
The tourist office in Moissac holds discovery visits to the Cloisters and other parts of Moissac especially for children, offering them guided tours to find the hidden treasures of the town. Also for children, the tourist office suggests that a family boat trip on the Tarn towards St-Nicolas-de-la-Grave would be interesting, learning about the locks system and the birds of the river. Another idea is donkey riding at Lauzerte farm, 8km out of town.

Farmers' markets
These are held on Saturday and Sunday mornings in Moissac's town centre at pl. des Récollets. A covered market offering fish, meat, cheese, bread and other goods takes place Tue–Sun.

Festivals
The first major annual festival in Moissac's calendar is in late April when the two-day Arts Festival is held. Arts and crafts are demonstrated in the r. Jean Moura. Street entertainments, music, merrymaking, special events and regional food are enjoyed.

More than 100 attractions are staged for the three-day Feast of Pentecost in late May, with bread blessed and distributed and a parade of decorated boats.

For four days in mid-July Moissac holds its Festival of the Voice, with singing, classical music and various events, and July and August bring free Saturday night music events on the square.

September marks the three-day Feast of the *Chasselas* exhibition, with awards for the most beautiful and best-flavoured grapes. The *Chasselas*, with its sweet taste and fine skin, has had the rare distinction for a fruit of being entitled to an *appellation controlée*. Its juice and other fruit juices can be sampled at the Uvarium, a 1930s kiosk decorated in art deco style at 2 av. de l'Uvarium, Moissac, by the River Tarn (closed in winter) (*tel: 05 63 04 53 16*).

Hiking
The waymarked Pilgrims' Route to Compostela in Spain passes through Moissac and two villages in the area, Lauzerte and Auvillar. This is the GR65, now used as a long-distance footpath, considered the most important cultural path in Europe. Hundreds of kilometres of signposted walks and country lanes are available for walkers, mountain bike riders and horse-riders. Information is available at local tourist offices.

Leisure afloat
Summer cruises aboard the péniche *Grain d'Or* provide a leisurely way of experiencing the countryside (*Moissac Navigation Plaisance, Port de*

Plaisance, Moissac; tel: 05 63 04 48 28. Times vary). Alternatively, you can provide your own paddle power in a canoe or kayak (*tel: 05 63 04 10 42).*

Historic villages

For the visitor who likes to potter around a town's historic sites and arts scene and do a little gentle motoring to explore old towns and villages, Moissac makes an agreeable holiday base. You'll find much of interest at some of the places within an easy distance along the Tarn and Garonne valleys.

The two rivers join together near Moissac at **St-Nicolas-de-la-Grave**: pilgrims on their way to Compostela waited for the ferry here. Base de Loisirs is a watersports centre on a 400-hectare stretch of water with an extensive campsite (*tel: 05 63 95 50 00; e-mail: guedj@grand-sud.com; www.grand-sud.com/nicolas).* A sailing school welcomes learners and individual sailing enthusiasts. If you fancy getting afloat, you also have a choice of canoes and kayaks, pedalos and electric boats. Trip boats take passengers by Bird Island, a stopover for migratory species.

Richard Coeur-de-Lion's castle (12th and 13th centuries) is in the village of St-Nicolas-de-la-Grave: an exhibition of paintings and sculptures is held here in July and August.

The birthplace of the man who founded Detroit in the USA, and who had cars named after him nearly two centuries later, is now a museum. Antoine Laumet de Lamothe Cadillac was born in St-Nicolas-de-la-Grave in 1658. His home became a small museum.

A farmers' market is held in the village on Monday mornings.

To the northeast of Moissac is medieval **Lauzerte**, a halt for the Compostela pilgrims, fêted as one of the loveliest villages in France. (Several southwestern towns make this claim, usually with some justification.) Lauzerte sits high on a rock, and has narrow streets, old mansions and an art colony whose works blend in with those from past ages. Several studios are open to the public. The market is on Saturday morning. Lauzerte Tourist Office is at *pl. des Cornieres; tel: 05 63 94 61 94; e-mail: lauzerte.tourisme@quercy-blanc.net; www.quercy-blanc.net*

Lauzerte's Museum of Archaeology has exhibits from the palaeolithic age to the 17th century. There are guided tours in French and English. The museum is in *r. de la Gendarmes; tel: 05 63 94 62 40. Open 1430–1830 weekends and public holidays in May; daily except Tue in Jun and Sept and daily, 1030–1230 and 1400–1700 Jul and Aug.*

Producing quill pens from goose feathers was a major industry in **Auvillar**, southwest of Moissac on the Garonne river, in the 18th century. In the 19th century the local economy was based on earthenware pottery, and some fine examples can be seen in the Musée d'Art et Traditions Populaires. Auvillar pottery is greatly prized by collectors.

Picturesque houses of the 16th and 17th centuries, the site of a castle destroyed in the Wars of Religion in 1572 – providing a wonderful view of the Garonne Valley – and the 17th-century clock-tower on the site of one of the old wall's gates make this a pleasant place to stroll in. It is a fine example of an old Ocitan market town with its river port. The triangular 'square', in which stands a circular covered market, is unique in France; the medieval grain measures are still in place.

A farmers' market is held on Sunday mornings. The tourist office is at *pl. d'Horloge; tel: 05 63 39 89 82; e-mail: office.auvillar@wanadoo.fr; www.webpan.com/auvillar*

Just north of Auvillar is **Valence d'Agen** where old *lavoirs* – predecessors of today's launderettes – may be seen.

Accommodation and food

Hôtel Aube Nouvelle €–€€ *Durfort-Lacapelette; tel: 05 63 04 50 33; www.chez.com/aubenouvelle.* Set in *Chasselas* grape country, with a shady garden, the hotel is 12km from Moissac on the road towards Lauzerte. Nine rooms.

Le Chapon Fin €€ *pl. des Recollets, Moissac; tel: 05 63 04 04 22; www.lechaponfin-moissac.com.* Each room in the 2-star hotel near the market has a bath or shower, TV and direct-dial telephone – and there's a honeymoon suite. Cuisine in the restaurant ranges from traditional regional fare to the innovative.

Hotel des Crêtes de Pignols €–€€ *route de Lafrançaise, Moissac; tel: 05 63 04 04 04; www.cretesdepignols.com.* A small, quiet country hotel 4km from Moissac town centre. The comfortable rooms are en suite; regional cuisine is served in the restaurant. Swimming pool.

La Ferme de Lamouroux € *tel: 05 63 04 27 32.* Stay on a farm on the Pilgrims' Route to Compostela on a *chambre d'hôte* basis. The farm, 5km from Moissac, is a convenient overnight stop for long-distance walkers and all-terrain cyclists. Pets are allowed and horses and riders can be accommodated by prior arrangement. Breakfast is included in the price. Gastronomic meals can be provided at other times of the day.

Le Luxembourg € *av. Pierre Chabrie, Moissac; tel: 05 63 04 00 27; www.hotelluxembourg82.com/Page1.html.* This traditional hotel two minutes from the Abbey was founded in 1883. All rooms are sound-proofed.

Le Pont Napoléon €€–€€€ *2 allées Montebello, Moissac; tel: 05 63 04 01 55; www.canal-du-midi.org/pont-napoleon/main-hebergement.htm.* Beside the River Tarn and close to the town centre, the 2-star hotel has 12 peaceful and attractive en suite rooms. Michel Dussau's acclaimed 3-star restaurant (*closed Wed*) is mentioned in several good eating guides.

Hôtel de la Poste €€ *pl. de la Poste, Moissac; tel: 05 63 04 01 47.* The hotel building is a former convent in the heart of Moissac. Tea dances are sometimes held.

Lou Grill € *3 r. de Mare, Moissac; tel: 05 63 04 32 80. Closed Mon.* Meat and fish grilled on a wood fire, buffet of hors d'oeuvres.

Pub Murrayfield € *4 r. de la Republique, Moissac.* Bar with snacks and ice cream, popular with the sporty set.

Restaurant de l'Abbaye €–€€ *pl. Roger Delthil, Moissac; tel: 05 63 04 81 01; e-mail: j-p.jalin@restaurant-de-labbaye.com; http://restaurant-de-labbaye.com.* The restaurant on the square in front of the abbey is open daily for lunch and dinner, serving grills and regional dishes such as breast of duck, duck *confit* and *cassoulet*.

Camping: *l'Ile du Bidounet, Moissac; tel: 05 63 32 52 52; e-mail: camping.bidounet@wanadoo.fr. Open Apr–Sept.* On an island site 2km from Moissac town centre, the campground offers furnished tents sleeping four people, and places for caravans. Hot showers, laundry facilities and a swimming pool are on site. Canoes, pedalos and electric boats can be hired. 100 pitches.

Below
The Abbaye de St-Pierre

Suggested tour

Total distance: The main route totals 126km. The detour covers 45km, adding 22km to the main route.

Time: Allow 3 hours' driving time for the main route. The detour will take about an hour to drive.

Links: From Lafrançaise you can head south on the D927 to reach Montauban (*see pages 202–11*) in 17km. From Montcuq, the D653, heading northeast, will take you to Cahors (*see pages 182–91*) in about 24km, and from Valence-d'Agen you can take the N113 west for 28km to Agen (*see pages 222–3*).

Route: From **MOISSAC** ❶ head east on the D927 for 14km, turn left on to the D2 and in less than 400m turn right on to the D68.

Detour: Continuing on the D927 towards Montauban for a further 3km brings you to **Lafrançaise**, where you can take the D20 northeast. This road runs more or less parallel with the D68 on the main route, never more than 10km away, but leads to the old *bastide* villages of **Molières** (*see page 146*) and **Montpezat-de-Quercy** (*see page 210*). At Montpezat, noted for its covered arcades, half-timbered houses and 15th-century town gate, head northwest on the D38 for 3.5km, then continue on the D4 for a further 8.5km to rejoin the main route at Castelnau-Montratier.

From the D2 on the main route, follow the D68 for 25km to **Castelnau-Montratier** ❷, passing through typical Quercy Blanc countryside – a narrow, sparsely populated but fertile valley of chalky soil. Castelnau-Montratier, a hilltop *bastide* founded in the 13th century, has a triangular main square and three old windmills, one still working. Leave the village on the D74, which crosses a number of *serres* – rows of long plateaux separated by narrow valleys – and reaches **Montcuq** ❸ in 19km.

Montcuq has a long and violent history. It dates from the 12th century and during the Albigensian Crusade, the Hundred Years' War and the

Wars of Religion suffered numerous battles. A 12th-century castle keep stands as a reminder of those terrible times. From Montcuq take the D953 to **Lauzerte 4**, 11.5km to the southwest. Founded as a *bastide* in 1241 and once occupied by the English, Lauzerte is a peaceful village with a mixture of half-timbered, Gothic and Renaissance houses.

Continue on the D953 for a further 25km, following the course of the River Barguelonne to **Valence-d'Agen** on the north bank of the Canal Latéral à la Garonne. Cross the canal to reach the attractive hilltop village of **Auvillar 5**, overlooking the Garonne river just a few km downstream of its confluence with the Tarn. A promenade at the top of the village has picnic sites and is a good place for a rest and to enjoy the view.

From Auvillar continue east for 11km on the D12, then take the D158 for 3.5km, crossing the Autoroute des Deux-Mers to reach **St-Nicolas-de-la-Grave 6** at the confluence of the Tarn and Garonne. Take the D26 south of St-Nicolas and return to the D12 (3.5km), which leads to the canalside town of Castelsarrasin. From here head north on the N113 for 8km, crossing the Tarn to return to Moissac.

Around Agen and Condom

Ratings

Countryside	●●●●●
History	●●●●●
Villages	●●●●●
Châteaux	●●●●○
Food and drink	●●●●○
Markets	●●●●○
Architecture	●●●○○
Outdoor activities	●●●○○

Couth of the Garonne river and west of the city of Agen, the *département* of Gers is truly French – even though many of its small towns and villages had their beginnings as English *bastides* in the Middle Ages. It is a rural area, producing more garlic than anywhere else in the country, as well as vast quantities of *foie gras*, *confit*, chickens, eggs and cereals. It has rolling hills, sweetly running rivers, ancient churches and abbeys and stately châteaux. And as you might expect of the homeland of that dashing Musketeer d'Artagnan, it is peopled with a breed of individuals who are prepared to take direct action when confronted by awkward authority – dumping with great élan a wagonload of dung on the steps of the town hall, for example. They also have spirit in another sense, for this is where that great brandy Armagnac is produced.

AGEN✦✦

ⓘ **Agen** *107 blvd Carnot; tel: 05 53 47 36 09; e-mail: otsi.agen@wanadoo.fr; www.ot-agen.org. Open all year. Guided tours of the city can be arranged.*

Maybe it's the 35,000 tonnes of prunes they produce each year or the fact that they have one of the best rugby teams in France – whatever the reason, a national poll has decreed that the citizens of Agen are the most contented in the country. Sprawling along the banks of the River Garonne and set on a fertile plain halfway between Toulouse and Bordeaux, Agen is a busy but pleasant city earning its living largely from the surrounding area of market gardens and orchards of peach and plum trees. The old town has some interesting squares and streets with noteworthy houses, shops and public buildings dating from the 14th to 19th centuries.

Cathédrale St-Caprais, founded as a collegiate church in the 11th century, was granted cathedral status in 1802. Frescoes on the walls inside the building portray the city's patron saints. Esplanade du Gravier, fronting the river, is a pleasant area for a walk, with a pond and lawns in the shade of plane trees.

Musée des Beaux-Arts €€ *pl. du Docteur Esquirol, Agen; tel: 05 53 69 47 23; e-mail: musee@ville-agen.fr; www.ville-agen.fr/musee. Open 1000–1800. Closed Tue.*

The city's pride and joy is the **Musée des Beaux-Arts✦✦**, housed in three stately mansions dating from the 16th and 17th centuries, though the cellars of one were once used as a prison and the iron rings to which prisoners were shackled are still fixed to the walls of the museum's prehistoric section. The museum contains a collection of fine paintings, including works by Corot, Goya and Watteau. Its finest possession is the Vénus de Mas, on show in the Gallo-Roman archaeology department. The gracefully proportioned Greek marble statue, dating from the 1st century BC, was found at nearby Mars d'Agenais in 1876.

CONDOM✦✦✦

Condom *pl. Bossuet; tel: 05 62 28 00 80; e-mail: otsi@condom.org; www.condom.org. Open all year 0900–1200 and 1400–1800.*

Boat trips €€ *Gascogne Navigation, Condom; tel: 05 62 28 46 46. Cruises Jul–Aug daily.*

The attractive country town of Condom stands on the River Baïse and its fine 17th- and 18th-century mansions speak of its importance as a centre for the trade in Armagnac, Gascony's rival to Cognac brandy. You can take a **boat trip✦✦** along the river, which was turned into a canal to ship Armagnac to Bordeaux, and rowing boats and motor boats are available for hire.

The town's focal point is the **Cathédrale de St-Pierre✦✦** (*tel: 05 62 28 12 23*), completed in 1531 and battered about a bit over the centuries. In 1569, during the Wars of Religion, the people of Condom paid a ransom of 30,000 francs to prevent the Huguenot army from demolishing it. Inside, there are big gallery windows – some of the stained glass is original, but most dates from the 19th century – and

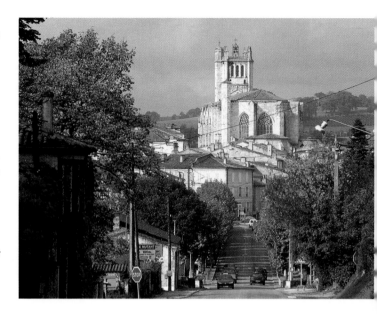

Musée de l'Armagnac €€ *2 r. Jules Ferry, Condom; tel: 05 62 28 31 41. Open daily except Tue, Apr–Oct 1000– 1200 and 1500–1800; Nov–Mar 1500–1700.*

Abbaye de Flaran €€ *off the D142, Valence-sur-Baïse; tel: 05 62 28 50 19; e-mail: mhue@cg.32.fr. Open daily 0930–1200 and 1400–1800, except Jul–Aug 0930–1900; closed mid-Jan–mid-Feb.*

Château du Busca-Maniban €€ *off the D229, 3km south of Cassaigne, near Condom; tel: 05 62 28 40 38. Open (guided tour) Apr–Nov daily 1400–1800. Closed Sun.*

Château de Cassaigne €€ *Cassaigne, near Condom; tel: 05 62 28 04 02; e-mail: chateaudecassaigne@ teleparc.net; www. chateaudecassaigne.com. Open (guided tour) mid-Feb–late Jan daily 0900–1200 and 1400–1900. Closed Mon mid-Oct–mid-Mar.*

complex vaulting. Outside, the 16th-century cloisters, restored in the 19th century, now serve as offices for the Mairie.

The **Musée de l'Armagnac*** houses a collection of vintage tools and machinery once used in local vineyards and features the history of the region's special spirit. **Abbaye de Flaran****, 7km south of Condom, was founded by the Cistercians in 1151. Restored and extended over the centuries, it now serves as a regional cultural centre where concerts, dramatic performances and exhibitions are staged, but guided tours are available. Visitors are shown the abbey church, built 1180–1210, the 14th-century cloisters, the living quarters built to accommodate the prior and guests in the 18th century, the monastic buildings, monks' dormitory and dining room and the kitchens. Outside, there is a formal French garden with a herb plot.

Just over 10km southwest of Condom is the grand **Château du Busca-Maniban****, which is fronted by an expansive courtyard and has a terrace from which on a clear day you can see the Pyrenees. A splendid staircase leads from the imposing hall to a gallery supported by columns. Elegant pieces of period furniture are on show. **Château de Cassaigne****, 7km southwest of the town, was built in the 13th century, though the present façade dates from the 1700s. For many centuries it served as the country residence of the Bishops of Condom. A tour of the castle includes the 16th-century kitchen, with big solid tables and benches, earthenware pots and jars and lots of copper and pewter utensils. For some visitors, however, the highlight will be the store where Armagnac is aged in oak barrels. An audio-visual

Opposite
Condom

presentation features the production of the brandy and there is a tasting session.

LABASTIDE-D'ARMAGNAC✦✦

ℹ️ **Labastide-d'Armagnac** pl. Royale; tel: 05 58 44 67 56; www.labastide-d-armagnac.com/eng/index.php3. Open all year.

🏛️ **Ecomusée de l'Armagnac** €€ Château Garreau, Labastide-d'Armagnac; tel: 05 58 44 88 38; e-mail: chateau.garreau@wanadoo.fr. Open Mon–Sat 0900–1200 and 1400–1800; Sun and public holidays 1500–1800.

This small town of half-timbered houses built on a typical gridiron of streets probably looks much the same as it did when it was founded as an English *bastide* at the end of the 13th century. Its central square, pl. Royale, with its arcaded buildings, is said to have inspired Henri IV to build the pl. des Vosges in Paris. Henri spent some time in Labastide-d'Armagnac before he was enthroned.

The **Ecomusée de l'Armagnac**✦✦ focuses on the famous liquor but also deals with the region's ecology, and nature trips into the surrounding terrain can be arranged. Off the D626, 3km south-east of the town, is **Notre-Dame-des-Cyclistes**✦ €€ (*off the D626, 3km southeast of Labastide-d'Armagnac. Open Tue–Sun 1430–1800; Jul–Aug 1000–1200 and 1430–1800*), the official chapel for France's racing cyclists. It also houses a small museum of cycling memorabilia. The full story is told on the website of the tourist office (in English).

LECTOURE✦✦

ℹ️ **Lectoure** Mairie, pl. de l'Hôtel-de-Ville; tel: 05 62 68 76 98; e-mail: ot.lectoure@wanadoo.fr; www.lectoure.fr. Open all year.

🏛️ **Musée Lapidaire** €€ Open Jul–Aug daily 1000–1200 and 1400–1900; rest of year 1000–1200 and 1400–1700. Visits arranged through the tourist office.

Until the French Revolution Lectoure was always on the centre stage of the nation's history – and frequently suffered for it. It was built on a cliff for reasons of defence, which meant it repeatedly invited attack from invading armies. Its first occupants were the Lactoratii, a Celtic tribe who collaborated with the Romans at a time when other Gauls were at war with them. The Lactoratii were rewarded by being allowed to form a semi-independent republic and the city of Lactora became one of the most important in the region during Roman times.

Later it was knocked about by both the Visigoths and Normans and in the Middle Ages it became the capital of the counts of Armagnac. After the Hundred Years' War the army of Louis XI attacked Lectoure and there was a long siege, which ended in an agreement that the Armagnacs would accept the king's authority while their own rights and those of the town would be guaranteed. But when the town gates were opened, the king's troops set fire to the town and murdered the count and most of the citizens.

The **Cathédrale St-Gervais et St-Protais**✦ dates from 1488. On a clear day there is a stupendous view from the top of the bell tower. The **Musée Lapidaire**✦✦ is in the Mairie, formerly the episcopal palace. It houses a collection of Gallo-Roman funeral monuments in the form of altars decorated with bulls' heads, which were found in the 19th century by workmen excavating under the cathedral. There is also a collection of Roman and Merovingian jewellery.

Accommodation and food

Atlantic Hôtel €€ *133 av. Jean Jaurès, Agen; tel: 05 53 9616 56. Open 2 Jan–24 Dec.* No restaurant but breakfast is available. Each of the hotel's 44 rooms has direct-dial telephone and television, but three do not have en suite facilities. There is a swimming pool. Cars may be garaged or left in the private car park.

Hôtel de Bastard €€–€€€ *r. Lagrange, Lectoure; tel: 05 62 68 82 44.* Don't worry about the name – this is a legitimate, friendly hotel with 29 en suite rooms in a tasteful 18th-century mansion. Each room has a direct-dial telephone and television. There is a swimming pool and garage parking. Traditional Gascon and Italian-inspired dishes appear on the menu in the restaurant (**€€–€€€**), which has an outside dining area.

Bastide-Gascogne €€€ *av. des Thermes, Barbotan-les-Thermes; tel: 05 62 08 31 31.* Gracious living in a restored Carthusian monastery. There is a swimming pool, a garden with a dining terrace and each of the 22 en suite rooms has a direct-dial telephone and a television. Wine is available by the glass in the restaurant (**€€€**), one of the best in an area renowned for its cuisine.

Hôtel de Bordeaux €–€€ *8 pl. Jasmin, Agen; tel: 05 53 68 46 46. Open all year.* The hotel has 22 rooms, but only nine have en suite facilities. There is a restaurant.

Hôtel Château des Jacobins €€€ *1 ter, pl. des Jacobins, Agen; tel: 05 53 47 03 31. Open all year.* The hotel has 15 en suite rooms with direct-dial telephones and television and there is an enclosed car park. Tennis court. No restaurant, but breakfast is available.

Ferme de Flaran €€ *route Condom, Valence-sur-Baïse; tel: 05 62 28 58 22. Closed mid-Nov–mid-Dec and Jan.* Good accommodation and food (**€€–€€€**) in rural surroundings. There are 15 rooms with direct-dial telephones and television, a garden, dining terrace and a swimming pool.

Hôtel Hélène Darroze €€€ *57 Grand Rue, Villeneuve-de-Marsan; tel: 05 58 45 20 07. Closed first three weeks in Jan.* Three well-justified stars have been awarded to this hotel-restaurant, which has 14 well-appointed en suite rooms and a restaurant (**€€–€€€**) specialising in seafood and regional duck and game dishes. The hotel has a garden, dining terrace and swimming pool.

Hôtel Hervé Garrapit €€€ *pl. de la Boiterie, Villeneuve-de-Marsan; tel: 05 58 45 20 08; www.herve-garrapit.com. Open all year.* Nine en suite rooms, a restaurant and swimming pool.

Opposite
Lectoure's early morning market

Hôtel des Trois Lys €€€ *38 r. Gambetta, Condom; tel: 05 62 28 00 80; e-mail: hoteltroislys@minitel.net. Closed Feb. Restaurant closed Sun and*

Mon midday. An elegant 18th-century mansion, the hotel has 10 en suite rooms with direct-dial telephones and television. Wine is available by the glass in the restaurant (€€–€€€). Swimming pool; enclosed parking.

Logis des Cordeliers €€–€€€ *r. de la Paix; Condom; tel: 05 62 28 03 68; www.logisdescordeliers.com. Closed Jan.* The hotel has no restaurant, but breakfast is available. Its 21 en suite rooms have direct-dial telephones and television. Swimming pool; private parking.

Camping l'Oasis *1120 av. des Pyrénées, Villeneuve-de-Marsan; tel: 05 58 45 36 23. Open all year.* Here's a rarity – a campground that's open all year. It has only 16 pitches but you can rent a tent, mobile home or chalet and there are spaces for motor homes. The site has a takeaway food service and bar.

Stim'Otel €€ *105 blvd Carnot, Agen; tel: 05 53 47 31 23. Open 2 Jan–24 Dec.* There are 58 en suite rooms with direct-dial telephones and television. The restaurant (€€) is air conditioned and wine is available by the glass.

Chez Simone €€ *opposite the church, Montréal; tel: 05 62 29 44 40. Closed Sun lunch and all day Mon, except Jul–Aug.* A pleasant restaurant offering good-value food, with a budget meal available at lunchtime.

Restaurant Bohème €€–€€€ *14 r. E. Sentini, Agen; tel: 05 53 68 31 00; e-mail: la-boheme2@wanadoo.fr; www.laboheme-france.com. Closed 15–30 Sept.* A simple, inexpensive (€) meal is served at lunchtime in this pleasant establishment, which has a terraced dining area and serves wine by the glass.

Table des Cordeliers €–€€€ *r. Cordeliers, Condom; tel: 05 62 68 43 82.* Closed Oct–mid-Nov and 2–16 Jan. A comfortable restaurant with a dining terrace and private car park.

Suggested tour

Total distance: The main route covers a total of 147km. The detour totals 37km.

Time: Driving time for the main route is about 3 hours. Allow an hour's driving for the detour.

Links: Agen is on the main route between the Atlantic Ocean and the Mediterranean, with the A62 – the Autoroute-des-Deux-Mers – providing a fast link between Bordeaux and Montauban. North of Agen the N21 travels 28km to Villeneuve-sur-Lot (*see page 197*).

Opposite
Labastide-d'Armagnac

Route: From **AGEN** ❶ head south on the N21 for 36km to **LECTOURE** ❷ then take the D7 west for 16km to the village of Caussens.

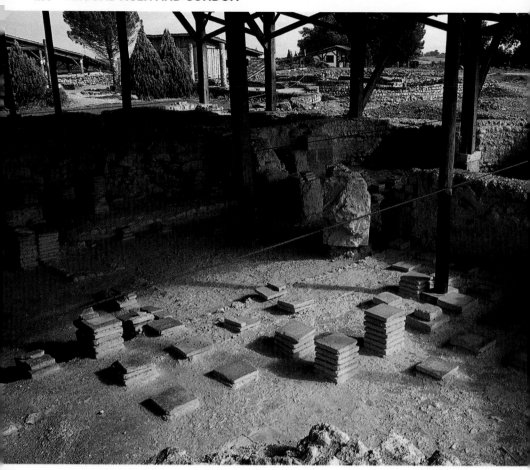

Above
Montréal's Roman villa

🚩 **Château de Monluc €€** *St-Puy;* tel: 05 62 28 94 00. Open (guided tours) daily 1000–1200 and 1500–1900. Closed Sun am, public holidays and Jan.

Detour: From Caussens take the D204 south for 4km to St-Orens, a hilltop fortified village. Take the D232 west for 2km and turn left on to the D654, which in 4km reaches St-Puy, where you can visit the **Château de Monluc**, home of the cocktail ominously known as *pousse-rapière* – 'the rapier thrust'. It's made by steeping oranges in Armagnac then adding dry sparkling wine. Leave St-Puy by the D42 south and after 1.5km turn right on to the D142, which reaches **Valence-sur-Baïse** in 8km. With a typical gridiron of streets, Valence is a *bastide* founded in 1274. Continue on the D142, passing the **Abbaye de Flaran** to reach **Cassaigne** after 4.5km. Take the D208 west for 3km to **Mouchan**, an attractive village with a church dating in part from the 10th century. From Mouchan head north on the D931 for 10km to **CONDOM ❸**.

On the main route, from Caussens continue on the D7 west for 5km to Condom and leave on the D15 west. After 5km it's worth straying

Musée Archéologique €€
pl. de la Mairie, Montréal du Gers; tel: 05 62 29 42 85. Open Mar–Nov 1000–1200 and 1400–1800.

Gallo-Roman Villa €€
Séviac; tel: 05 62 29 48 57; www.seviac-villa.fr.st. Open Mar–mid-Nov daily 1000–1900.

just off the road to visit **Larressingle**, a 13th-century walled village reached by a bridge over a moat. You can take a walk around the ramparts to see the fortified church and a ruined keep. Further west, 10km on, the D15 reaches picturesque **Montréal**, founded as an English *bastide* in 1256. It has arcaded houses surrounding a central square. A collection of Gallo-Roman pottery and metal artefacts and a striking mosaic of trees are displayed in the **Musée Archéologique**. At **Séviac**, just outside Montréal, is the impressive archaeological site of a 4th-century **Gallo-Roman Villa**, with the ruins of the baths and a pool, some fine mosaics and two 7th-century skeletons.

From Montréal, head south on the D29 for 14km to the flourishing market town of Eauze, leaving on the D30 and after 3km heading northwest on the D626. After a further 2.5km bear right on to the D10, which soon becomes the D37. Turn left in 9km on to the D15 then left again after 2.5km on to the D656, reaching in 2km the spa town of **Barbotan-les-Thermes**, known since Roman times for the therapeutic properties of its mud.

Leave the spa town on the D656 and at Cazaubon, 3km away, follow the D626 for 11km to **LABASTIDE-D'ARMAGNAC** ❹. Next, take the D11 southwest for 14km to **Villeneuve-de-Marsan**, noted for its *foie gras* markets. From here, the D1 west reaches Mont-de-Marsan in 17km.

Northern Gascony and the Landes Regional Nature Park

Ratings

Museums	●●●●●
Nature	●●●●●
Outdoor activities	●●●●●
Children	●●●●○
Food and drink	●●●●○
Art and craft	●●●○○
Villages	●●●○○
Historic sites	●●○○○

The Landes has two distinctions based on size: it is the second largest *département* in France and it contains the largest forest in Europe – 600,000 hectares of cultivated trees, mostly maritime pines. And within that forest is the massive Parc Naturel Régional des Landes de Gascogne – 290,000 hectares set aside for the protection of wildlife and the environment and for humans to enjoy. Within its boundaries are way-marked tracks, footpaths, bridle paths and cycle routes and there are opportunities galore for canoeing, cycling, fishing, hiking and riding. It's all very green and very healthy, but until the second half of the 19th century the Landes was a region to avoid, where a few permanent inhabitants struggled to make a living as they went about on stilts tending miserable flocks of sheep in a desert of marshy moorland. Few landscapes have undergone a more dramatic transformation.

BELIN-BELIET✤✤

ⓘ Parc Naturel Régional des Landes de Gascogne *Maison du Parc 33, route de Bayonne, Belin-Béliet; tel: 05 57 71 99 99; e-mail: info@parc-landes-de-gascogne.fr; www.parc-landes-de-gascogne.fr*

Belin-Béliet *Office de Tourisme, 6 av. Aliénor; tel: 05 56 88 06 14. Open Jul–Aug.*

Until the 11th century Belin was the capital of Gascony and a serious rival to Bordeaux. In 1122 the powerful Eleanor of Aquitaine, mother of Richard Coeur-de-Lion, was born here. In one sense, at least, this modest village on the banks of the Leyre river is a capital once again, for here is the headquarters of the **Parc Naturel Régional des Landes de Gascogne✤✤✤**. Today, a plaque on a low mound near the village centre identifies all that is left of the castle in which Eleanor was born. One survivor of her time, though, is l'Eglise St-Pierre-de-Mons, on the edge of Belin, a stop for pilgrims on the road to Santiago de Compostela. Its bell tower was fortified during the Hundred Years' War. Inside the church itself are four elaborately carved capitals.

About 3km out of the village, off the D110 west, is **Vieux-Lugo**, an ancient village that was abandoned in 1869 when the inhabitants decided to relocate on to a healthier site to the west. Its fortified,

Centre d'Animation du Graoux *Centre du Graoux 31 route du Graoux, Belin-Béliet; tel: 05 57 71 99 29; e-mail: centre-graoux@parc-landes-de-gascogne.fr; www.parc-landes-de-gascogne.fr. Open all year.*

Romanesque church of St-Michel contains 16th-century frescoes illustrating the Seven Deadly Sins and the Works of Mercy. The **Centre d'Animation du Graoux***, just north of Belin, offers courses in environmental studies and such outdoor activities as archery, canoeing, cycling and rambling.

Right
Belin-Béliet

LUXEY**❖❖**

Ecomusée de la Grande Lande €€
Sabres (administration); tel: 05 58 08 3 31; e-mail: ecomusee-marqueze@parc-landes-de-gascogne.fr. The museum has sections at Luxey, Marquèze and Moustey, each illustrating a different aspect of daily life in the region during the 18th and 19th centuries. It was the first open-air folk museum in France when it opened in 1968. You can buy a discounted combination ticket for the three sections, even if you plan to visit them on different days.

This attractive little village illustrates the dramatic changes that occurred as the ancient moorlands of the Landes gave way to the vast pine forest of today. The shepherds who had traditionally followed their flocks for centuries adapted to their new environment by becoming *gemmeurs* – resin tappers. The sticky discharge from the pine trees is the raw material for turpentine and rosin and was very much in demand from the beginning of the Industrial Revolution until the introduction of synthetic products after World War II.

The story of the *gemmeurs* and their way of life is told at the **Atelier de produits résineaux Jacques et Louis Vidal**, part of the **Ecomusée de la Grande Lande** (*Luxey; tel: 05 58 07 56 85. Open Jun–Sept daily 1000–1200 and 1400–1900; Apr–May Mon–Fri 1000–1200, Sat 1400–1900, Sun 1000–1200 and 1400–1900; Oct Sun only 1000–1200 and 1400–1900. Closed Nov–Mar and public holidays*). Located in an old resin distillery founded in 1859 and in operation until 1954, the workshop demonstrates the various stages in the traditional production of turpentine and other products. The industry's heyday was during the American Civil War (1861–5) when imports from the United States were cut off and the price of resin rose by more than 600 per cent. Today, there are about 50 *gemmeurs* still working in the forest, compared with an estimated 30,000 at the beginning of the 20th century.

MARQUEZE✦✦✦

Ⓗ Le Quartier de Marquèze €€
Sabres; tel: 05 58 08 31 31; www.parcs-landes-de-gascogne.fr. Jun–Sept train departures from Sabres daily every 40 minutes 1000–1210 and 1400–1720 (last train returns from Marquèze 1900); Apr–May Mon–Fri 1500, returning 1730, Sat 1400–1720, Sun as Jun–Sept; Oct Mon–Fri 1500–1640, Sat 1400–1640, Sun 1010–1210 and 1400–1640. Closed Nov–Mar.

There's only one way you can get to Marquèze, and that is by special steam train from Sabres. The 5km journey takes 10 minutes. This section of the folk museum is called **Le Quartier de Marquèze**.

In the past, *communes* in the Landes were divided into *quartiers*. One would contain the church, school, local government offices and shops, and others would contain farm workers' cottages, agricultural buildings and particular areas of farmland. Marquèze covers 70 hectares and is a reconstruction of an abandoned *quartier* of Sabres.

Most of the 30 or so traditional buildings date from the late 19th century, and a few were recovered from *quartiers* elsewhere. They are spaced around an *airial*, a clearing in the forest, with the *Maison du Maître* – the landowner's house – taking the central position. In addition to houses for the tenant farmer and labourers, there are pigsties, barns, beehives and hen houses built on stilts to keep foxes out. A way-marked trail leads through woodland to the miller's house and the mill itself and ends where the charcoal burners work.

There are daily demonstrations of baking, the miller grinds grains Mon, Wed and Fri, and resin-tapping is demonstrated on Tue. Exhibits on the Landes, documents, maps and models are on show in an information centre. In a separate area there is a model orchard with more than 1600 varieties of apple, cherry, medlar, plum, quince and other fruit trees native to the region. A snack bar and restaurant are on the site.

MOUSTEY✦✦

ⓘ Syndicat d'Initiative *pl. de la Mairies; tel: 05 58 07 70 00.*

Standing at the confluence of the Grand and Petite Leyre rivers, the village of Moustey has two 13th-century churches in its central square: St-Martin was built as the parish church; Notre-Dame, a stop for the Santiago de Compostela pilgrims, now houses the **Musée du Patrimoine**

Right
Moustey's Museum of Religion and Popular Beliefs

Musée du Patrimoine Religieux et des Croyances Populaires
€€ *Moustey; tel: 05 58 07 70 01. Open Jun–Sept daily 1000–1200 and 1400–1900, Sat 1400–1800, Sun 1000–1200 and 1400–1800; rest of year visits by appointment.*

Eglise Notre-Dame *Tel: 05 58 07 70 01. Open daily Jul–Aug 1000–1200 and 1400–1900; Jun, Sept at weekends.*

Right
Moustey's Notre-Dame

Opposite
Roquefort

Religieux et des Croyances Populaires✢✢, the third part of the Grande Lande folk museum. There are regularly changing exhibitions illustrating local religious beliefs and superstitions and the conflicts that sometimes arose between local churchgoers and the pilgrims.

ROQUEFORT✢

Syndicat d'Initiative *pl. du Soleil d'Or; tel: 05 58 45 50 46.*

Musée de la Chasse €€
Pouydesseaux, on the D934, 8km south of Roquefort; tel: 05 58 90 18 69. Open 0900–1200 and 1400–1700 daily.

This is **not** the place where they make the famous cheese. This Roquefort is in the Landes, about 22km northeast of Mont-de-Marsan, and its towers and ramparts, dating from the 12th and 14th centuries, testify that it was once a fortified town. Its Gothic church, with a square tower and arrow slits, was founded in the 11th century by the Benedictine monks of St-Sever. The church was later used by a hospitaller order of Antonites who looked after people suffering from 'St Anthony's Fire' or ergotism, a type of food poisoning caused by eating diseased cereal.

The tiny hamlet of Pouydesseaux, 8km to the south, is noted for its **Musée de la Chasse**✢, a museum dedicated to pigeon shooting, a popular pastime in the Landes and a major contributor to the region's dining tables.

SOLFERINO❖❖

Napoléon III founded Solférino in 1863 as a model village and social experiment and named it after a battle his army had won four years earlier. Cottages were built that the occupants could own with 2 hectares of land after working free for 75 days a year for 10 years.

From desert to oasis

The French word *landes* means 'moors' but even that conveys an image too verdant for the fearsome region of marshland and barren ground that was known as the desert of France. In wintertime it was swept by terrible storms that raged in from the Bay of Biscay, bringing from the coast tons of sand that choked the watercourses and rendered the land even more sterile. In summertime the fetid marshes were a breeding ground for millions of mosquitoes, and malaria flourished.

Little wonder that few people, other than brigands and those on the run, wanted to settle in the area; nor that the natives of the Landes were said to be destined not to grow old.

Destiny took a turn for the better when Napoléon III, who had bought 7400 hectares around what is now the village of Solférino, launched a programme of drainage and irrigation, ordering the creation of a forest of maritime pines across the region. At first the locals were suspicious of the scheme, but they soon latched on to the benefits and eagerly embraced their new roles as lumberjacks, resin-tappers and turpentine producers.

Today the forest serves the needs of France's leisure-seekers, but it also provides the raw materials for the nation's lumber, paper and chemical industries. The desert has become an oasis.

Accommodation and food

Communities are small and scattered in Northern Gascony and the Landes, so the accommodation net has been cast rather wider than usual to include places that may not be included in the Gazetteer but at least have somewhere to eat and enjoy a night's rest. Here, more than anywhere else, perhaps, it might be wise to plan your trip and book accommodation well in advance. The Parc Régional will provide a list of hotels, holiday homes, bed-and-breakfast establishments, holiday villages and campgrounds. Self-catering accommodation in the form of *gîtes rurals* (renovated traditional homes), and *gîtes forestiers* (individual bungalows of local pine) are also available.

Hotels

Hôtel l'Auberge des Pins €€–€€€ *Sabres; tel: 05 58 07 50 47. Open all year.* Only one of the hotel's 24 rooms does not have en suite facilities. Restaurant.

Hôtel Bellevue €€–€€€ *2 r. Carnot, Morcenx (11km south of Solférino); tel: 05 58 07 85 07. Open 7 Jan–20 Dec.* The hotel has 20 rooms, 19 of which have en suite facilities. There is a restaurant and tennis is available.

Hôtel le Colombier € *Roquefort; tel: 05 58 45 50 57. Open all year.* There are 15 en suite rooms and a restaurant.

Hôtel du Commerce €–€€ *14 av. Foch, Morcenx; tel: 05 58 07 80 25. Open all year.* Seven of the hotel's 10 rooms have en suite facilities. There is a restaurant.

Hôtel Relais Napoléon III €–€€ *Sortie 15, N10, Solférino; tel: 05 58 07 20 52. Open all year.* The hotel has a restaurant and 15 rooms with en suite facilities.

Chambres d'hôtes

Guy and Cathy Bonneaud € *Broy, St-Symphorien (25km north of Luxey); tel: 05 56 25 74 46; e-mail: julianjordon@claranet.fr.* Two en suite rooms – one double, one triple – in a century-old house in the middle of a country park. There is also a *gîte rural*, sleeping three, with bathroom, kitchenette and private garden. English spoken.

Monique Labri € *Les Arbousiers Le Gaille Sabres; tel: 05 58 07 52 52; e-mail: contact@lesarbousiers.com. Open all year.* A traditional Landaise house in a forest clearing with five double rooms, each with en suite facilities. *Table d'hôte* dinner is taken with the proprietors. English spoken.

Le Plaisy € *Sabres; tel: 05 58 07 50 29. Open all year.* Three double rooms with en suite facilities in a large house in 5 hectares of land; TV room, swimming pool. Breakfast in the dining-room or on the terrace.

Le Volcelest € *Joué, Belin-Béliet; tel: 05 56 88 02 68.* Six en suite rooms, each accommodating up to three persons at an equestrian centre in a clearing in the Landes forest. Central heating. *Table d'hôte (€€).*

Suggested tour

Total distance: The route covers 190km.

Time: Driving time is about 4 hours, but plan to take at least a day over the trip, especially if you intend to visit Marquèze.

Links: From Roquefort the D932 runs southwest for 22km to Mont-de-Marsan (*see page 250*) and north for 60km to Langon, a junction

---

Camping

Camping l'Arriu *route de Sore, Pissos (19km north of Sabres); tel: 05 58 08 90 38. Open Jul–mid-Sept.* Mobile homes and chalets may be rented on this 69-pitch site. Bar.

Camping Cap de Pin *Sortie 15, N10, Solférino; tel: 05 58 07 20 52. Open May–end Sept.* The site has 25 pitches. There is a bar and takeaway meals are available; mini-golf.

Camping Municipal *Nauton, Roquefort; tel: 05 58 45 59 99. Open Apr–Oct.* A simple campground with 36 pitches.

Camping du Peyricat *route de Luglon, Sabres; tel: 05 58 07 51 88. Open mid-Jun–mid-Sept.* The site has 69 pitches and mobile homes and chalets are available for rent. Takeaway meals, bar, nursery, launderette, tennis.

ⓝ Musée Napoléon III € *av. du Centenaire, Solferino; tel: 05 58 07 24 92.*

Airial Artisanal € *Pissos; tel: 05 58 08 90 66. Open Apr–Sept daily. Rest of year closed Mon.*

Carlos Viera's Glassblowing Workshop € *Pissos; tel: 05 58 08 97 42. Open Jul–Aug daily 1000–1200 and 1500–1900; Apr–Jun and Sept daily 1500–1800; Mar and mid-Oct–Dec Thur–Tue 1500–1800; mid-Jan–Feb Mon, Tue and Thur–Sat 1500–1800.*

for routes west to Bordeaux (*see pages 42–53*), southeast towards Agen (*see pages 222–3*) and Montauban (*see pages 202–11*) and northeast towards the Dordogne.

Route: Starting at Roquefort, head west on the D626, passing through the villages of Cachen and Labrit to reach **Sabres** in 36km. Hardly more than a dot on the map today, Labrit was the seat of the powerful d'Albret family who remained faithful to the French crown at a time when most of Aquitaine paid homage to the English: Henri d'Albret became king of Navarre.

At Sabres you can join the steam train for the 5km trip to **MARQUEZE ❶**, part of the Ecomusée de la Grande Lande. Continue west on the D44 for 14km to **SOLFERINO ❷**. The **Musée Napoléon III** is 2km east of the village near the intersection with the D325.

Take the D402 north for 7km to Labouheyre, a market town that grew along a Roman road and has a medieval town gate. From Labouheyre head east on the D626 for 12.5km to **Commensacq**, where 15th-century paintings of Adam and Eve decorate the vaults in the 11th-century Eglise St-Martin. There's also an intriguing frieze, which shows a rather sexy mermaid, a pig playing bagpipes and a rabbit playing the violin: evidence, some people believe, of a pre-Christian cult.

Follow the D34 north to **Pissos**, 12km away. The village is a centre for *gîtes forestiers* (*see Accommodation and food, page 238*). The **Airial Artisanal**❖ here is a showplace for contemporary art, regional gourmet products, jewellery and craft items in copper, ceramics and wood. Nearby is the **Pissos Glass-blowers' Workshop**❖, run by master glass-blower, Carlos Viera.

Head north on the N134 for 6km to **MOUSTEY ❸**, then continue north on the D134 for 14km to Joué, where a left turn on to the D110 will take you to **BELIN-BELIET ❹** in a further 5km. Leave Belin-Béliet on the N10 north and after 2km head east on the D3, which in 12km reaches Hostens where the **Domaine départemental**❖❖, a 500-hectare leisure park with a nature trail, has been developed on the site of a former open-cast lignite mine: its two lakes were formed by flooding the old quarries.

From Hostens head south for **Belhade**, 13.5km along the D651. Set beside the Petite Leyre river and surrounded by ancient oaks, Belhade – the name is Gascon for 'beautiful fairy' – has an 11th-century church where the porch has columns intriguingly carved with the figures of a mermaid, sailors, animals and birds. Just outside the town is the moated **Château de Rochefort-Lavie**, which has three round crenellated towers.

Continue south on the D651 for 11km to **Sore** where a moat and a gate are all that remains of the d'Albret castle that stood here until the Wars of Religion. The village also has a 12th-century fortified mill. Another 11km south along the D651 bring you to **LUXEY ❺** and from here the D9 heads southeast, returning you to Roquefort in 31km.

Dax–Biarritz

Ratings

Art	●●●●●
Pelota	●●●●●
Surfing	●●●●●
Beaches	●●●●○
Nightlife	●●●●○
Spa treatments	●●●●○
History	●●●○○
Architecture	●●○○○

Biarritz, originally a small whaling port, has developed into the foremost seaside resort of Southwest France. It has good bathing and surfing, a couple of casinos, a Museum of the Sea and about a dozen golf courses. Drive northeast from Biarritz, at the threshold of the Basque Country, to the urban sprawl of the French Basque capital, Bayonne, on to the Landes spa city of Dax, with its hot springs, to the bullfighting centre of Mont-de-Marsan. Bayonne, an administrative and industrial centre, is a major port on the wide River Adour. One of its famous products is Bayonne ham. The Musée Bonnat is a mecca for art lovers, displaying works by some of the world's greatest painters. The Fontaine Chaude in Dax gushes 2400 cubic metres of water daily, and its constant temperature is 64°C: several hotels offer thermal treatments.

BIARRITZ✦✦✦

ⓘ Agence Touristique du Pays Basque 1 r. Donzac, Bayonne; tel: 05 59 46 46 64; e-mail: paysbasque@tourisme.com; www.tourisme64.com. Open all year.

Office de Tourisme 1 square d'Ixelles; tel: 05 59 22 37 00; e-mail: biarritz.tourisme@biarritz.tm.fr; www.biarritz.tm.fr. Open daily Jul–Aug 0800–2000; Sept–Jun Mon–Sat 0900–1800, Sun 1000–1700. Tourist offices also at Gare de Biarritz and Antennes (exit A63) open mid-Jun–mid-Sept.

History

This great playground of the Southwest was a small whaling port until sea bathing became popular in the 19th century. It was Eugénie de Montijo, the future wife of Napoléon III, who launched the fashion for sea bathing, and Biarritz – with its fine sandy beaches, its setting between the ocean and the foothills of the Pyrenees and its gentle climate – soon developed as a glittering holiday resort. In 1854 Napoléon and Eugénie had a summer villa built there (where the Hôtel de Palais is today), and many followed their example.

Today much of the coast is lined with smart villas and homes and about a quarter of the population are retired residents. Biarritz has become an important conference venue. A buzzing nightlife centred on the gaming tables, and other late-night spots, attracts holiday-makers all year. As well as family beaches there are some of the

**Le Phare/
Lighthouse** (€
*Pointe St Martin, Biarritz.
Open daily Jul–Aug
1000–1200 and
1500–1900). Closed Mon.*
For a view of Biarritz and
beyond it to the Basque
Pyrenees climb the steps
up to the top of the
lighthouse, which stands
73m above sea level.

Fast play

Every Basque town and village has its *fronton* where *pelota*, involving a wall
and a ball – it's described as the world's fastest ball game – is played. There
are various forms of the game, the most spectacular being one in which
wicker 'gloves' are worn. Guides to the big matches can be obtained from
the Agence Touristique du Pays Basque. Children learn to play from a
young age. The very fast version of *pelota* that has become popular in the
USA and Central America in the past 35 years, Cesta Punta (or jai alai), is
played in summer contests in Biarritz.

⊙ Hippodrome de la Cité des Fleurs⁺
(€€ *Allée Dulac Marion, Biarritz. For information on events and race days, tel: 05 59 23 11 56 or contact the tourist office*). This is where competitive riding events take place and trotting races are held regularly.

⊙ Musée de la Mer
€€ *esplanade du Rocher de la Vierge, Biarritz; tel: 05 59 22 75 40. Open daily all year, mid-Jun–mid-Sept 0930–1900 (to midnight mid-Jul and all of Aug), rest of year 0930–1230 and 1400–1800. (Feeding time 1030 and 1700.)*

Musée Historique de Biarritz €€ *r. Broquedis, Biarritz; tel: 05 59 24 86 28; e-mail: avb.mhb@laposte.net. Open Tue–Sat 1000–1200 and 1430–1830.*

Institut Louison Bobet (Thalassotherapy) €€€ *11 av. Louison-Bobet; tel: 05 59 24 20 80. One of the many Thalassotherapy centres in Biarritz.*

The surf also rises

Surfing in the waves on the Biarritz beaches was popularised by film scriptwriter Peter Viertel during the shooting of *The Sun Also Rises* in the 1950s. Viertel, husband of actress and film star Deborah Kerr, introduced some of surfing's pioneers to Biarritz, and they found it an ideal location for the sport. The pounding Atlantic waves have made Biarritz a world-class surfing centre ever since.

world's best surfing beaches and rocky headlands on which Atlantic rollers crash dramatically.

Surfing is just one of the sports at which the Basques excel. They are passionate about rugby and have a great reputation for ball games such as *pelota*, bred into them by a pedigree of generations of *pelota* players. Golf is an obsession, with a good choice of courses for visitors and locals: the first course in Biarritz was opened in 1888. Sea-water treatments (thalassotherapy) are a speciality in Biarritz, recommended for good health and mental stability.

Musée de la Mer⁺⁺⁺

This is a combined museum, aquarium and scientific research centre, which was founded in 1835. A display on whaling, a study of the ocean in the Biarritz area, conservation matters, boat models, navigational aids and fishing methods, many fish species in a series of aquaria, and seals and sharks in an underwater tank – these are just some of the exhibits that make this an interesting place to visit. Shore birds and sea birds of the area, and birds of the Pyrenees may be seen in the ornithology gallery, where recordings of their calls are played. From a terrace visitors can watch seals having their twice-daily feed and get a great view along the coast.

Musée Historique de Biarritz⁺⁺

In the early days when sea bathing first became fashionable in the 19th century, Biarritz grew from a small whaling port into a resort favoured by the crowned heads of Europe, the rich and the famous. This was before the days of the railway. Some made the journey across country. A wicker seat was mounted on the back of a donkey or mule, enabling ladies in elaborate gowns to lounge gracefully aboard while a young maiden led the animal. Between the two World Wars dinner parties and casinos were attended by such celebrated visitors as Winston Churchill, Charlie Chaplin and Ernest Hemingway. Later visitors included the Duke and Duchess of Windsor, Frank Sinatra and Rita Hayworth. All these times and other aspects of old Biarritz are recalled through pictures and paraphernalia at the small museum.

Plateau de l'Atalaye⁺⁺ *(for more information, contact the tourist office)*

The last of the Biarritz watchtowers is here. From it, centuries ago, smoke signals were sent to announce that a school of whales had been sighted, and the men would take to the boats in pursuit. The area can be explored by a series of reefs, causeways and tunnels between rocky islands. A footpath leads to the Virgin's Rock landmark. The Plateau provides a view of the Port des Pêcheurs – now used by pleasure craft rather than fishing boats.

A marble statue of the Virgin Mary stands on the largest rock on the Plateau de l'Atalaye. Choose a calm day to walk to it – in windy weather great waves crash aggressively over the footbridge leading to Virgin's Rock.

Thalassotherapy*

Sea-water baths and allied treatments were introduced in the Hôtel Miramar in 1979 by champion cyclist Louison Bobet. There are other centres along the Basque coast. Warm sea-water baths, mud and seaweed baths are administered with advanced techniques for the treatment of stress, rheumatism and back problems, poor circulation, overweight and tobacco dependency. New mothers are said to benefit from post-natal treatments.

Below
Biarritz seafront

BAYONNE

ⓘ Bayonne *pl. des Basques; tel: 05 59 46 01 46; e-mail: infos@bayonne-tourisme.com. Open daily in high season 0900–1900, Sun 1000–1300; off-peak Mon–Fri 0900–1800 and Sat 1000–1800, closed Sun. Guided tours take place in July and August for individuals and groups, in French, English, German and Spanish. Information from the tourist office.*

ⓗ Cathédrale de Ste-Marie € *Grand Bayonne; tel: 05 59 59 19 84. Open Mon–Sat 0700–1230 and 1500–1900.* **Cloisters €€** *open Jun–Sept 0930–1230 and 1400–1800, rest of year to 1700.*

Musée Bonnat €€ *9 r. Bastiat, Bayonne; tel: 05 59 59 08 52. Open daily 1000–1830.*

ⓜ Markets take place in Bayonne every morning except Sun (all day on Fri) in modern covered market premises along the quai de Cdt Roquebert.

ⓡ River cruises (€€; *tel: 05 59 59 21 93. Half-day cruises are from 1400–1800 and full-day excursions are from 1030–1630.)*

River boat cruises are available in the season on the River Adour, departing from allées Boufflers.

History

The capital of the French Pays Basque is a sprawling commercial and administrative centre and an important port. It is worth a visit for the old quarters of Grand Bayonne, with its pedestrianised shopping streets, and Petit Bayonne. To the east of Petit Bayonne is the Château Neuf, a great fortification built around 1460 at the end of three centuries of English rule: it is not open to the public. Adjacent to the Château Neuf, outside the walls built by Vauban, is the Parc de Mousserolles, a pleasant place to walk or relax, which has a lake and a children's playground.

Between the old quarters flows the River Nive, at right angles to the much wider River Adour. Big cargo ships berth on the Adour, and visitors are also catered for, with half-day and full-day river boat cruises. The front elevation of Bayonne's Gothic cathedral, dating from the 13th century, is reminiscent of the Cathedral of Reims, and attracts many people. The town is known for its Bayonne ham and its bullfights. In the six-day festival at the beginning of August, bullfights take place and there's dancing in the street and general merrymaking.

Cathédrale de Ste-Marie✦✦

The majestic Gothic-style cathedral in the old town was built between the 13th and 16th centuries; its twin steeples are 19th-century additions. The cathedral was one of the stopping places on the pilgrimage route to Compostela. There is some fine Renaissance stained glass in the nave and la Chapelle St-Jerome. The remaining cloisters are from the 14th century.

Izarra Distillery✦ (€ *9 Quai Bergeret, Quartier St-Esprit, Bayonne. Open Mon–Fri 0900–1130 and 1400–1830, also Sat in peak season)*. Visitors can learn about the history and production of Bayonne's sweet liqueur, from the gathering of Pyrenean herbs to the final alcoholic delight with its hint of brandy and spices.

Jambon de Bayonne✦ (€ *Pierre d'Ibaialde Cannery, 4 r. des Cordelier). Open Tue–Sat 1000–1300 and 1430–1830.* Learn about the curing process and other aspects of the celebrated local ham, and enjoy a sample.

Musée Bonnat✦✦

Léon Bonnat, the portraitist, was born in Bayonne in 1833. He was an ardent collector of paintings and sculptures and when he died in 1922 he left his priceless collection to Bayonne. Musée Bonnat is regarded by many as the most important art museum of Southwest France, with works by Botticelli, Degas, Delacroix, El Greco, Goya, Rembrandt, Rubens, Van Dyck and other all-time greats. The basement is devoted to archaeology, the nucleus of the exhibits having come from Bonnat's collection, which included Greek statuettes, amphora and Italian glass.

DAX

ℹ **Dax** pl. Thiers; tel: 05 58 56 86 86; e-mail: tourisme.dax@wanadoo.fr; www.dax.fr. Open all year, Jul–Aug daily 0930–1900; Apr–Jun & Sept–Oct 0930–1230 and 1400–1830, Sun 1000–1200 and 1500–1700; Nov–Mar 0930–1230 and 1400–1800 but closed Sat pm and all day Sun.

Musée de Foie Gras €€ 1 r. des Jardins. Open Mar–Oct Mon–Sat 1000–1200 and 1400–1800.

Musée de l'Aviation € Base Navelet, 58 av. de l'Aerodrome, Dax; tel: 05 58 74 66 19. Open Feb–Nov.

Health Spa, Calicéo € r. du Centre Aere, St-Paul-les-Dax (across the river from Dax); tel: 05 58 90 66 00; e-mail: caliceo@ thermesdous.com

Les Arènes €€ parc Theodore Denis, Dax. The cow fights calendar is available from the Departmental Tourist Board of the Landes; tel: 05 58 90 99 09.

Cathédrale Notre-Dame € (donations welcome) r. St-Pierre, Dax. Open daily.

Musée de Borda and Crypte Archeologique €€ r. Cazade, Dax; tel: 05 58 74 12 91. Open Mar–Nov daily except Tue, Sun and public holidays.

River cruises⁺⁺ (€€ Adour Plaisance, quai du 28th Batallion de Chasseurs; tel: 05 58 74 87 07).

A four-hour boat trip on the Adour embarks from Dax at 1400.

Upstream of Bayonne, the River Adour graces Dax, just over the Pyrénées-Atlantiques border in Landes. Dax is one of France's premier thermal spa towns, a centre for bullfighting and an attractive place to visit, with its hot water fountain, riverside walks and its 17th-century buildings in the r. Neuve. It has **museums** of *foie gras* and **aviation**, and another displaying curiosities from Roman times to the 20th century.

Many people go to Dax to take the cure for a range of conditions. This usually means a three-week stay, but you can take a week-long 'get into shape' fitness course. One-day stress relief treatments are another option. The hot mud treatments are said to be particularly beneficial for rheumatism sufferers. A dozen hotels in Dax are connected to thermal establishments.

Les Arènes⁺

This grand building from the early 1900s is where bullfights and cow fights are staged between March and October. In cow fights the *escarteur* (from the word 'swerve') has to pit his last-minute swerving skills against the brute strength of the cow, or leap over its horns as it charges. Portuguese-style *corridas* – bullfighting on horseback – take place here. A festival week of celebration centred on bulls and cows is held in August.

Bois de Boulogne⁺⁺

This old oak forest in the west of Dax has been put to good use as a leisure park. It stretches for 6km and contains a golf driving range, jogging circuit, riding school, lake, woodland paths and a restaurant.

Cathédrale Notre-Dame⁺

This is the third cathedral to have been built on the same site: one was destroyed in 1295 by the English; another collapsed in the 17th century. Some of the material was used in the present building. Choir stalls and a fine doorway in the north transept are among treasures retrieved from earlier centuries.

Fontaine Chaude⁺⁺

Dax is worth visiting for this wonder alone. The natural hot spring was known to the Romans; now, channelled through a trio of ornate 'taps' in the town centre, it dispenses 2400 cubic metres of 64°C water a day into a vast basin.

Musée de Borda⁺⁺

This fascinating museum of curiosities, coins and collectables from diverse times and places is named after a seaman who was also a great marine engineer, mathematician and maker of navigational instruments,

Jean Charles de Borda. He was born in Dax in 1733. A statue of him stands in pl. Thiers. Opposite the museum is the **Crypte Archéologique** – the foundations of a Gallo-Roman temple discovered in the 1970s.

Below
Market day in Dax

MONT-DE-MARSAN❖

ⓘ Mont-de-Marsan 6
pl. de General Laclerc;
tel: 05 58 05 87 37;
e-mail: tourisme@mont-de-marsan.org;
www.mont-de-marsan.org.
Open in high season Mon–Sat
0900–1830; off-peak
0900–1230 and
1330–1800. Guided tours
available by appointment.

ⓜ Musée Despiau-
  Wlérick €€ *pl.*
Mauguerite de Navarre,
Mont-de-Marsan; tel: 05 58
75 00 45. Open all year
Wed–Mon 1000–1200 and
1400–1800. Free entry Mon.

Below
Mont-de-Marsan

As well as being an administrative centre for the southeast region of the Landes, Mont-de-Marsan is a noted bullfighting centre and also a famous horse-racing venue. There are 12 events a year at the racecourse – steeplechase meetings, flat racing or trotting races. The foremost bullfighters of Spain and the French Basque country compete in bull and cow events in Mont-de-Marsan, and visitors are assured that the animals are not killed. In July these human-versus-bovine events and other activities and entertainments are presented in the **Fêtes de la Madeleine**, in which the whole town celebrates.

Mont-de-Marsan lies at the confluence of the rivers Douze and Midou, known as Midouze, and has some lovely old riverside houses. Information on guided tours of the town is available at the tourist office.

Named after two sculptors who were born in Mont-de-Marsan within eight years of one another and who died in the mid-1940s, the **Musée Despiau-Wlérick**❖❖ is in two sections; linking them is a central gallery where temporary exhibitions are staged. Charles Despiau and Robert Wlérick each have a floor devoted to their works. Two other floors present sculptures by their contemporaries.

Accommodation and food

Camping Airotel *la Cheneraie, Chemin Cazenove, Bayonne; tel: 05 59 55 01 31. Open Apr–Sept.* The riverside campground has 257 pitches for tents and caravans. There are mobile homes and caravans on site, a foodstore, takeaway food, bar and laundry facilities, swimming and tennis.

Biarritz Camping *28 route d'Harcet; tel: 05 59 23 00 12. Open May–Sept.* Waterside setting with 196 pitches, grocery store, takeaway food and bar. Mobile homes and chalets can be rented.

Camping Les Chênes *Bois de Boulogne, Dax; tel: 05 58 90 05 53; e-mail: camping-chenes@wanadoo.fr. Open late Mar–early Nov.* Well-equipped site with chalets and mobile homes. Amenities include grocery store, takeaway food, bar, swimming pool and launderette.

Hôtel Climat de France €€ *N10, Aéroport de Parme, Biarritz; tel: 05 59 23 40 41.* All 74 rooms are en suite. The restaurant is gratifyingly easy on the pocket in this 2-star hotel.

Club Hippique € *Bois de Boulogne, Dax; tel: 05 58 74 09 14. Open Mar–Oct.* Gîte sleeping 30 in the spacious recreational woodland park, offering riding on site or long distance. Individuals or groups.

Hôtel Frantour €€–€€€ *Lousrau, Bayonne; tel: 05 59 55 08 08. Open all year.* A 3-star hotel with 44 en suite rooms and a restaurant.

Grand Hôtel-Citadel Adour €€ *blvd des Sports, Dax; tel: 05 58 90 53 00. Open all year.* The 3-star hotel has 137 en suite rooms in different styles and a restaurant.

Hôtel Monbar €€ *24 r. Pannecau, Bayonne; tel: 05 59 59 26 80. Closed mid-Sept–mid-Oct.* Small 1-star hotel with 10 rooms, all with facilities.

Hôtel Peyroux € *8 av. Victor Hugo, Dax; tel: 05 58 90 49 49. Open Mar–Nov.* The hotel has 19 en suite rooms.

Hôtel de Renaissance €€–€€€ *route de Villeneuve, Mont-de-Marsan; tel: 05 58 51 51 51. Open all year.* The 3-star hotel has 30 rooms, all but one with en suite facilities. There is a restaurant (€€) and a swimming pool.

Sofitel Mirimar €€€ *13 r. Louison Bobet, Biarritz; tel: 05 59 41 30 00. Open all year.* Modern 4-star hotel with 126 en suite rooms, a good restaurant (€€–€€€), swimming pool and a thalassotherapy centre.

Hôtel Thermal Miradour €€ *av. E. Millies Lacroix, Dax; tel: 05 58 56 77 77. Open all year.* The Miradour has 120 en suite rooms and a restaurant.

Hôtel Tulip Inn Louisiane €€ *r. Guy Petit Biarritz; tel: 05 59 22 20 20; e-mail: hotel.louisiane.biarritz@wanadoo.fr; www.louisiane-biarritz.com. Open all year.* 77 rooms in a modern hotel close to the city centre with easy access to the motorway system, rail station and airport. Secure underground car parking. Excellent restaurant, **Le Baton Rouge €€**, specialising in Cajun style dishes.

Chez Albert €–€€ *Port des Pêcheurs, Biarritz; tel: 05 59 24 43 84.* Locals and visitors go here for the good seafood and value for money.

Restaurant du Bois de Boulogne €€ *allée du Bois de Boulogne, Dax; tel: 05 58 74 23 32.* Regional fare and good seafood give this restaurant much repeat business.

Restaurant de la Tour €–€€ *5 r. des Faures, Bayonne; tel: 05 59 59 05 67.* One of the towers in Bayonne's wall has been utilised to form a cool setting in which to choose a meal from an innovative menu.

Suggested tour

Musée de la Chalosse €€
Domaine de Carcher, Montfort-en-Chalosse; tel: 05 58 98 69 27; e-mail: musee.chalosse@libertysurf.fr. Open Apr–Oct 1000–1200 and 1400–1830; Nov–Mar Tue–Fri 1400–1800.

Abbaye d'Arthous €€
Peyrehorade; tel: 05 58 73 03 89; e-mail: arthous@cg40.fr. Open Wed–Mon 0930–1200 and 1400–1700. Closed Nov and public holidays.

Total distance: The main route covers 125km. The detour totals 47km.

Time: Allow at least 3 hours for driving the main route, but give yourself a whole day to make the most of it – or take in an overnight stop.

Links: From Mont-de-Marsan you can head northeast towards Agen (*see pages 222–3*) on the D933, north towards Bordeaux (*see pages 42–53*) on the D932 or northwest through the Parc Régional des Landes de Gascogne towards Arcachon (*see pages 262–4*) or Bordeaux.

Route: From **MONT-DE-MARSAN ❶** take the D933 southwest for 14km to St-Sever, which looks out over the Adour river and the huge expanse of the Landes pine forests to the north. The Benedictine abbey church here, founded in 988, has marble columns that originally graced the palace of a Roman governor.

Head west from the town on the D32, which rolls through some lovely countryside, reaching Mugron after 17km and Montfort-en-Chalosse after a further 9km. Founded as an English *bastide* in the 13th century, Montfort is a small hill town where the **Musée de la Chalosse** features country life in the 19th century. Continue on the D32 for 18km to reach the outskirts of **DAX ❷**. Follow the D106 west for 2km, then head south on the D6 for 16km, joining the D33 for 5km into Peyrehorade, once a major river port and now enjoying a new life as a centre for leisure boating.

On the south side of the river, off the D19, is the restored **Abbaye d'Arthous**, founded in 1167, a staging post on the road to Santiago de Compostela and used as farm buildings after the Revolution. Take the D19 south for 10km to Bidache then head west on the D936.

Above
Scenic coastline

ℹ Musée Grévin €€
7 rue Mazarin, St-Jean-de-Luz; tel: 05 59 51 24 88.
Open Apr–Jun and Sept–Oct 1000–1200 and 1400–1830;
Jul–Aug 1000–1230 and 1400–2000.
www.basquexplorer.com/pbe/musee-grevin.htm

ℹ St-Jean-de-Luz
Office de Tourisme pl. du Maréchal Foch; tel: 05 59 26 03 16; www.saint-jean-de-luz.com. Open all year Mon–Sat 0900–1230 and 1400–1800, Sun and public holidays 1000–1300.

Detour: Leave Bidache on the D936 and after 10km, just beyond the hamlet of Nogues, turn left on to the D10: a winding, hilly road reaches La Bastide-Clairence, founded by the king of Navarre in 1314, in 5km and Hasparren in a further 5km. Workaday Hasparren is on the Route Impériale des Cimes, a military road constructed on the orders of Napoléon I to link Bayonne and St-Jean-Pied-de-Port. It is a lovely road with views of the Pyrenees and of the Basque coastline. From Hasparren to St-Pierre-d'Irube, along the Route Impériale (now the D22) is 24km. The D936 covers the final 3km into Bayonne.

Continuing the main route from Bidache, follow the D936 east for 17km to Briscous, then the D312 for 14km to **BAYONNE ❸**. There are a number of routes you can take from Bayonne to **BIARRITZ ❹**, which are less than 8km apart as the crow flies, but you can follow the Adour for 6km to its mouth on the D309, south of the river, then follow the road along the coast for 7km into Biarritz.

Also worth exploring

Continuing south along the coast from Biarritz brings you to **St-Jean-de-Luz**, a whaling port from as early as the 11th century, but a popular resort since the 1840s. Basque history is featured at the **Musée Grévin**.

Ratings

Beaches	●●●●●
Children	●●●●●
Outdoor activities	●●●●●
Food and drink	●●●●○
Villages	●●●●○
Architecture	●●●○○
Boat trips	●●●○○
Museums	●●●○○

The Southern Côte d'Argent

The southern half of the Côte d'Argent – between Biarritz and Arcachon – is a paradise for watersports enthusiasts, especially surfers. Those who feel the rolling waters of the Atlantic Ocean might be a bit too much, however, will still be able to enjoy themselves in the cool, clear – and tranquil – waters of the lakes and lagoons a short distance inshore. On lake or sea you can join in a host of waterborne activities: sailing, surfboarding, canoeing – or simply relaxing in the sun. There are sandy beaches on the lake shores as well as at the seaside. There are splendid seaside resorts and quaint old villages of traditional houses and ancient churches to be discovered, and for cyclists and ramblers a network of trails and paths crisscross the pine woods fringing the coast. Campers will find no shortage of places to pitch a tent, caravan or motor home.

BISCARROSSE✦✦✦

ℹ Office de Tourisme
55 pl. G.Dufau; tel: 05 58 78 20 96; e-mail: biscarrosse@biscarrosse.com; www.biscarrosse.com. Open Jul–Aug daily 0900–2000; off-peak 1000–1200 and 1400–1700.

About 10km inland, Biscarrosse nonetheless has a waterfront setting, located as it is between two lakes – Petit Etang de Biscarrosse and the very much larger Etang de Biscarrosse et de Parentis. A 2km canal at the northern end of the town forms a link with another large lake, Etang de Cazaux et de Sanguinet. Before World War II Biscarrosse was an important seaplane base and its story is told in the **Musée Historique de l'Hydraviation✦✦**. The museum exhibits models, documents and parts of original aircraft, both civil and military. There is a section on the early days of France's airmail service, and seaplanes and flying boats can be viewed in a giant glass hangar. The pioneer airmail pilot and writer Antoine de Saint-Exupéry used to enjoy sitting in the shade of the ancient elm tree standing in the town's main square. In the past, unfaithful wives were brought to the tree to be shamed, but legend has it that when an innocent woman was brought forward the tree formed a crown of white leaves over her head – a

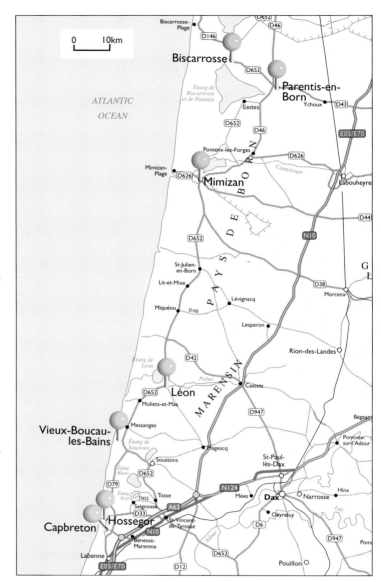

Musée Historique de l'Hydraviation
€€ 332 ave. Louis Breguet, Biscarrosse; tel: 05 58 78 00 65; e-mail: musée.hydraviation@ ville-biscarrosse.fr; www.latecoere.com/ expos/hydra.htm. Open Jul–Aug daily 1000–1900; Apr–Jun and Sept 1500–1900; rest of year daily 1400–1800. Adapted for disabled and blind people.

Bisca Surf Club
197 chemin de Mathiou, Biscarrosse; tel: 05 58 78 27 29; e-mail: bisca.surfclub@free.fr; http://bisca.surfclub.free.fr. Open Apr–Oct, daily in Jul–Aug. A lively club for surfing and body-boarding in the Atlantic breakers on the beaches south of Biscarrosse, with a surf school and qualified instructors.

phenomenon it now displays each year. **Biscarrosse-Plage✧✧**, on the coast as you might guess, is a modern seaside resort offering the usual beach and watersports. The advantage here is that if the Atlantic rollers are coming in too fiercely you can move inland to enjoy the calm of the sandy beaches around the lakes.

CAPBRETON✦✦

🛈 **Office de Tourisme**
av. Georges Pompidou;
tel: 05 58 72 12 11;
e-mail: tourisme.capbreton@
wanadoo.fr or otsi.capbreton
@wanadoo.fr;
www.tourisme.fr/capbreton.
Open all year.

🏛 **Ecomusée de la Mer**
€€ Casino Municipal, pl.
de la Liberté, Capbreton; tel: 05
58 72 40 50; e-mail:
ecomusee.capbreton@
wanadoo.fr; www.chez.com/
asmlandes/capbreton.htm.
Open Jun–Aug daily 0930–
1200 and 1430–1900; Apr–
May and Sept 1400–1800;
rest of year Sun, school and
public holidays 1400–1800.

Until the 14th century Capbreton was an important whaling and fishing port, then the River Adour changed course and left the place high and dry. It got a new lease of life in the 19th century when Napoléon III began to farm oysters, but the real boost came in the 1930s when property developers started to move in and Capbreton achieved popularity as a resort. Today, it is very much a modern seaside town, separated from neighbouring Hossegor (*see below*) by the Boudigau canal. Bathers are warned to swim only from those designated areas of beach which are protected by lifeguards. Elsewhere there are dangers from the pounding Atlantic rollers. Capbreton's main shore-based attraction is the **Ecomusée de la Pêche et de la Mer**✦✦, which features the history of the local fishing industry and marine geology with an aquarium, fossils, shells and model ships. From the museum's terrace you can enjoy a panoramic view of the coast. Offshore, just outside the harbour, lies the **Fosse de Capbreton**, an underwater chasm more than 60km long, up to 10km wide and some 3000m deep.

HOSSEGOR

🛈 Pl. des Halles,
Hossegor; tel: 05 58
41 79 00; e-mail: hossegor.
tourisme@wanadoo.fr;
www.hossegor.fr. Open all
year.

Capbreton's next-door neighbour became a colony for writers and artists in the early 1900s and has since benefited from careful development which has preserved its natural wooded setting of pines and cork oak. Today there are gardens, hotels, a casino, parks and a golf course. Thanks to the powerful groundswell produced by the Fosse de Capbreton (*see above*), the town has become a mecca for surfers, especially during the second half of August each year when the Hossegor Rip Curl championship for professional surfers is staged. For those who prefer calmer conditions, especially toddlers, the tidal salt water Lac d'Hosseger is ideal. There are sandy beaches and canoeing, sailing and windsurfing are available.

LEON✦✦✦

🛈 **Office de
Tourisme** 65 pl. Jean
Baptiste Courtiau; tel: 05 58
48 76 03; e-mail: ot.leon@
wanadoo.fr; www.ot-leon.fr.
Open all year.

Tranquil Léon, with its traditional Landes houses faced with diagonal brickwork, stands 6km inland at the southern end of **Etang de Léon**✦✦. Picturesquely set among peaceful countryside, the lake attracts watersports enthusiasts to the village. The area between the lake and the sea is a nature reserve. But the chief attraction in the area is the **Courant d'Huchet**✦✦, a meandering river that winds its way for 14km from the lake to the sea through trees garlanded with ivy, water lilies, wild hibiscus and other lush vegetation that give the terrain a sub-tropical appearance. There are **boat trips**✦✦ along the river from

ⓘ Les Bateliers du Courant d'Huchet
€€€ *Léon; tel: 05 58 48 75 39. Departures daily Apr–Oct.*

Léon to Huchet beach on the coast, but they are very popular and reservations are essential, especially in August when you may have to book two weeks ahead.

MIMIZAN-LES-BAINS✦✦

ⓘ *38 av. Maurice-Martin, Mimizan-Plage; tel: 05 58 09 11 20; e-mail: O.T.MIMIZAN@wanadoo.fr; www.mimizan-tourism.com. Mimizan-Plage Pavillon de Tourisme open summer 0900–1900.*

ⓜ Musée d'Histoire de Mimizan €€ *tel: 05 58 09 00 61. Open mid-Jun–mid-Sept 1030–1900, closed Sun; rest of year by appointment. Closed on Sundays.*

Woolsack Manor *Not open to the public, but can be seen from the lake.*

Thanks to the planting of grasses, rushes and pine trees, Mimizan's footing is much more secure now than in the past when the town was repeatedly engulfed by shifting sands. In Roman times it was a port named Ségosa, which the sands buried in the 6th century. Rebuilt in the 10th century, it was inundated again in 1342, along with a 12th-century Benedictine abbey of which only the belfry and sculpted Gothic portal survived. The ruins are still standing and can be seen beside the D626, on the way to Mimizan-Plage. Nearby is the **Musée d'Histoire de Mimizan✦** which has exhibits on the area's ancient and medieval history. On the northwest shore of the picturesque Etang d'Aureilhan, which provides Mimizan with an inshore waterfront, are the ruins of **Woolsack**, a Tudor-style manor built in 1910 by the then Duke of Westminster. Winston Churchill, Coco Chanel and King Gustav II of Sweden were among the celebrities who stayed there before World War II. The mouth of the Courant de Ste-Eulalie divides the long wide beach of **Mimizan-Plage**, but a bridge across the river provides access to both sides. There are four bathing areas, each with lifeguards. The resort is 6km from the main town.

Right
Mimizan-les-Bains

PARENTIS-EN-BORN✦

ⓜ Musée du Pétrole €€ *Route des Lacs, Parentis-en-Born; tel: 05 58 78 54 20; www.ville-parentis-en-born.fr/en/Museum.htm. Open for 1-hour guided tours Jul–early Sept daily 1000–1230 and 1500–1900.*

The pre-war philosopher, writer and pioneer pilot, Antoine Saint-Exupéry, described Parentis as a place 'where life flows like honey'. Today, he might be tempted to substitute the word 'oil' for 'honey', for the Etang de Biscarrosse et de Parentis, on which the town stands, is dotted with platforms exploiting the biggest oilfield in France. The story of oil, from prospecting to processing, is told in the **Musée du Pétrole✦**.

VIEUX-BOUCAU-LES-BAINS❖

ⓘ Office de Tourisme
Port d'Albret; tel: 05 58 48 13 47; e-mail: officedetourisme.vieuxboucau@wanadoo.fr; www.ot-vieux-boucau.fr. Open all year 0900–1300 and 1430–1900; times vary out of season.

ⓝ Tropica Parc €€
signposted off the D652 in the direction of Soustons; tel: 05 58 48 04 99. Open July–Aug 1000–dusk; May–Jun and Sept–Oct 1000–1200 and 1400–1900.

Until the 16th century this coastal town was known as Port d'Albret. In 1578 the Adour river changed course, shifting its mouth from Port d'Albret to Bayonne, some 30km to the south. As the ancient harbour town sank into decline, its pragmatic citizens sadly renamed it Vieux-Boucau – Old Mouth. Happily, however, the town's fortunes have been revived along with its old name, now applied to a purpose-built tourist resort developed around a 50-hectare lagoon. The old and new parts of the town are connected by an attractive esplanade. Just inland from Vieux-Boucau, **Tropica Parc❖❖** is an open-air tropical garden with aviaries and a small zoo. There are lots of exotic Asian plants and trees and spices are grown in glasshouses. It's a pleasant, restful place.

Accommodation and food

Alienor €€ *r. Madrid, Capbreton; tel: 05 58 41 00 18. Open all year.* There are 20 en suite rooms. No restaurant, but breakfast is available.

Hôtel les Allées Marines €–€€€ *20 al. Marines, Capbreton; tel: 05 58 72 10 13. Open all year.* The hotel has eight en suite rooms and a restaurant.

Hôtel Aquitaine €–€€ *66 av. de Lattre de Tassigny, Capbreton; tel: 05 58 72 38 11. Open throughout the year.* The hotel has a swimming pool and restaurant. Its 24 guest rooms are all en suite.

Hôtel Atlantide €€–€€€ *pl. Marsan, Biscarrosse; tel: 05 58 78 08 86. Open all year.* No restaurant, but breakfast is available. The hotel's 33 rooms are all en suite, with direct-dial telephones and television.

Le Beauséjour €€€ *333 av. du Tour du Lac, Hossegor; tel: 05 58 43 51 07. Open May–mid-Oct.* In a tree-shaded lakeside setting, with a garden and swimming pool, the hotel has 45 en suite rooms with television and direct-dial telephones.

Hôtel Bellevue €€ *av. G. Pompidou, Capbreton; tel: 05 58 72 10 30. Closed early Jan–mid-Feb.* It has 16 rooms, 12 of them en suite, all with television and direct-dial telephones. This is also a restaurant (**€€**).

Au Bon Coin du Lac €€€ *34 av. du Lac, Mimizan; tel: 05 58 09 01 55. Open all year.* Nine luxurious en suite rooms overlook the Etang d'Aureilhan. The restaurant (**€€€**) is noted for its seafood and beef dishes and there is a dining terrace outside.

Hôtel Côte d'Argent €€ *r. Principale, Vieux Boucau; tel: 05 58 48 13 17. Open mid-Nov–Sept.* The hotel has 36 en suite rooms with television and direct-dial telephones. The restaurant (**€€–€€€**) has an outdoor dining terrace.

Hôtel Emeraude des Bois €€–€€€ *68 av. Courant, Mimizan; tel: 05 58 09 05 28. Open Apr–Sept (hotel).* There are 15 en suite rooms with television and direct-dial telephones. There is a dining terrace, but the restaurant (**€–€€**) does not serve lunch.

Hôtel–Restaurant la Forestiere €–€€€ *2 av. du Pyla, Biscarrosse; tel: 05 58 78 24 14. Open Apr–Oct.* There are 34 en suite rooms and the hotel has a swimming pool.

Les Hélianthes €–€€€ *av. de la Côte d'Argent, Hossegor; tel: 05 58 43 52 19. Open Apr–mid-Oct.* No more than a kilometre from the beach, this friendly, family-run establishment has 17 rooms, 14 of them with en suite facilities. There is a swimming pool but no restaurant. However, breakfast is available.

Hôtel de la Plage €€–€€€ *2 av. de la Plage, Biscarrosse; tel: 05 58 78 26 69. Open Apr–mid-Oct.* The hotel has 34 en suite rooms and a restaurant.

Hôtel St-Hubert €–€€€ *588 av. G. Latécoère, Biscarrosse; tel: 05 58 78 09 99; e-mail: le.saint-hubert@wanadoo.fr. Open year round.* There are 16 en suite rooms, each with television and direct-dial telephone. No restaurant but breakfast is available.

Camping

There are a great many campgrounds along the coast between Biscarrosse and Capbreton, some with hundreds of pitches and full facilities, including tent, mobile home and chalet hire, bars, restaurants, grocery stores, launderettes, discos and sports amenities. Here are a few suggestions.

Camping lou Broustaricq *route de Langeot, Sanguinet; tel: 05 58 82 74 82. Open all year.* With 555 pitches, the site has a full range of facilities. No disco.

Camping Campeole Navarrosse *712 chemin de Navarrosse, Biscarrosse; tel: 05 58 09 84 32. Open Apr–Oct.* The site has 640 pitches with mobile homes and chalets for hire.

Camping Club Marina *Plage Sud, Mimizan; tel: 05 58 09 12 66; e-mail: contact@clubmarina.com; www.clubmarina.com. Open mid-May–mid-Sept.* This site has 580 pitches and tents, caravans, mobile homes and chalets for hire. It offers the full range of amenities and sports facilities.

Camping le Grandes Pins *route du Lac; Sanguinet; tel: 05 58 78 61 74. Open all year.* Tents, caravans, mobile homes and chalets may be hired on this 260-pitch site which has all amenities, except a disco.

Camping Municipal les Sableres *blvd du Marensin, Vieux Boucau; tel: 05 58 48 12 29; e-mail: lessableres@wanadoo.fr. Open Apr–mid-Oct.* A simple but huge campground with 591 pitches. Launderette.

Camping la Pointe *off the D652, Capbreton; tel: 05 58 72 14 98. Open Jun–Sept.* The site has 283 pitches, with facilities for motor homes. Tents, caravans, mobile homes and chalets may be rented. Amenities include a shop, takeaway food, bar and launderette.

Camping de la Rive *Lac de Sanguinet, Biscarrosse; tel: 05 58 78 12 33; e-mail: info@camping-de-la-rive.fr. Open Apr–Oct.* A massive site with 640 pitches, facilities for renting tents, caravans, mobile homes and chalets, hook-ups for motor homes, shop, takeaway food, bar, nursery, launderette, swimming, tennis and mini-golf. No disco.

Suggested tour

Total distance: Without side trips to the beach resorts associated with some inland places – never more than half a dozen kilometres each way – the main route covers 134km. The detour totals 28km.

Time: The main route can be driven comfortably in under 3 hours. Allow an hour for the detour.

Links: From Capbreton the D652 south leads in 5.5km to Labenne, where it joins the N10, the main route into Bayonne and Biarritz to the south and Dax to the northeast. From Biscarrosse-Plage you can continue north along the D218 through the Forêt de la Teste and past the Dune du Pilat to reach Arcachon (*see pages 262–4*) in 30km.

Route: From **CAPBRETON** ❶ travel north for 3km to **HOSSEGOR** ❷, then turn east on to the D33. After 2km take a left turn on to the D652 for 3.5km to reach the quiet old village of **Seignosse**, nestled at the southern end of Etang Noir, so called because of its black mud. Follow the road around the west side of the lake, then turn right after 1km to pass between Etang Noir and Etang Blanc, named for the colour of its sandy bottom. Another 3km and you reach the village of **Tosse** with its 11th-century church. Next, head north on the D652, which reaches **Soustons** after 9km. Soustons, a major market town, makes corks that go into bottles of Bordeaux wine. Follow the D652 west for 8km to **VIEUX-BOUCAU** ❸ and on for a further 4km to **Messanges**, where vines planted among the sand dunes produce *vin des sables*, a rare red wine with an aroma of violets. Another 4km along the D652 brings you to **Moliets-et-Maa**, which has a challenging golf course. Continue along the D652 for a further 5km and you will reach **LEON** ❹. From here keep on the D652 for a further 15km then turn right at the hamlet of **Miquéou** on to the D105 for 10km to **Lévignacq**, a delightful village, typically Landaise with timber-framed houses, an old water mill and a 13th-century fortified church. The church has frescoes from the 15th century and a wooden ceiling covered with 18th-century paintings of the Nativity, the Ascension and the Holy Trinity. Leave Lévignacq by the D41 north, rejoining the D652 at **St-Julien-en-Born** after 8km. Follow the D652 north for 16km to **MIMIZAN** ❺, where you can visit

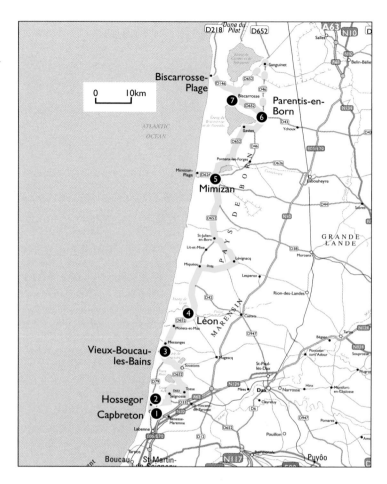

Musée des Sites Lacustres €€ *pl. de la Mairie, Sanguinet; tel: 05 58 78 54 20. Open July–Aug daily 1000–1200 and 1430–1900.*

Mimizan-Plage by heading west for 6km on the D626. **PARENTIS-EN-BORN ⑥** is reached 24km beyond Mimizan, but before that you can enjoy a good view of Etang de Biscarrosse et de Parentis from Gastes.

Detour: From Parentis head north on the D46 for 15km to **Sanguinet**, where Iron Age dugout canoes and other finds from excavations in the area are displayed in the **Musée des Sites Lacustres✦✦**. Sanguinet stands on the site of a Gallo-Roman village and a stone temple can be seen submerged 4m below the lake's surface. From Sanguinet the D652 heads south for 13km to **BISCARROSSE ⑦**.

On the main route, from Parentis the D652 skirts the eastern shore of the lake, reaching Biscarrosse in 9km. From here follow the D146 for 9.5km to **Biscarrosse-Plage**.

Arcachon

Ratings

Beaches	●●●●●
Seafood	●●●●●
Sports facilities	●●●●●
Children's interests	●●●●○
Coastal villages	●●●●○
Ornithology	●●●●○
Architecture	●●●○○
Walks	●●●○○

Developed in the 19th century, Arcachon, with its pine woods, its sandy beaches, its carefully nurtured architecture and its almost land-locked triangular bay, is not just a pretty face. The resort, on Aquitaine's lovely Silver Coast, presents a range of activities for the many thousands of people who swarm into Arcachon (resident population 12,000) from Easter to autumn and beyond. Golf, gambling, surfing, hang-gliding, climbing Europe's biggest sand dune and eating oysters are some of the options. Arcachon is one of the most popular yachting centres in Europe, with 2500 boats in its harbour and a 10-year waiting list for moorings. The town, less than an hour's drive or a pleasant train ride from Bordeaux, has four quarters, each named after a season of the year. Oyster parks, which can be visited by boat or on foot, produce 15,000 tons of oysters a year.

ARCACHON✦✦✦

ℹ Office de Tourisme d'Arcachon *Esplanade Georges Pompidou, Arcachon; tel: 05 57 52 97 97; e-mail: tourisme@arcachon.com; www.arcachon.com. Information kiosks also at the railway station and Arcachon harbour. Open all year. Bookings taken for guided walking tours of Winter Town.*

Arcachon has four main quarters, each named after a season of the year. La Ville de Printemps includes Pereire Park and Pereire Beach. Tennis, bowling, golf, swimming, jai alai and horse riding are among the pursuits enjoyed in the park. The stretch of the seafront, with its pavement cafés and boating events, is in La Ville d'Eté. La Ville d'Automne takes in the fishing port, fish market and marina. A large sculpture here, by Claude Dousceau, appears as an anchor from the side and as a cross from the front. The sculpture is a memorial to fishermen who died at sea.

La Ville d'Hiver, on a higher level, with fine views of the ocean, is where grand houses in an amazing range of architectural styles were built in the 19th and early 20th centuries for the rich and famous. The Winter Town development was started by the two Pereire brothers

Apart from a pharmacy and a newspaper outlet, Winter Town has no shops. Residents use a lift in the Parc Mauresque above Summer Town for easy access to and from the business and social area of Arcachon.

Gujan-Mestras Office de Tourisme *19 av. de Lattre de Tassigny; tel: 05 56 66 12 65; e-mail: otgujan@wanadoo.fr*

when the Bordeaux–la Teste railway line was extended to Arcachon in the 1840s. The sea air and the scent of pine trees planted around the homes enhanced the town's reputation as being beneficial to people suffering from lung diseases. Guided walks around Winter Town from mid-June to mid-September can be booked at the tourist office.

Les Abatilles € *la Source, Ste-Anne-des-Abatilles, Société des Eaux Minérales d'Arcachon 157 blvd De la Côte d'Argent, Arcachon; tel: 05 56 22 38 50. Open for visits to the mineral water production centre Jul–Aug.*

Les Abatilles⁺

A search for oil in Arcachon was unsuccessful. Instead a mineral water spring was discovered. Visitors can taste the water and learn from guides about its history, production and qualities.

Aqualand⁺

(€€€ *Gujan-Mestras, Bassin d'Arcachon, la Hume; tel: 05 56 66 39 39; e-mail: gujanmestras@aqualand.fr; www.aqualand.fr. Open daily mid-Jun–mid-Sept.*) A place to splash around and cool off, with water chutes and attractions for all the family in a 10-hectare park. You can have a restaurant meal or enjoy a picnic in the shade of pine trees.

Aquarium Tropical✦

(€ *Maison des Jeunes, 8 allée José Maria de Hérédia; tel: 05 56 83 19 52; e-mail: aquarium.tropical@free.fr. Open daily 1400–1800.*) Fascinating displays of tiny and not-so-tiny fish in glorious colours and shapes, from various tropical parts. Information in French and English, and video presentation.

Right
Arcachon oyster boat

BASSIN D'ARCACHON✦✦✦

ⓘ La Teste-de-Buch Office de Tourisme
pl. Jean Hameau; tel: 05 56 54 63 14; e-mail: ot.la.teste.de.buch@ wanadoo.fr; www.latestedebuch.com. Open all year Mon–Fri 0900–1230 and 1400–1800, Sat to 1700. Closed Sun and public holidays. Summer season Pavillon du Marché open 1000–1300 (not Mon am).

Fishing trawlers' catches are unloaded at the dockside. Lying at their moorings are 2500 yachts representing millions of pounds. In summer boat trips go to l'Ile aux Oiseaux (Bird Island), the only island in the bay. At low tide it is 15 times as big as at high tide. Oyster parks are revealed at low tide and can be visited by boat or on foot (*see page 269*). Guided **sea kayak trips✦** to places of interest are also available, along with other watersports (*Centre Nautique du Port d'Arcachon, quai de Goslar, Arcachon; tel: 05 56 22 36 83. Open all year*).

Fashionable Cap Ferret is at the tip of a narrow peninsula opposite Arcachon, and the two towns are connected by a boat service. You can explore villages, oyster parks and nature study sites along the road around the bay, where there is also a 54km cycle path running alongside between Cap Ferret and le Teich.

The salt marshes of the **Parc Ornithologique✦** at le Teich, which has 260 bird species, are used by huge numbers of migratory birds as a

Parc Ornithologique de le Teich € and other natural history venues and activities around the bay: *Maison de la Nature; tel: 05 56 22 80 93. Open all year 1000–1800 (2000 in Jul–Aug); www.parc-ornithologique-du-teich.com*

Boat trips €–€€ Catamaran, *Arcachon Croisiere Ocean; tel: 05 56 54 36 70.* Pinasses, *Les Bataliers Arcachonais; tel: 05 56 54 60 32. Atlantic Princess restaurant boat; tel: 05 56 83 39 39.*

La Dune du Pilat Syndicat d'Initiative Maison du Tourisme *rd-point du Figuier; tel: 05 56 54 02 22; e-mail: pyla002@attglobal.net; www.pyla-sur-mer.com. Open all year.*

Pavillon de la Grande Dune *tel: 05 56 22 12 85. Open in high season daily 1000–1300 and 1430–1830; rest of year Mon–Fri 0830–1330 and 1400–1700.*

VSM L'Oceana Diving School €€€ *14 Quai du Capitaine Allegre Arcachon; tel: 05 56 83 98 95; e-mail: vsmplonge@wanadoo.fr; http://vsmplonge.free.fr. Open all year. Qualified instructors offer dive training in a pool or the natural settings of Caraux lake, Arcachon Bay or the open sea.*

Centre SubAquatique au Bassin d'Arcachon (CSBA) €€€ *Centre Nautique de Bassin d'Arcachon; tel: 05 56 22 36 83.*

stopping place. Guided birdwatching visits with an expert ornithologist are offered, using a series of hides in the park.

Boat trips✦✦✦
From Arcachon public boat services go across the bay to Cap Ferret, l'Ile aux Oiseaux, Andernos and Banc d'Arguin. There is also a service between le Moulleau and Cap Ferret. Information: **Union des Bateliers, Arcachonais** (*tel: 05 56 54 60 32*).

In summer you have a choice of boat trips, by catamaran or the traditional Bassin d'Arcachon flat-bottomed 'pinasse', to the Dune de Pyla, the oyster parks or to do a 35km circuit of the Ile aux Oiseaux. A smart restaurant boat more than 30m long, the *Atlantic Princess*, offers popular luncheon and dinner cruises.

Casino de la Plage✦✦
(*163 blvd de la Plage, Arcachon; tel: 05 56 83 41 44. Open 1000–0400*). The chips are down every day as roulette, blackjack and 80 slots go into action at the casino in the Château Deganne. Bowls, a disco, restaurant and bars are added attractions on the premises.

Deep-sea diving✦
(€€€ *Centre SubAquatique au Bassin d'Arcachon (CSBA), Centre Nautique de Bassin d'Arcachon; tel: 05 56 22 36 83*) This is available in the bay for novices and people of various levels of ability. Equipment is provided. Exploration dives are an option.

La Dune du Pilat✦✦✦
Europe's largest sand dune was listed as a national site in 1978. A century ago it was 60m high. Today it is almost twice that height, more than 2.5km long and 1km wide. It has been formed over a period of about 6000 years from layers of dune systems. The dune is constantly on the march, moving 6m or more a year.

It can be approached from a few kilometres out of town via Pyla-sur-Mer and Pilat-Plage. People like to get there for the sunset view from the top – well worth the climb – or by narrated boat trip from the Bassin d'Arcachon (*see Boat trips above*). There are campsites and places to eat around the edge of the dune.

Galleries✦
Arcachon has more than half a dozen art galleries, most of which are on the blvd de la Plage. Some others include **L'Espace 2000** (€€ *pl. Lucien de Gracia; tel: 05 57 52 98 98*) and **Galerie Municipale** (€ *Centre Socio-Culturel, 51 cours Tartas; tel: 05 57 52 98 98, ext. 52*).

Hang-gliding✦
Take a course at the **Ecole Pyla Parapente** (€€€ *1 r. Aurelien, Daisson, Gujan-Mestras; tel: 05 56 22 15 02*), or experience hang-gliding in tandem with a professional pilot.

Le Jardin de Papillons✱✱ (€€ *le Teich (15km from Arcachon on the RN 250 road to Bordeaux); tel: 05 57 52 32 32; e-mail: info@jardindespapillons.com. Open daily mid-Apr–1 Nov).* Visitors can wander in exotic gardens, seeing hundreds of butterflies of numerous species flying freely among tropical vegetation and trees. The 2000m² of the park includes an orchid garden, a butterfly boutique and a shady picnic area.

Labiland Park✱✱

As well as a great maze and a children's mini-maze set in the 5-hectare park, a large area is devoted to games: mini-golf, volleyball, basket ball, badminton, mini-tennis, water fun and other pursuits are provided. Costumed entertainers keep youngsters amused with fairy-tales and legends of the Middle Ages.

Musée Aquarium d'Arcachon✱

Many species of marine life from the Bassin d'Arcachon and the open sea beyond the bay are displayed in large glass tanks. The museum also has sections showing discoveries from archaeological excavations in the area, aspects of oyster farming and local natural history collections.

Parc Animalier 'La Coccinelle'✱✱ (€€€ *La Hume; tel: 05 56 66 30 41; http://perso.wanadoo.fr/touristom2000/t5v9b.html. Open daily late May–late Aug. Children under 90cm free).* A delight for the little ones – and grown-ups, too. The 'Ladybird Park' has 800 domestic pets and small farm animals: you can watch some of them being bottle-fed. Amusements include a little train, water to play in and a carousel.

Sports fishing✱

Mar–May there is migration of several species of fish, notably mackerel and whiting, across the Gasgogne Gulf. Jun–Sept shark fishing is possible in larger boats with professional fishermen based in Arcachon. All gear is provided for people going on sea-fishing trips by boat. Jul and Aug are the peak months. Night-time trips can be arranged.

Village Médiéval de la Hume✱✱✱ (€€ *tel: 05 56 66 16 76. Open 1000–1930 mid-Jun–early Sept).* A back-in-time experience, seeing costumed craftspeople making farm implements, jewellery and various artefacts and crafts. Knights, jugglers and torture at the pillory add to the medieval atmosphere. Arts and crafts are on display.

Accommodation and food

Arc Hotel sur Mer €€€ *89 blvd de la Plage, Arcachon; tel: 05 56 83 06 85; www.arc-hotel-sur-mer.com. Open all year.* The 4-star hotel, right on the beach, has a large swimming pool, solarium and sauna. Most of the 30 rooms have a balcony. There is no restaurant, but a brasserie is open Mar–Oct. There is private enclosed parking.

Right
Grand villa in Arcachon

More than 80 hotels – small by international standards – and a generous assortment of house rentals and guesthouses welcome visitors in Arcachon and its environs. But if you plan a holiday here in July or August, it's wise to book your accommodation months in advance.

Auberge Basque € *la Coquille, 55 cours de Verdun, Gujan-Mestras; tel: 05 56 66 08 60. Open all year.* 1km from the beach, the 23-room hotel has its own restaurant.

Marinette €€ *15 allée Jose Maria de Hérédia, Arcachon; tel: 05 56 83 06 67. Open mid-Mar–Oct.* In Winter Town, the hotel is within 1km of the beach and the town. Each room has its own breakfast terrace.

Hôtel du Parc €€€ *5–7 av. de Parc, Arcachon, tel: 05 56 83 10 58. Open May–Sept.* Each of the 30 en suite rooms has its own spacious covered terrace. The 3-star hotel, set among pine trees, has private parking.

Ttiki Etchea €€ *2 pl. Louis Gaume, Pyla-sur-Mer; tel: 05 56 22 71 15. Open May–Sept.* An attractive hotel with terrace and garden, which welcomes cats and dogs as well as their owners. Traditional cuisine.

Camping Club d'Arcachon €–€€ *allée de la Galaxie, Abatilles, Arcachon; tel: 05 56 83 24 15. Open all year.* One of well over a dozen campsites

🌙 Thinking of renting accommodation for a week, fortnight or month? Local renting agencies include **Dazens Immobilier**, *43 av. des Violettes, Pyla-sur-Mer; tel: 05 56 54 54 26*, **Agence du Littoral**, *151 blvd de la Republique, Andernos; tel: 05 56 82 02 68* and **Agence Reichert**, *29 av. du Vieux Bourg, Audenge; tel: 05 56 26 84 81*.

Opposite
Oyster boat in the Bassin d'Arcachon

Below
Oysters

in Arcachon and around the bay: it has well-maintained sites within 2km of the town and beach. 250 pitches.

Camping de la Dune €–€€ *route de Biscarrosse, Pyla-sur-Mer; tel: 05 56 22 72 17*, is one of the campsites around the Dune du Pilat.

Les Baguettes d'Or € *43 bis, r. Mal de lattre de Tassigny, Arcachon; tel: 05 56 83 84 79. Open all year, closed Monday lunchtime.* Asian food, including Vietnamese specialities, at remarkably good prices.

Le Bistrot € *3 av. du Gal de Gaulle, la Teste; tel: 05 56 66 30 14.* Traditional bistro fare with *prix fixe* menus at modest levels and a children's menu.

Cap Pereire *1 av. du Parc Pereire, Arcachon; tel: 05 56 83 24 01.* Seafood specialities in a colonial-style building by the ocean.

Chez Yvette €€–€€€ *59 blvd du Gal Leclerc, Arcachon; tel: 05 56 83 05 11. Open daily all year.* The restaurant specialises in oysters, *fruits de mer* and fish and offers a good choice of Bordeaux Blanc wines.

Pizzeria Azzurra € *13 r. du Professeur Jolyet, Arcachon; tel: 05 56 83 00 39.* Good pizzas with Italian wine, and a children's menu. Close to the beach.

Tracking down oysters

Commercial breeding of oysters has taken place around the Bassin d'Arcachon for 150 years. Today some 600 families are involved in oyster farming in the area. They are dependent on the tides, the oyster parks being submerged by the twice-daily high tides. Low tide is the time to see the few remaining traditional cabins on stilts.

Obviously, boat trips to the oyster beds are equally dependent on the tides, but there are many points around the bay where you can visit oyster farms on foot. Tracks at right angles to the road lead to places where oyster farmers unload their *pinasses*, the sleek flat-bottomed boats traditionally used in the Bassin, and you can taste and buy the oysters.

There are nearly 20 of these little ports – Arès, Andernos-les-Bains, Audenge, Gujan-Mestras, la Teste-de-Buch, Meyran, the village of l'Herbe and others.

Workshops where the pinewood *pinasses* are built can be seen at Gujan-Mestras and la Teste-de-Buch.

Most of the oysters farmed around Arcachon today are a deep-shelled Japanese variety (*gigas*), introduced about 30 years ago. The flat-shelled (*gravette*) Arcachon oyster is now found only in its wild state. The Portuguese deep-shelled oyster (*angulate*) disappeared from the region in the early 1970s.

Much time, effort and skill are involved in the breeding and farming of oysters. To visit the people and places producing these quality products is a fascinating experience.

Suggested tour

The Parc de Loisirs, which includes Aqualand, la Coccinelle and the Village Médiéval, stands at the intersection of the N250 and the D652.

La Maison de l'Huitre *€€ Port de Larros, Gujan-Mestras; tel: 05 56 66 23 71. Open all year 1000–1200 and 1430–1830; closed Sun Oct–Mar.*

Total distance: Staying close to the water's edge on its way around the Bassin d'Arcachon, the route covers 67km, plus a 3km ferry crossing between Cap Ferret and Arcachon. You can, of course, complete the circuit in the opposite direction to that suggested here.

Time: Leaving aside the ferry crossing (about 30 min, frequent services during summer), the driving time for the route is around 2 hours, but allow a full day for a relaxed tour and serendipitous stops.

Links: From Le Moulleau and la Teste-de-Buch, the D218 leads south to Biscarrosse and other seaside resorts along the southern Côte d'Argent (*see pages 254–61*). Just east of le Teich you can take the D3 south towards Belin-Béliet, the Parc Régional des Landes and Northern Gascony (*see pages 232–41*). From this point you can follow the N250 to Bordeaux (*see pages 42–53*), which can also be reached by way of the D106 east from Arès.

Route: From **ARCACHON** ❶ follow the N250 for 6km to la Teste-de-Buch, capital of the Buch family kingdom in medieval times and now the seat of one of the largest municipalities in France, which includes the resorts of Pyla-sur-Mer and Pilat-Plage, as well as the massive **DUNE DU PILAT** ❷ and Lac de Cazaux, the second largest in the country. Continue on the N250 for 4½km, then turn left on to the D652, and at the waterfront at la Hume (3km) turn right on to the D650, which reaches **Gujan-Mestras** in a further 3½km.

Picturesque Gujan-Mestras is the Arcachon Basin's main oyster farming centre and there are many kiosks where the tasty molluscs may be sampled and purchased. Here, the story of oyster farming is told at **La Maison de l'Huitre❖❖**.

Passing the **PARC ORNITHOLOGIQUE** ❸, continue on the D650 through le Teich and after 9km turn north on to the D3 to skirt the eastern edge of the Basin. Audenge, another oyster-farming port, where

ⓘ Cap Ferret *Office de Tourisme 1 av. du Général de Gaulle, Lege-Cap-Ferret; tel: 05 56 03 94 49; e-mail: info@lege-capferret.com; www.lege-capferret.com*

ⓡ Petit Train Touristique €€ *Jetée Bélisaire, Cap Ferret; tel: 05 56 60 60 20. Departures daily 1000–1810 (Jul–Aug); 1100–1745 (Jun and Sept); 1415–1645 (Apr–May).*

ⓕ Cap Ferret Lighthouse €€ *Tel: 05 56 03 94 49 or 05 57 70 33 30 (Lighthouse). Open Jul–Aug 1000–1900; closed Nov–Dec; rest of year 1000–1230 and 1400–1800.*

the retreating tide traps the catch in special reservoirs, comes after 5km. Lanton, 3km further along the pine-fringed road, has a long beach and a Romanesque church with a 12th-century apse. An ancient community, Andernos-les-Bains, 7km beyond Lanton, is now a popular summer resort, thanks to its sheltered position and 4km of beach.

A further 6km along the D3 brings you to Arès, another former oyster port now reincarnated as a resort. At the northern end of Arès head left on to the D106 to round the top of the **BASSIN D'ARCACHON**. The road passes through a cluster of tiny oyster ports, including l'Herbe, a quaint hamlet of wooden homes, which was founded in the 17th century. Excellent views across the basin can be enjoyed from Villa-Algérienne, the site of a building in North-African style that was demolished in the 1960s.

Cap Ferret✦✦✦, 23km from Arès, is an attractive pine-clad resort that offers surf-riding, a narrow-gauge **railway ride**✦✦✦ to the oceanside beach and a climb of 258 steps to enjoy the view from the top of the **Cap Ferret lighthouse**✦✦.

The Northern Côte d'Argent

Ratings

Beaches	●●●●●
Wine	●●●●●
Children	●●●●○
Coastal resorts	●●●●○
Outdoor activities	●●●●○
Walks	●●●●○
Boat trips	●●●○○
Food and drink	●●●○○

The northern end of the Côte d'Argent, with the Bassin d'Arcachon at its base, the Atlantic Ocean to the west and the Médoc wine region to the east, ends dramatically at Pointe de Grave, which curls inland as if to protect the mouth of the Gironde river. Soulac-sur-Mer, the last town of any size on the coast, has been important for hundreds of years. This was where many pilgrims setting out on the road to Santiago de Compostela started the final overland section of their trek to Spain, and because large numbers of them came from England this part of the journey came to be called 'the English Way'. Today's visitors will be seeking physical rather than spiritual refreshment and they will find much to satisfy their quest among the dunes and beaches, pine forests and lakes of this delightful region.

HOURTIN✦✦✦

ⓘ **Office de Tourisme d'Hourtin** *pl. du Port; tel: 05 56 09 19 00; e-mail: tourisme@hourtin-medoc.com; www.hourtin-medoc.com. Open all year.*

This small village at the northern end of Lac d'Hourtin-Carcans is very much a place for outdoor types – a notion underscored by the fact that while official literature lists only one hotel for the area, there are more than 2000 camping pitches – one site alone, at Hourtin-Plage, has 750 spaces. It is also a centre for canoe trips into a labyrinth of waterways and lagoons and there are watersports facilities

Pte de
la Coubre

D25

D14

D733

0   10km

Royan Semussac

Coz

Pte de Grave

Le-Verdon-sur-Mer

Gironde

Soulac-sur-Mer
l'Amélie-sur-Mer

Grayan-et-l'Hôpital

St-Vivien-de-Médoc
Vensac

Montalivet-
les-Bains

Vendays-
Montalivet

Queyrac

St-
M

N215

Gallian-en-Médoc

D101

Lesparre-Médoc

St-G
d'Est

D204

Hourtin-
Plage

D101 E7

Vertheuil

Le Contaut
Cartignac

Hourtin

Pauill

Étang d'Hourtin
et de Carcans

St-Laurent-Médoc

D3

N21

Carcans-
Plage

D207

Carcans

Listrac-Médoc

Maubuisson

Castelnau-de-
Médoc

D6 E1

Lacanau-
Océan

D6

Lacanau

Étang de Lacanau

D6

Ste-on the lake as well as on the coast. Surrounded by moorland, forest and massive dunes and fringed by marshes, the lake covers an area of more than 6000 hectares and has plenty of room for those who like seclusion. Opposite Hourtin, on the lake's northwestern shore is le Contaut, a training centre for the French navy, where visitors can join a tour through protected wetlands (*details from the tourism office*).

LACANAU-OCEAN✧✧

ⓘ Lacanau-Ocean Office de Tourisme *pl de l'Europe; tel: 05 56 03 21 01; e-mail: lacanau@ lacanau.com; www.lacanau.com. Open all year except 1 Jan and 25 Dec. Tourist office at rail station open Jun–Sept.*

A surfer's paradise, with the Atlantic Ocean pounding on to wide beaches of fine sand, the resort is in an idyllic setting of sand dunes and plantations of sea pines. Lac de Lacanau, a lovely stretch of fresh water, offers an extensive range of water activities and is popular with families. Boat rentals are available. Its great shoals of fish – especially eels, perch and pike – make it a favourite with anglers. Cycle trails and footpaths circle the lake.

MAUBUISSON✧✧

ⓜ Musée des Arts et Traditions Populaires €€ *Maubuisson; tel: 05 56 03 33 96. Open May–Sept Sun–Fri 1500–1900.*

Etang de Cousseau *tel: SEPANSO (Society for the protection of nature in the southwest) 05 56 91 33 65, or tourist office Lacanau-Ocean 05 56 03 21 01; e-mail: rncousseau@wanadoo.fr; http://assoc.wanadoo.fr/ federation.sepanso/pages/ reserves/cousse.htm*

Maubuisson, at the southwestern end of Lac d'Hourtin-Carcans, lies on the edge of the extensive pine forest that fringes the coast, and the forest's influence on local life is featured in the **Musée des Arts et Traditions Populaires des Landes✧✧**. A little over 2km north of the village is **Bombannes✧** (*tel: 05 56 03 95 95*), an open-air leisure centre covering 200 hectares. Visitors can take part in archery, boating, swimming, tennis and a host of other activities. There are attractive picnic areas among the pines and overlooking the lake.

A fascinating nature trail follows the western shore of the 2km long **Etang de Cousseau✧✧**, a nature reserve just south of Maubuisson and about halfway between Lac d'Hourtin-Carcans and Lac de Lacanau. You can access the reserve only by a footpath through the Forêt de Lacanau or on paved cycle trails. Bikes are not allowed into the reserve, and must be left in designated areas. The area surrounding the lake – the eastern shore is marshy and inaccessible – has an interesting range of flora and fauna, including wild boar. There are guided tours daily mid-Jun–mid-Sept, when you can see demonstrations of resin-tapping. Reservations for the tours must be made at the Lacanau tourist office (*see above*).

PHARE DE CORDOUAN✧✧

There has been a lighthouse of sorts guarding the Gironde estuary since the 14th century. When the Black Prince ordered a fire to be kept going 24 hours a day on an octagonal tower, the rocks on which it stood were part of the mainland at Pointe de Grave, but by the 17th century they

Phare de Cordouan
€€ *The lighthouse is accessible by boat from Pointe de Grave (Jul–Aug), Royan and le Verdon-sur-Mer (weather permitting). Guided tours of the lighthouse and its museum in high season 1030–1200 and 1400–1800; off-peak at weekends 1400–1800, by appointment only, tel: 05 56 09 62 93; http://perso.wanadoo.fr/cordouan*

had become separated. The lighthouse now stands some 8km offshore. The Black Prince's tower was replaced by an ornate wedding-cake structure designed by Louis de Foix, the engineer who diverted the River Adour. In 1788 the upper levels were remodelled to a more practical shape, but the lighthouse today retains some of its old extravagant style. Reaching a height of 66m, it contains a King's Apartment and a chapel. Reaching the lamp involves a climb up 301 steps.

POINTE DE GRAVE❖❖

ⓘ *A tourist information booth opposite the Pointe de Grave landing stage is open Jul–Aug daily. Tel: 05 56 73 37 73.*

Boat trips
€€–€€€ la Bohême II, landing stage, Pointe de Grave; tel: 05 56 09 62 93; e-mail: richardgrass@netup.com or vedettelaboheme@aol.com; www.edv.fr/boheme2/boheme2.html. Trips to Cordouan lighthouse and along the Gironde estuary.

Scenic railway €€€
Departure times and other information from the tourist offices at le Verdon, tel: 05 56 09 61 78 and Soulac, tel: 05 56 09 86 61. This little train runs between the Pointe de Grave and Soulac, with splendid views of the coastline and the forests. Journey time about 1 hour.

The most northerly point of the Côte d'Argent, overlooking the mouth of the Gironde, has been of strategic importance in World Wars I and II. It is marked by a monument commemorating the landing of American troops in 1917 – the original, a 75m pyramid, was destroyed by the Germans in 1942. Allied forces landed in France in June 1944, but it took them nearly a year to shake the Germans from Pointe de Grave.

It's a peaceful enough spot today, however, with magnificent views of the Phare de Cordouan, the Gironde estuary and le Verdon-sur-Mer. A lighthouse on the point serves as the **Musée de Phare de Courdouan**❖❖, featuring the old structure's history and the life of a lighthouse keeper. There is also an aquarium. **Boat trips**❖❖ may be taken from Pointe de Grave, which is also a terminus for a 10km **scenic railway**❖❖ trip along the pine-fringed shore to Soulac-sur-Mer.

Right
Sunrise at Pointe de Grave

ROYAN❖❖❖

ⓘ Office de Tourisme
Rond-Point de la Poste;
tel; 05 46 05 04 71; e-mail:
info@royan-tourisme.com;
www.royan-tourisme.com
Open Jul–Aug Mon–Sat
0900–1930, Sun 1000–
1300 and 1500–1800;
Sept–Jun Mon–Sat
0900–1800.

ⓜ Zoo de la Palmyre
€€€ tel: 05 46 22
46 06; e-mail:
admin@zoo-palmyre.com;
www.zoo-palmyre.fr. Open
Apr–Sept daily 0900–1900;
Oct–Mar daily 0900–1200
and 1400–1800.

Five kilometres across the mouth of the Gironde from Pointe de Grave – a 30-minute ferry boat trip – Royan, in Charente-Maritime *département*, is a popular coastal holiday centre. Almost flattened by bombing during the closing months of World War II, the town, which had been the archetypal Victorian French resort, had to be rebuilt after losing many of its overblown villas and grand hotels. Despite its post-war architecture, Royan is a lively and fitting capital for the Côte de Beauté, as the coastline that runs north from here is known.

The town is graced with 2km of crescent-shaped beach – the **Front de Mer**❖❖ – fringing the large cove which holds the main harbour. This is where ferryboats depart for Pointe de Grave. Four smaller coves also on the west side of the harbour have fine sandy beaches. The town's main church, **Eglise Notre-Dame**❖, was completed after three years in 1958 and is strikingly built of reinforced concrete coated with resin to protect it from wind and weather. It is noted for its glass walls and 65m belfry.

The coast on the Atlantic side of Royan invites exploration. **St-Palais-sur-Mer**❖❖, only 5km away, is a small, elegant resort. **Zoo de la Palmyre**❖❖❖, in a forest of pines and oaks 15km from Royan, is an extended nature trail through 14 hectares of lakes and hills where some 1500 animals from all parts of the world live in habitats as near-natural as possible. Among the zoo's stars are families of gorillas, flying foxes and lion cubs. Just beyond la Palmyre is the **Forêt de la Coubre**❖❖❖ where deer roam – and you can enjoy a guided tour – among 8000 hectares of pine and ilex trees. Enquire at tourist office.

SOULAC-SUR-MER❖❖

ⓘ Office de Tourisme
68 r. de la Plage; tel:
05 56 09 86 61; e-mail:
tourismesoulac@wanadoo.fr;
www.soulac.com. Open daily
in high season 0900–1900;
off-peak Mon–Sat 0900–
1230 and 1400–1730.

ⓜ Fondation Soulac-
Médoc €€ *Soulac-*
sur-Mer; tel: 05 56 09 83
99. Open Jul–mid-Sept daily
1700–1930.

The town has had at least three incarnations. Until the 6th century it was the ancient city of Noviomagus, then the sea swept over it. Next, it was an important port with a large natural harbour where pilgrims would disembark before setting off overland on the road to Santiago de Compostela. This time, in the 17th century, the fickle sea ran out and the harbour became marshland. Now it's a popular seaside resort at the southern end of the scenic railway to Pointe de Grave (*see page 275*).

A survivor from Soulac's second life is the **Basilique Notre-Dame-de-la-Fin-des-Terres**❖❖ (Our Lady of Land's End), which was uncovered and restored in the 19th century after being almost totally buried in

Musée d'Artet d'Archéologie €
av. El Burgo de Osma, Soulac-sur-Mer; tel: 05 56 09 83 99. Open Jul–Aug daily 1500–1900; rest of year daily 1500–1800. Closed Wed.

sand. There are traces of 12th-century Romanesque architecture and its belfry dates from the 14th century. Among the decorated capitals inside the church is one depicting the tomb and shrine of St Veronica, who died in Soulac. Another portrays Daniel in the lions' den and a third shows St Peter in prison.

Paintings and sculptures by contemporary artists from the area are displayed in the **Fondation Soulac-Médoc**. A collection of tools and weapons from the neolithic and Bronze Ages and artefacts from the Gallo-Roman period – including ceramics and glassware – are on show in the **Musée d'Archéologie**.

LE VERDON-SUR-MER

Office de Tourisme *r. François Lebreton; tel: 05 56 09 61 78; e-mail: tourismeleverdon-sur-mer@wanadoo.fr; www.littoral33.com/ Le_Verdon.htm. Open Mon–Sat 1000–1200 and 1500–1900.*

Apart from being a departure point for boat trips along the estuary and to Phare de Cordouan, le Verdon-sur-Mer is a deep-water port and container terminal handling huge container vessels and oil tankers on their way to and from various parts of the world.

Accommodation and food

Biche au Bois €–€€ *141 blvd Côte de Beauté, route de St-Palais, Vaux-sur-Mer; tel: 05 46 39 01 52; e-mail: hotel.biche-au-bois@wanadoo.fr. Closed Oct–Nov.* The restaurant offers very reasonably priced meals and wine is available by the glass. Accommodation (**€€**) is in 12 en suite rooms with direct-dial telephones and television. Garden; enclosed parking.

Hôtel la Dame de Cœur €–€€ *103 r. de la Plage, Soulac-sur-Mer; tel: 05 56 09 80 80; e-mail: la.dame.de.coeur@wanadoo.fr. Open all year.* The hotel has 12 en suite rooms and a restaurant.

Hôtel le Dauphin €€ *17 pl. de l'Eglise, Hourtin; tel: 05 56 09 11 15. Open all year.* The hotel has 20 en suite rooms and a restaurant.

L'Etoile d'Argent €€–€€€ *pl. de l'Europe, Lacanau-Océan; tel: 05 56 03 21 07. Open Feb–Nov.* This hotel–restaurant offers accommodation in 14 en suite rooms with direct-dial telephones and television and there is private parking for customers. The restaurant (**€–€€€**) offers a menu with house wine included.

Family Golf Hôtel €€€ *28 blvd Garnier, Royan; tel: 05 46 05 14 66. Open mid-Mar–Oct.* No restaurant, but breakfast is available. The hotel has 33 en suite rooms with direct-dial telephones and television. Private parking.

Hôtel du Golf €€€ *Domaine de l'Ardilouse, Lacanau-Océan; tel: 05 56 03 92 92. Open all year.* Adjoining an 18-hole golf course, the hotel has 50 en suite rooms, each with direct-dial telephone and television, and a restaurant (**€€–€€€**) where you can buy wine by the glass. There is a terraced dining area and amenities include a swimming pool and garden.

Hôtel Lescorce €–€€ *36 r. Trouche, Soulac-sur-Mer; tel: 05 56 09 84 13. Open mid-Apr–Oct.* A simple hotel with 18 en suite rooms. No restaurant; tennis court.

Hôtel Michelet €€–€€€ *1 r. Bernard Baguenard, Soulac-sur-Mer; tel: 05 56 09 84 18. Open all year.* No restaurant, but breakfast is available at this hotel with 20 en suite rooms.

Ocean Hôtel Loisirs €€–€€€ *l'Amélie, Soulac-sur-Mer; tel: 05 56 09 78 05. Open early Jun–mid-Sept.* The hotel has 21 en suite rooms, a swimming pool and restaurant.

Hôtel des Pins €€–€€€ *l'Amélie, Soulac-sur-Mer; tel: 05 56 73 27 27; e-mail: hotel.pin@wanadoo.fr; www.hotel-des-pins.com. Closed Feb and two weeks in Nov.* The restaurant (€€) here offers terraced dining and wine by the glass. The hotel's 31 en suite rooms have direct-dial telephones and television. Private parking for guests.

Résidence de Rohan €€€ *7 av. de Rohan, Vaux-sur-Mer; tel: 05 46 39 00 75; e-mail: info@residence-rohan.com. Open Apr–mid-Nov.* Situated in a park setting overlooking the beach, the hotel has 41 en suite rooms with direct-dial telephones and television. Swimming pool, tennis and private parking. No restaurant, but breakfast is available.

Résidence de Saintonge €€–€€€ *allée des Algues, Pontaillac, Royan; tel: 05 46 39 00 00. Open Apr–Sept.* House wine by the carafe is available at the hotel's restaurant, Pavillon Bleu (€–€€). There are 40 en suite rooms with direct-dial telephones and television; private parking.

Résidences Domaine Aplus €€€ *route de Baganais, Lacanau-Océan; tel: 05 56 03 91 00; e-mail: info@aplus-lacanau.com. Open early Mar–mid-Nov.* There are two swimming pools – one indoors, one outside – at this hotel, which also has a restaurant (€€€) with terraced dining area, where wine is available by the glass. There are tennis courts and a fitness room, and 59 en suite rooms with direct-dial telephones and television.

Camping

Airotel Côte d'Argent *Hourtin-Plage; tel: 05 56 09 10 25; e-mail: info@camping-cote-dargent.com; www.camping-cote-dargent.com. Open mid-May–mid-Sept.* A massive campground with 750 pitches, including spaces for motor homes. Caravans, tents, mobile homes and chalets are available for hire. Launderette; swimming pool.

Airotel de l'Ocean *r. du Repos, Lacanau-Océan; tel: 05 56 03 24 45; e-mail: airotel.lacanau@wanadoo.fr; www.lacanau-airotel.com/gb/ airotel.htm. Open late April–Sept.* A disco and swimming pool are among the amenities at this 550-pitch site which has tents, caravans, chalets and mobile homes for rent and facilities for motor homes.

Les Genêts *l'Amélie, Soulac-sur-Mer; tel: 05 56 09 85 79. Open Apr–Sept.* The site has a launderette and swimming pool and there are 250 pitches, with spaces for motor homes. Caravans, chalets, mobile homes and tents for hire.

Les Grands Pins *Lacanau-Océan; tel: 05 56 03 20 77; e-mail: reception@lesgrandspins.com; www.lesgrandspins.com. Open May–mid-Sept.* Spaces for motor homes are among the 560 pitches, and mobile homes and chalets may be rented. Launderette; pool.

Le Lilhan *l'Amélie, Soulac-sur-Mer; tel: 05 56 09 77 63. Open Jun–mid-Sept.* Caravans, chalets, mobile homes and tents may be hired at this site, where there are 170 pitches including spaces for motor homes. Launderette; pool.

La Mariflaude *off the D4, Hourtin; tel: 05 56 09 11 97. Open mid-May–mid-Sept.* Mobile homes and chalets may be rented at this 166-pitch site, which has places for motor homes. Launderette; swimming pool.

Les Sables d'Argent *blvd de l'Amélie, Soulac-sur-Mer; tel: 05 56 09 82 87. Open Apr–Sept.* The site has spaces for motor homes on its 152 pitches. Caravans, tents, chalets and mobile homes are available for hire. Launderette.

Talaris Vacances *route de l'Océan, Lacanau-Océan; tel: 05 56 03 04 15; e-mail: talarisvacances@free.fr. Open June–mid-Sept.* The site has 200 pitches, including spaces for motor homes. Caravans, tents, chalets and mobile homes for hire. Launderette; pool.

Suggested tour

Moulin de Vensac
€€ Tel: 05 56 09 45
00; http://perso.wanadoo.fr/
gilles.coutreau/region/
a-visiter/sfmoulin.htm.
Guided tours (30 mins)
Jul–Aug daily 1000–1230
and 1430–1830; Jun and
Sept Sat–Sun same times;
Mar–May and Oct–Nov
Sun 1430–1830. Closed
Dec–Feb.

Total distance: The round trip covers 192km. From Soulac to Lacanau the distance is 89.5km.

Time: Driving time for the total route is about 4 hours.

Links: The N215 from the outskirts of Soulac is the main route to Bordeaux (*see pages 42–53*). From Lacanau the D3 south reaches the northern part of the Bassin d'Arcachon (*see page 264*) in 24km.

Route: The route begins, as it did for many pilgrims setting out on the road to Santiago de Compostela, at **SOULAC-SUR-MER** ❶. The route took those pilgrims right down to Spain, but we're following the 'English Way' only as far as Lacanau, then returning through the Médoc with a chance perhaps to try some of the region's splendid wines. From Soulac take the D101, which runs behind the dunes, and follow the road for 4.5km to l'Amélie-sur-Mer. From here, those on foot or bicycle can continue along a coastal path to Hourtin-Plage. In a car, turn away from the sea on the D101, joining the D101 after 2.5km.

Turn right and continue for 6.5km to Grayan-et-l'Hôpital, where a hospital, which no longer exists, was founded in the 12th century to receive pilgrims coming from Soulac. The D101 continues south for 11km to Vendays-Montalivet, where there are a number of hotels and campgrounds. Montalivet-les-Bains, a seaside resort, is 8km west on the D102. From Vendays-Montalivet continue south along the D101 for 17km to the hamlet of Cartignac, where you turn right on to the D101, crossing the Marais dit Palu, an area of marshland, and passing through **le Contaut** to reach **Hourtin-Plage** in 8.5km. The small town of **HOURTIN** ❷, a focal point of campgrounds, is 3km south of Cartignac.

From Hourtin, continue south on the D3 for a further 12km and at Carcans turn right on to the D207, skirting the southern end of Lac d'Hourtin-Carcans to reach **MAUBUISSON** ❸ in 8.5km. Carcans-Plage is a further 4.5km along the D207, but 3.5km out of Maubuisson the D6 leads off to the south to form a very scenic route through the Forêt de Lacanau. After 9km it joins the D6 on the edge of **LACANAU-OCEAN** ❹. Head inland on the D6, which follows the northern shore of Lac de Lacanau, reaching the town of **Lacanau** in 12km.

Continue east on the D6 for 16km to Ste-Hélène, then follow the D5 northeast for 10km to Castelnau-de-Médoc, where the D105 heads east for 7km to Margaux, home of the noted wine château. The D2 goes north for 21km, following the Gironde to Pauillac (*see pages 58–9*), then continues for another 8km to Vertheuil, passing the great châteaux of Mouton-Rothschild and Lafite-Rothschild on the way. From Vertheuil take the D204 for 10.5km to Lesparre-Médoc, where it joins the N215, which continues north, returning you to Soulac in 30km. On the way, stop off at the village of **Vensac**, where you can watch corn being ground in the traditional way in an 18th-century stone-built mill.

Language

Although English is spoken in most tourist locations it is courteous to attempt to speak some French. The effort is generally appreciated, and may even elicit a reply in perfect English! The following is a very brief list of some useful words and phrases, with approximate pronunciation guides. For driver's vocabulary, see page 28. The *Thomas Cook European 12-Language Phrasebook* (£4.99) lists more than 350 travel phrases in French (and in 11 other European languages).

- **Hello/Goodbye**
  Bonjour/Au revoir *Bawngzhoor/Ohrervwahr*

- **Good evening/Goodnight**
  Bonsoir/Bonne nuit *Bawngswahr/Bon nwee*

- **Yes/No**
  Oui/Non *Wee/Nawng*

- **Please/Thank you (very much)**
  S'il vous plaît/Merci (beaucoup) *Seelvooplay/Mehrsee (bohkoo)*

- **Excuse me, can you help me please?**
  Excusez-moi, vous pouvez m'aider s'il vous plaît? *Ekskewzaymwah, voo poovay mahyday seelvooplay?*

- **Do you speak English?**
  Vous parlez anglais? *Voo pahrlay ahnglay?*

- **I'm sorry, I don't understand.**
  Pardon, je ne comprends pas. *Pahrdawng, zher ner kawngprawng pah.*

- **I am looking for the tourist information office.**
  Je cherche l'office de tourisme. *Zher shaersh lohfeece de tooreezm.*

- **Do you have a map of the town/area?**
  Avez-vous une carte de la ville/région? *Ahveh-voo ewn cart der lah veel/rehzhawng?*

- **Do you have a list of hotels?**
  Vous avez une liste d'hôtels? *Vooz ahveh ewn leesst dohtehl?*

- **Do you have any rooms free?**
  Vous avez des chambres disponibles? *Voozahveh deh shahngbr deesspohneebl?*

- **I would like to reserve a single/double room with/without bath/shower.**
  Je voudrais réserver une chambre pour une personne/pour deux personnes avec/sans salle de bain/douche. *Zher voodray rehsehrveh ewn shahngbr poor ewn pehrson/poor der pehrson avek/sawns sal der banne/doosh.*

- **I would like bed and breakfast/(room and) half board/(room and) full board.**
  Je voudrais le petit-déjeuner/la demi-pension/la pension complète. *Zher voodray ler pewtee-dehjewneh/lah dermee-pahngsyawng/lah pahngsyawng kawngplait.*

- **How much is it per night?**
  Quel est le prix pour une nuit? *Khel eh ler pree poor ewn nuwy?*

- **I would like to stay for . . . nights.**
  Je voudrais rester . . . nuits. *Zhe voodray resteh . . . newyh.*

- **Do you accept traveller's cheques/credit cards?**
  Vous acceptez les chèques de voyages/les cartes de crédit? *Voos aksepteh leh sheck der vwoyazh/leh kart der krehdee?*

- **I would like a table for two.**
  Je voudrais une table pour deux personnes. *Zher voodray ewn tabl poor der pehrson.*

- **I would like a cup of/two cups of/another coffee/tea.**
  Je voudrais une tasse de/deux tasses de/encore une tasse de café/thé. *Zher voodray ewn tahss der/der tahss der/oncaw ewn tahss der kafeh/teh.*

- **I would like a bottle/glass/two glasses of mineral water/red wine/white wine, please.**
  Je voudrais une bouteille/un verre/deux verres d'eau minérale/de vin rouge/de vin blanc, s'il vous plaît. *Zher voodray ewn bootayy/ang vair/der vair doh mynehral/der vang roozh/der vang blahng, seelvooplay.*

- **Could I have it well-cooked/medium/rare please?**
  Je le voudrais bien cuit/à point/saignant s'il vous plaît? *Zher ler voodray beeang kwee/ah pwahng/saynyang, seelvooplay?*

- **May I have the bill, please?**
  L'addition, s'il vous plaît? *Laddyssyawng, seelvooplay?*

- **Where is the toilet (restroom), please?**
  Où sont les toilettes, s'il vous plaît? *Oo sawng leh twahlaitt, seelvooplay?*

- **How much does it/this cost?**
  Quel est le prix? *Kehl eh ler pree?*

- **A (half-)kilo of . . . please.**
  Un (demi-) kilo de . . . s'il vous plaît. *Ang (dermee)keelo der . . . seelvooplay.*

Index

Acknowledgements

Project management: Cambridge Publishing Management Limited
Project editor: Karen Beaulah
Series design: Fox Design
Cover design: Liz Lyons Design
Layout and map work: Concept 5D/Cambridge Publishing Management Ltd
Repro and image setting: PDQ Digital Media Solutions Ltd/
                          Cambridge Publishing Management Ltd
Printed and bound in India by: Replika Press Pvt Ltd

We would like to thank Image Select International/Chris Fairclough Colour Library for the photographs used in this book, to whom the copyright in the photographs belongs, with the exception of the following:

Front cover: Castelnaud, Simeone Huber/Getty Images
Back cover: Four French specialities, Robert Harding Picture Library Ltd/Alamy

J Allan Cash (pages 102, 104, 112, 122, 212, 214, 219 and 257); **John Heseltine** (page 18); **David Martyn Hughes/images-of-france.com** (pages 112–13); **Spectrum Colour Library** (pages 98, 100, 108, 110, 114, 118, 121, 125, 126, 128 and 220); **Pictures Colour Library** (page 27).

Picture research: Image Select International

Feedback form

If you enjoyed using this book, or even if you didn't, please help us improve future editions by taking part in our reader survey. Every returned form will be acknowledged, and to show our appreciation we will give you £1 off your next purchase of a Thomas Cook guidebook. Just take a few minutes to complete and return this form to us.

When did you buy this book? ....

....

Where did you buy it? (Please give town/city and, if possible, name of retailer)

....

....

When did you/do you intend to travel in Dordogne? ....

....

For how long (approx)? ....

How many people in your party? ....

Which cities, national parks and other locations did you/do you intend mainly to visit?

....

....

....

....

Did you/will you:
❑ Make all your travel arrangements independently?
❑ Travel on a fly-drive package?
Please give brief details: ....

....

Did you/do you intend to use this book:
❑ For planning your trip?   ❑ Both?
❑ During the trip itself?

Did you/do you intend also to purchase any of the following travel publications for your trip?
A road map/atlas (please specify) ....
Other guidebooks (please specify) ....

Have you used any other Thomas Cook guidebooks in the past? If so, which?

....

....

....

Please rate the following features of Drive Around Dordogne and Western France for their value to you (circle VU for 'very useful', U for 'useful', NU for 'little or no use'):

The Travel Facts section on pages 14–22	VU U NU
The Driver's Guide section on pages 23–29	VU U NU
The Touring itineraries on pages 40–41	VU U NU
The recommended driving routes throughout the book	VU U NU
Information on towns and cities, National Parks, etc	VU U NU
The maps of towns and cities, parks, etc	VU U NU

Please use this space to tell us about any features that in your opinion could be changed, improved, or added in future editions of the book, or any other comments you would like to make concerning the book:

....

....

....

....

....

....

Your age category: ❏ 21–30   ❏ 31–40   ❏ 41–50   ❏ over 50

Your name: Mr/Mrs/Miss/Ms ....

(First name or initials) ....

(Last name) ....

Your full address: (Please include postal or zip code)

....

....

....

....

....

Your daytime telephone number: ....

Please detach this page and send it to: The Series Editor, Drive Around Guides, Thomas Cook Publishing, PO Box 227, The Thomas Cook Business Park, 15–16 Coningsby Road, Peterborough PE3 8SB.

Alternatively, you can e-mail us at: *books@thomascook.com*

We will be pleased to send you details of how to claim your discount upon receipt of this questionnaire.